CASE STUDIES IN
CULTURAL ANTHROPOLOGY

GENERAL EDITORS

George and Louise Spindler

STANFORD UNIVERSITY

YUQUI

Forest Nomads in a Changing World

Figure 1.   Yuquí study area

YUQUI

Forest Nomads in a Changing World

ALLYN MACLEAN STEARMAN

University of Central Florida

HOLT, RINEHART AND WINSTON

NEW YORK   CHICAGO   SAN FRANCISCO   PHILADELPHIA
MONTREAL   TORONTO   LONDON   SYDNEY   TOKYO

Library of Congress Cataloging-in-Publication Data
Stearman, Allyn MacLean, 1943–
 Yuquí : forest nomads in a changing world.
 (Case studies in cultural anthropology)
 Bibliography: p.
 Includes index.
 1. Yuqui Indians. I. Title. II. Series.
F3320.2.Y78S74 1988   984′.00498   88-8428

ISBN 0-03-022702-X

Printed in the United States of America.
9 0 1 2 016 9 8 7 6 5 4 3 2 1

Holt, Rinehart and Winston, Inc.
The Dryden Press
Saunders College Publishing

To Mike

Foreword

These case studies in cultural anthropology are designed to bring to students, in beginning and intermediate courses in the social sciences, insights into the richness and complexity of human life as it is lived in different ways and in different places. They are written by men and women who have lived in the societies they write about and who are professionally trained as observers and interpreters of human behavior. The authors are also teachers, and in writing their books they have kept the students who will read them foremost in their minds. It is our belief that when an understanding of ways of life very different from one's own is gained, abstractions and generalizations about social structure, cultural values, subsistence techniques, and the other universal categories of human social behavior become meaningful.

ABOUT THE AUTHOR

Allyn MacLean Stearman was born in Los Angeles, California, in 1943, one of two children. She is a fourth-generation Californian, descended from Bartolo Ballerino, one of the early Spanish settlers of Los Angeles. She resided in both southern and northern California, attending high schools in North Hollywood and Burlingame. She attended the University of California at Santa Barbara, where she graduated with honors in Spanish in 1964. As a student at UCSB, Stearman traveled during her junior year to Bogota, Colombia, where she studied Spanish language and literature at the Instituto Caro y Cuervo.

Immediately following graduation, Stearman joined the Peace Corps and was sent to lowland Bolivia with a group of 44 volunteers to work in a frontier settlement program. She ultimately was assigned to a small peasant village on the edge of a colonization zone, where she remained four years working in community development. While in Bolivia, she married a fellow volunteer, Michael Stearman, who had extended his term of service to complete a project with the Bolivian Ministry of Agriculture.

The Peace Corps experience not only fostered a lifelong involvement with the Bolivian Amazon, but also inspired an interest in anthropology. Returning with her husband to his home state of Florida, Stearman enrolled in the anthropology program at the University of Florida. While in graduate school, she conducted two field projects in applied anthropology: one a study of public housing for the elderly in Gainesville, Florida, and the other a study of land tenure patterns of a rural black community near the university. In 1975, she received a Social Science Research Council fellowship for dissertation research in lowland Bolivia. For her doctoral thesis, Stearman returned to the Santa Cruz region, where she had worked as a Peace Corps volunteer, to study changing patterns of migration and development on the Bolivian frontier.

Following the awarding of her Ph. D. in 1976, Stearman was invited to join the faculty of the University of Central Florida, where she is presently an associate professor. She has published several books and monographs on Bolivia and numerous articles in professional and popular journals. Since 1975, Stearman has returned on numerous occasions to Bolivia and other areas of Latin America to serve as a consultant and to conduct fieldwork. She was recently awarded grants from the Lindbergh Fund, the Explorer's Club, the Leakey Foundation, and the National Science Foundation to continue her research among the Sirionó and Yuquí.

The Stearmans reside in rural Florida with their two children.

ABOUT THIS CASE STUDY

Allyn Stearman has succeeded in interweaving several themes in this case study. Her personal fieldwork experience, the history of contact with the Yuquí, the influence of the missionaries, relationships with the outside world, the traditional social and cultural life of the Yuquí, and the many changes taking place all come together in her analysis.

The Yuquí in their totality, including both those still living as nomadic foragers in the Bolivian rain forest and those living at the mission station, number not more than 150 persons. They are the remnant of a once larger population, and their present traditional culture shows evidence of cultural loss, or "deculturation." So small a group with such a culture scarcely merits much attention, some might say, but a close scrutiny of their present predicament and their adaptations to it provides insight into what is happening around the world as powerless, small societies (and some large ones) are overrun by outsiders desirous of exploiting their land base and its presumed resources. And no other as yet undeveloped part of the world is under greater pressure than the great tropical forests of South and Central America. This pressure has consequences that will affect us all in the long run, but peoples like the Yuquí are directly in the path of destruction. Their case is instructive.

Some Yuquí are still in the process of being contacted, as the mission group were in the 1950s. Their traditional technological culture is very simple, and Stearman describes it in detail. Nor is their traditional social organization very complex. Their political organization is almost nonexistent. And yet the processes of change and adaptation are representative of such processes everywhere. In particular it is noteworthy that the Yuquí, who seem to have little to give up, resist attempts to change them and cling to their own ways. The deep-seated need of humankind to retain and celebrate ethnic and cultural identity is apparent.

There is a widespread tendency among nonanthropologists to regard anthropology as the study of the remote and exotic, or the study of "bones and stones." The study of the Yuquí makes it clear that anthropology is more than this. It is the study of change and response to events and pressures put in motion during our time, which in one way or another we all will encounter. Students who read this case study will enlarge their concept of anthropology and its role in the modern world as well as learn about the Yuquí and their situation.

GEORGE AND LOUISE SPINDLER
Series Editors
Calistoga, California

Preface

In no region of the earth is the demand for land more intense than in the great tropical forests. The original inhabitants of these immense wilderness areas are frequently small bands of foragers or village horticulturalists who supplement their hunting and gathering with gardens of plantains, manioc, and sweet potatoes. Unfortunately, in the minds of many, this way of life is seen as backward and unproductive. It stands in the way of development, of progress, of national destiny. A tropical forest is considered by most developing nations to be an untapped resource that will ultimately solve problems of overpopulated cities, poverty, hunger, and political restiveness. As has been the case in other places and times, wilderness areas are designated as vacant land, awaiting only the civilizing forces of the pioneer. It is seldom recognized by governments or the colonizers themselves that indigenous populations have any rightful claim to the wilderness they depend on for their existence. Rather, aboriginals are defined as savage and, like the land they inhabit, are considered to need taming. Nor is it conceded that foraging is a rational adaptation, one often more compatible with the fragile environment of the tropical rain forest than are the accepted patterns of intensive farming.

Once wilderness tracts are opened for settlement, peasants move across the landscape like locusts, leaving in their wake the devastation of slash-and-burn agricultural methods abused to their limit. Many indigenous peoples are simply swallowed up in the process, unwittingly but eagerly trading a simpler life for the glitter of cheap gadgetry, processed foods, and alcohol as a swift escape from pressures never before experienced.

Others may fight back, albeit in a war they have no chance of winning. They are labeled savages, beasts, animals. Because they have become impediments to the claiming of the wilderness, their demise has been swift: a well-aimed rifle; a bag of poisoned sugar placed along a trail; or a flu-infected shirt dropped from an airplane (Davis 1977).

Those indigenous groups that do manage to survive are usually large enough to withstand the initial decimation of their numbers from forced acculturation and disease. Anthropologists have found that most native peoples whose population is less than 500 have little chance for long-term cultural survival. Undoubtedly, there are other factors, such as intervention, that contribute to cultural survival. Conservationists, anthropologists, and missionaries, each with a different agenda but willing to bring to bear pressure on national agencies concerned with indigenous affairs, have been instrumental in fighting genocide and ethnocide. It is an ongoing struggle, however, and requires constant vigilance. Even in the case of the Yanomamö Indians, who number well over 10,000 and have received worldwide attention, the battle goes on to protect their homeland from outside interests (Bodley 1982).

This scenario is being enacted over and over again in South America's Amazon Basin. Bolivia is one of many nations sharing part of the region, in an area referred to as the east, or *oriente*. Although Bolivia is commonly considered an Andean country, with its governmental centers and well-known links to the Inca past resting in the highlands, almost two-thirds of its national domain lies in the *oriente*. The history of Bolivia has been marked by ongoing political struggles and turmoil that for generations have largely bypassed the eastern provinces. For highlanders, the *oriente* was the "green hell" described by author Julian Duguid in 1931 that harbored only savage Indians, half-civilized *mestizos*, wild animals, and tropical diseases. Governments of Bolivia found it a convenient dumping ground for political dissidents.

In the 1960s, increased political and economic pressures turned highland interests from the unprofitable tin mines and scarce farmland eastward, to the large expanses of lowland forest and plains. In other countries, such as Brazil, plans were being put in motion to begin to tap the presumed wealth of this largely unexplored region. Like its neighbors, the Bolivian government initiated programs to encourage pioneer settlement in its lowland territories. The movement began slowly at first; but as people increasingly braved the uncertainties of the lowland wilderness, more were encouraged to make the decision to relocate.

In the few remote regions of Bolivian rain forest that have eluded the axe and machete, nomadic foragers continue to exist. But the world is closing in on them as well, often with disastrous consequences as Indian and pioneer come face to face. One such people are the Yuquí, a group of hunters and gatherers forced to give up their way of life or perish at the hands of their enemies—the settlers.

The Yuquí do not have the advantage of strength of numbers. The one band now settled at the mission station on the Chimoré River consists of 73 individuals, only 30 of whom are adults. There are at least two additional groups still in the forest that are now in the process of being contacted by mission teams. From all reports, however, their numbers are few and growing smaller. In the fall of 1985, 11 forest Yuquí were killed in a skirmish with settlers. Even if these groups eventually are contacted and merged with those at the Chimoré, the total Yuquí population would barely reach 150. Thus the Yuquí, like so many foraging people before them, face the very real threat of extinction. Yet it remains my hope that this ethnography and a few scattered documents will not be their only legacy to the world, the only confirmation of their existence. This, then, is the story of the Yuquí, of their life as it once was and as it is now. It is also a study of the missionaries who first made contact with the Yuquí and their influence on the lives of these forest people.

Acknowledgments

Although this ethnography covers my field experiences among the Yuquí during 1982 and 1983, it is also the product of almost 25 years of involvement in lowland Bolivia. That now represents almost half of my life, a long time to acquire friends and colleagues who have contributed in many ways to my ongoing research efforts. I am therefore confronted with the impossible task of trying to list all of those individuals to whom I owe a great debt of gratitude. I hope they will forgive me in not doing this and will permit me instead to give everyone simply a collective, but heartfelt, thank-you.

In terms of this latest research effort, there are a few special people I would like to recognize for their assistance: Joan Burr of the Division of Sponsored Research of the University of Central Florida and Marianne Schmink of the Amazon Research and Training Program at the University of Florida for their funding support and encouragement of my work. I am also grateful to those individuals who furthered my research in Bolivia by assisting me with many of the logistical problems of working in the field, especially Ray Cowell, Jack Anderson, Hugo Daniel Ruíz, and the pilots of Alas de Paz. A number of people have contributed to the preparation of this ethnography by providing excellent critical commentary on the contents and suggestions for inclusions or elaboration: Bob and Mary Garland, David Jones, Linda Moore, Kent Redford, Warren Shapiro, George and Louise Spindler, Susan Stans, Tony Stocks, David Stoll, Dick Strickler, several anonymous readers, and the editors of Holt, Rinehart and Winston. I, of course, take full responsibility for the final version. A special thank-you to Karen Lynette and Jo Fields, who provided me with rapid and accurate wordprocessing throughout the development of the manuscript, and to Siglinde Quirk, for graphics.

Finally, my continuing work in Bolivia would not have been possible without the support of my family: my children Garrett and Erin, who have put up with a traveling mother since birth, and my husband, Mike, who miraculously manages to keep it all together during my oftentimes extended absences and to whom this ethnography is dedicated.

Contents

List of Illustrations

1/Fieldwork Among
the Yuquí

A PRELIMINARY VISIT

I first considered the possibility of doing research among the Yuquí while I was preparing to undertake a restudy of the Sirionó Indians. A colleague in Bolivia, German anthropologist Jürgen Riester, had been corresponding with me and suggested I look into the Yuquí as well. Riester wrote that it was believed the recently contacted Yuquí were related to the Sirionó but that few people other than missionaries had spent much time among this group. Since I was anticipating a preliminary site visit to Bolivia in 1982 prior to a more lengthy stay, he suggested I try to make a side trip to the Yuquí camp. Riester cautioned me, however, that the New Tribes Mission, the mission group working with the Yuquí, discouraged outsiders from coming to the Chimoré.

My initial contact with the New Tribes missionaries working with the Yuquí was at the mission home in Cochabamba. Although I had expected to leave the Yuquí segment of my research until the end of the trip, when I arrived in Bolivia I was told by a mission official in Santa Cruz that the senior couple at the Yuquí camp would be leaving shortly for a year's "furlough." If I wanted to visit the Chimoré, he explained, I would need their approval first. I quickly flew from Santa Cruz to Cochabamba, where I met John and Helen Porter, who were scheduled to leave Bolivia the following day. They interviewed me briefly and then arranged for the mission pilot to take me to the Chimoré on an already scheduled flight. By radio they were able to communicate with missionary Hank Monroe at the camp, and it was agreed I would stay at the home of Mike and Mary Daniels while they were away from the Chimoré. The Daniels, the camp's newest missionary couple, were to be gone for a week at a conference and would fly out on the plane that was taking me in. It was also decided that I would take my meals with the schoolteacher, Mariano Ichu, and his family.

After a short flight over the mountains from Cochabamba, I arrived at the Yuquí camp. The Daniels greeted me quickly as they boarded the plane for the return flight to Cochabamba. The only missionary remaining was Hank Monroe, a man I judged to be in his late 50s or early 60s.

I settled myself into a spare room on the first floor of the Daniels' two-story house, keeping an eye on things and checking to make certain the old

1

kerosene refrigerator had fuel and was operating properly. During the time I was alone in the house I met Monica,[1] a Yuquí woman about my age who had been twice widowed as a result of hostile encounters with outsiders. Recently, the Yuquí camp had been relocated to avoid seasonal flooding; as a woman without the assistance of a spouse, Monica had been unable to complete the move. Her eldest son, Jaime, had taken off about half the tin roofing from her old place and carried it to the new site, where he had erected support poles and a roof frame; but the house remained unfinished while he worked on his own dwelling. I volunteered to help Monica finish her house.

Monica knew a few words of Spanish, I was learning some Yuquí, and gestures filled in the gaps. I immediately determined that Monica knew how to use an axe, was strong as an ox, and would be a willing working companion. However, as the two of us began gathering materials for the house, our efforts were embarrassingly reminiscent of an old Laurel and Hardy movie. I took charge of designing the form the house would take, since I had had some previous experience in house construction. Monica's expertise lay in locating the materials we would require. Most of the wood we needed would come from a tall, stately palm called *pachiuba* (*Socratea exorrhiza*), which could be split into boards for walls and a sleeping platform. With axes, machetes, and Monica in the lead, we started off into the forest.

Monica found a stand of four *pachiuba* palms a short distance from her house site. I looked up into the crowns and saw that there was a good bit of tangle and growth there that might impede the trees' fall. I pointed out the problem to Monica, who seemed to understand but appeared unconcerned. I shrugged my shoulders. We took turns chopping and soon the pithy wood core was cut through. We heard the final crack as the tree gave way, both of us stepping away from the trunk. Nothing happened. Our tree was hanging there, swinging like a 30-foot pendulum. Monica plucked at her hair and muttered "*Eturā biti!*" a favorite Yuquí phrase used when things are not going well. We both grabbed the trunk to try to pull it free and soon were swinging back and forth like bell ringers. But the tree was stuck fast. Then Monica indicated we should chop down the next palm, using the weight of that tree to break loose the first. It seemed like a good idea so once again we began cutting. Our aim was perfect, and our second palm fell into the first but succeeded only in knocking it down to about a 45° angle. Now we had two trees hung up. The plan this time was to climb up the leaning trunks and jump on them. Many *Eturā biti*s later we decided that this technique was not going to work either. But Monica refused to give up. We cut down the last two trees, felling them on top of the others, having finally achieved a pile of four *pachiubas* inextricably entwined in the surrounding vegetation. By now we had spent most of the morning cutting down trees and had nothing to

1. All of the Yuquí have taken Spanish names now rather than continue to use their given names in Yuquí. These are the names they are known by, and so I will use them as well. The kinship chart (Figure 9) lists both names of those individuals who previously had Yuquí names. Children no longer are given names in their own language; hence younger individuals appear listed only in Spanish.

show for our labor. Monica motioned for me to follow. We would try a new location.

We moved to the edge of the small swamp behind the Yuquí camp that was filled with *chuchillo* (*Gynerium sagittatum*) reed and some large trees. There was a good-sized *pachiuba* among the trees, but I estimated that if we cut it properly, it would fall clear. True to form, Monica was swinging her axe harder than I and before we realized it, the tree was falling off center. We watched it drop into the crown of a tree nearby. Discouraged, I squatted down and rested my head in my arms. From a short distance away, I heard chopping. Looking up, I saw Monica attacking an enormous hardwood growing at the edge of the swamp.

Her plan again evidently was to use the weight of this tree to knock the *pachiuba* loose. But if this tree fell the wrong way, it would land in the middle of her half-completed house. I grabbed Monica's arm and indicated the problem. She nodded, smiled, and resumed cutting. At that moment, the schoolteacher's son appeared to tell me that lunch was ready and to come quickly before the food got cold. I needed little urging to leave Monica to her impending disaster.

After lunch with the Ichu family, I made my way with trepidation back to the Yuquí camp. As I came down the trail, I saw Monica busily roasting a plantain at a small fire in her unfinished house. I was greatly relieved to see that both she and the house were safe. She smiled at me and we walked back to where she had been cutting on the huge tree. As we stood on the edge of the swamp, my mouth fell open in wonderment. Monica had succeeded in dropping the big hardwood into the crotch of another large tree, pinning the *pachiuba* between them. I decided we would call it a day and returned to the Daniels' house.

The following day Monica and I were at it again, only now we had fortunately broken our streak of bad luck in felling trees. With several good *pachiubas* on the ground, Monica showed me how to make palm boards, a skill I had not learned in the region where I had previously worked. It was a laborious chore, taking strength and patience to pound the palm trunks with the broad head of the axe and to make hundreds of small vertical cuts along the trunk until it could be split open and flattened. Then the pithy core had to be peeled loose, leaving the hard palm wood exterior intact. The palm pith was full of needle-like fibers, and soon Monica's and my hands were sore from punctures. At this point, I walked back to the Daniels' house and borrowed a pair of cotton work gloves I had seen in the storeroom. The work was much easier with the gloves since not only was I protected from the spiny fibers, but I could get a better grip on the wet pith. After a while, I handed the gloves to Monica, who seemed delighted to try them. She struggled a moment before I realized she had never had on gloves before. While understanding how they worked, Monica was unable to get her fingers in the holes properly. Soon we were laughing uproariously as we both tried to get the gloves over those ten stubborn fingers.

By the end of the week, the house was progressing well but still needed a good deal of work. I was enjoying my time with Monica and the opportunity to get to know a few other Yuquí as well. Thus when the Daniels returned, I decided, with their consent, to remain a while longer. They were grateful for my efforts with the old refrigerator and that I had kept the house swept and clean during their absence. Mike and Mary Daniels were new to the field, this being their first assignment. They were pleasant people from my home state of California, and we seemed to find a number of shared experiences. I helped Mary around the house when I was not out with Monica, and assisted her with the clinic. She seemed overwhelmed by this responsibility since she had been given little training in medical work and was having to learn by experience. She was genuinely thankful one morning when I happened to be present to help out when Daniel, Monica's youngest son, sliced all of his toes across the bottom on a serrated *chuchillo* leaf while he was out hunting.

Mary expressed regret that I was not taking meals with them but explained that those arrangements had been made by others. I told her that I was enjoying eating with the Ichu family and was getting to know both Mariano and Leonarda quite well. They were a typical indigenous peasant family very much like the people I had worked with as a Peace Corps volunteer. At first, Leonarda was shy and embarrassed around me, fearful that I would scorn her food, which, she explained, was "not like what the missionaries eat." I laughed and said that I had spent many years eating food just like she prepared and enjoyed it very much. She relaxed and soon we were good friends. I tried to arrive for our main meal (at noon) early enough to help with the food preparation. There in the kitchen with Leonarda and the several Yuquí women who were always present, we would discuss the day's events. I have found that kitchens are always excellent places to do fieldwork since women are most at ease there and engage in free, unstructured conversation with few inhibitions. I also came to realize that Leonarda was very lonely at the Chimoré, having no one enough like her for her to feel comfortable. The missionary women were involved in their own activities and found Leonarda "native" like the Yuquí. Thus, while they were always kind to her, they had little in common. For Leonarda, the Yuquí were just as strange to her as she was to the missionaries. She spent a great deal of time with the Yuquí women teaching them to cook, sew, and bake, but did not understand them and found their ways and treatment of her savage at times.

Monica and I worked on her house for another week or so, finishing the roof, walls, and sleeping platform. During all this, the Daniels were enter- tained by my tales of Monica's and my exploits in house building. During the evening hours Mike would engage me in conversations of a religious nature, which after a while I found draining, especially after a long day of physical exertion in the heat and humidity of the forest. But he was also interested in broadening his own knowledge and of sharing my perceptions of the Yuquí. I found that both he and Mary were trying very hard to be "good missionaries" but still were struggling to learn Spanish. Yuquí, they said, seemed insur- mountable. Mike was a large man with a jovial nature but lacking in manual skills. He had brought in a piece of finished mahogany to try to repair the

Photo 1. Monica. After several false starts, we finally completed her house.

Yuquí's broken machete handles. When he saw that I was good with my hands, Mike asked if I would teach the Yuquí men to make the new handles. There was a big palm wood shed behind the Daniels' house that had a great many tools in maddening disarray, but in looking for a hammer and pliers to work on Monica's house, I had found what I needed. The Yuquí men had access to the tool shed as well, were frequently in there tinkering with their guns, and so had a knowledge of what was available. The old workshop served our purposes well, and before long I had a veritable production line of men cutting out handles, making rivets from nails, and wrapping the finished products with wire for additional strength. During all this, the young headman, Leonardo, asked me if I would teach him to make a canoe paddle. Mike found us a board of the right length and thickness, but it was a dense hardwood and seemed to take forever to cut out and shape. The result was a bit heavy but nonetheless a fine paddle, which Leonardo and I worked on diligently for several days until it was smooth to the touch. I was pleased when I returned a year later to see that he had the paddle in his house, now darkened from use but still intact.

Before leaving Bolivia, the Porters had told me of the existence of the mission's "Culture File," a compilation of cultural data on the Yuquí spanning almost ten years. When I had finished with Monica's house, I asked the Daniels if I could see the file. Hank brought it to the house one evening, and

I realized what a mine of information it was. I then began what was to be, between other chores, a ten-day task of copying verbatim all of the information the file contained. I remember pausing one morning, as writer's cramp began to take its toll, to reflect that with a few nickels and a photocopying machine, I could have completed the entire project in about 15 minutes.

I left the Chimoré to continue with a related research project after having spent five weeks with the Yuquí and the New Tribes missionaries. It had been an interesting experience in many respects and I was eager to return for a more lengthy stay.

PREPARING FOR FIELDWORK

Having completed a preliminary site survey, I applied for a leave from my university teaching duties the following year. Once funding was secured, I wrote to the Chimoré to tell them of my plans to spend half of my year's leave with the Yuquí. In a letter from Hank, I learned that the Daniels had taken another post and had been replaced by a different couple, Bill and Jane Brown. Hank also mentioned that the Porters would return in August.

I took a bush plane to the Chimoré camp on September 9, 1983 and was surprised to hear that the Porters had not yet arrived but would do so that same afternoon. Having been told by the other missionaries that the Porters would be there momentarily, I waited at the missionary end of camp to greet them. But the flight was delayed, and when the plane finally landed, it was dusk. By the time we had finished welcoming back the Porters so that Leonarda, Mariano, and several of the Yuquí were free to help me carry my gear back to the Yuquí camp, it was nearing sundown. I knew that it would now be impossible to cut *chuchillo* reed for tent poles (I had been forced to leave them behind because of weight limitations) so I settled for an abandoned house Leonarda and the Yuquí showed me. The former occupants, Humberto and Gloria, had squabbled with their neighbors and moved to another location, where they built a new house. Leonarda and the Yuquí helped me fashion a sleeping platform where I put up my mosquito net. Monica brought a burning brand from her house and started a fire. I made tea, shared the kilo of cheese I had brought as a gift with everyone present, and went to bed. A cold front had passed through earlier in the day and the night was chilly. I climbed onto my makeshift bed and zippered myself into my mosquito net. It was totally enclosed, giving me a sense of security that nothing would crawl in with me despite my poor shelter. Once inside my sleeping bag, I closed my eyes, trying to imagine that I was in more familiar surroundings. How many times before I had experienced the same sensation, as have other anthropologists on that first uncertain night in the field. I pondered what surely lay ahead of me: the good, the bad, the unknown. Also as before, I wondered what it was that brought me here, to give up the comforts of home and the warmth of my family in exchange for the small, nagging hardships and that hollow feeling of loneliness. Before falling asleep, I mused ruefully that anthropology was somehow much more romantic after the fact, when one was standing in the safe neutrality of a classroom.

After consulting with the missionaries and the Yuquí about a house site, I spent the next several days clearing brush. While I was busy preparing the area for my house, I received a visit from a young Bolivian man living with our only neighbor, a Yuracaré named Francisco Blanco. He needed work, he explained, and asked if I would consider hiring him to build my house. This seemed like a stroke of good fortune. We worked out an acceptable daily wage, and the young man, Oscar, began to cut and set palm posts. A few of the Yuquí men would stop by to help us now and then, but would take off without notice to hunt or fish. Oscar rapidly became disgruntled with their lack of dependability and was also beginning to suffer under the strain of the young girls' almost constant teasing while he was working. One day he failed to show up. I followed the trail upriver to Francisco's house, where I found Oscar. He looked embarrassed to see me but explained that he had found "other work" and would not be able to complete the house. I paid him for his labor and left. The Yuquí men and women helped me finish the house, and I moved in three weeks after construction had begun, much longer than I had anticipated. With the tent tied inside the house frame and off the ground, I had achieved a relatively bug-free, rain- and wind-resistant workplace. I could now begin fieldwork in earnest.

THE YUQUÍ

While doing fieldwork among the Ik (pronounced "eek") of Uganda, Africa, anthropologist Colin Turnbull challenged the old anthropological myth that the researcher will like and admire the people he or she is studying. A corollary of this assumption is that to the uninformed outsider who does not "understand" the culture, a group may seem hostile, unresponsive, or stoic, or may have any number of less admirable characteristics; but to the trained observer who truly knows "his or her" people, these attributes are only a façade presented to outsiders. What Turnbull finally had to concede, however, was that overall the Ik were not a very likable people. His portrait of the Ik as selfish, uncaring, and uninterested even in the survival of their own children is understandable when he describes their history of displacement, social disruption, and the constant threat of starvation. Nonetheless, an intellectual understanding of the factors contributing to Ik personality and behavior did not make it any easier for Turnbull to deal emotionally with the day-to-day interactions of fieldwork.

For me, knowing of Turnbull's situation alleviated some of my own anxieties in dealing with the Yuquí. As was Turnbull's, my previous field experiences among other peoples had been very positive. In the anthropologist's terms, this meant that I was accepted quite rapidly as a friend and that my informants were open and cooperative. The Yuquí did not fit any of these patterns. But like Turnbull, I understood something of the Yuquí past and

Photo 2. Victor prepares thatch for roofing.

Photo 3. Joel, putting thatch on my roof.

Photo 4. My house at Chimoré camp.

thus on an intellectual level could comprehend that since they were a hunted, beleaguered people being threatened with extinction I could not expect them to be warm, friendly, and welcoming. Still, on an emotional level it was very difficult to cope with my frequent feelings of anger and resentment at having to put up with their teasing, taunting, and testing on an almost daily basis. My only consolation was that while I was often the brunt of this activity, so were they themselves. I am uncertain whether I finally came to understand the Yuquí, or simply became hardened to their particular way of dealing with the world. By doing favors for people, I incurred their indebtedness, and these debts could be translated into favors owed. How I chose to collect was up to me. As favors mounted, I found that relationships with individual Yuquí were better. Then came the challenges. Could I be easily duped or taken advantage of? At first, I extended kindnesses gratuitously and was mocked. I learned to show my anger and stubbornness, to demand something in return for a tool lent or a service provided. Rather than alienate the Yuquí, this behavior (which I found difficult and distasteful throughout my stay) conferred prestige. The more I provided and then demanded in return, the more the Yuquí were willing to accept me. In the Yuquí world, as in any other, respect must be earned. But unlike many other peoples, for the Yuquí, kindness alone is not enough. In the end it is strength that is valued and that earns respect.

This lesson was driven home one day when I was physically assaulted by one of the young women, Susana. I had taught the children to sing a few old songs that I could play on a battered guitar given to one of the older lads by a colonist upriver. Their favorite was "Oh, Suzanna!" But because it was in English, Susana, the Yuquí woman, was uncertain if it was meant to tease her. One afternoon as we were all seated on a log singing, she suddenly leaped on me, laughing, but also quite serious about establishing her dominance. Although it was done in fun, I quickly realized that much more was at stake. Susana outweighed me by at least 30 pounds, and I soon found myself in the infamous Yuquí choke hold I had read about in the mission's "Culture File." Susana's strong thumb and fingers were wrapped around my windpipe. I could feel the tears well up in my eyes, the fear beginning to creep in that she would hold on until I passed out. If I did, I knew, I would be an object of ridicule. Still, I restrained myself, a lifetime of parental admonitions and the moral teachings of my own culture forbidding me to respond with violence. Then I experienced the sensation that everything was becoming quiet. I could see mouths laughing but the only sound was my own heart pounding. From some deep place within, the need to fight back overcame all of my inhibitions; I could feel the adrenaline begin to clear my head. I reached up with one hand and grabbed Susana just as she had me, but at the same time pulling her free arm behind her back. Now there was a different look in her eyes. The laughing stopped. I could feel her windpipe resisting my grip but tightened down even more. I was both exhilarated and disgusted by my actions. Finally, I rolled her off me, laughing as I did. There was no real victor, but at least I had held my own. For the next several days, the Yuquí admired the bruises on my neck like some badge of courage. We continued singing "Oh, Suzanna!" without further incident.

I also began to realize that my behavior was as carefully scrutinized by the Yuquí as theirs was by me. This scrutiny was more than just curiosity or even judgment. Once I had been accepted as a person of some worth and value, a status that took great energy on my part to achieve, the Yuquí began to consider my responses to given situations with thought and reflection. They are a people insecure in this new world of theirs. There is an innate comprehension that much of their old understanding of the world no longer applies. Because they are a very small group that has experienced long-term reduction in population and has lost much of its original culture, there is very little of their tradition that they are willing to fight for. Like the Ik of Africa, for many generations the Yuquí have had little time to do much other than try to stay alive. This in itself is a brutalizing experience, as Turnbull found in Uganda, a way of life that can rob people of much of their basic humanity.

Now that life for the Yuquí is more secure, they have begun to reassess themselves as human beings. It is a difficult period for them. They are attempting a kind of behavior modification in order to put themselves more in step with the values of the world around them, both missionary and Bolivian.

At times there is self-deprecation, something difficult to witness. An act of unkindness may be followed by the recriminations of others and then of self. There is a confusion about what "correct" behavior should be. In the past, the rules were different. Fights were common, and still are. But now there is negative sanction from missionaries and from other Yuquí for behavior that is considered inappropriate. The Yuquí have certainly mellowed since contact, and most seem to prefer this mellowing; but it is also quite superficial, as evidenced by the frequency of violent upheavals I witnessed in the group. They are fighting a battle with themselves to become "civilized," to measure up to different expectations. They are still uncertain what these are and do not quite understand how to achieve them, often blaming themselves when they fail. I was the first outsider to live with them in their camp. Naively, I thought this would bring instant acceptance. Yuquí reaction, however, was not delight at my decision. These highly status-conscious people thought I must be an undesirable, an outcast; otherwise, why wasn't I at the missionary end of camp with my own people? I was taunted about this for weeks. After a while, I suppose the novelty simply wore off, although I doubt that any of the Yuquí to this day understand my reasons for being in their camp. In spite of these constraints, my palm and *chuchillo* reed house, located in the center of the camp, became a point of interest, a place to gather now and then, and a bit of diversion from the routine of life. Since it was also the cleanest area, kept scrupulously free of weeds and brush to discourage snakes, the children liked to play there and, much to my chagrin, the camp dogs chose the area for nightly battles.

Being in the midst of the Yuquí camp had its drawbacks, however. Because I was an outsider, an *Abá*, it was assumed I would play a mediating role to settle disputes. I quickly dispelled this idea by refusing to take part or take sides in arguments. Finally, when fights occurred, I was simply ignored. My neutral role, nonetheless, did not keep stampedes through my yard from occurring on a regular basis. Because of the central location of my house, every major and many minor arguments brought everyone out of their homes, through my grounds, and to the place where the fight was occurring. At times it was like some mad comedy: screams and shouts from one house responded to by relatives shouting across camp to discern the nature and severity of the problem. If the outpouring of emotion continued, people would begin to gather like lemmings—men, women, and children all running toward the disturbance. Invariably, the group would merge at my house, shouting, waving arms, and raising dust as they rushed to their destination. A circle would form around the offending couple, usually a man and woman disagreeing about food, money, or unfaithfulness, and sides would be taken. This was always somewhat arbitrary, however, since everyone is related to everyone else. Normally, close relatives would defend their own, but not always. If a mother thought her daughter was in the wrong, she would be just as likely to side with her daughter's spouse, especially if he were a good provider of meat.

Much of the time, I had the impression that the Yuquí were simply tolerating me. Their relations with the missionaries tended to be of a similar nature in spite of their years together. Although the Yuquí have yielded to pacification and a sedentary existence out of a greater need to survive, they remain a proud, stubborn people. Much to the consternation of the missionaries, most have not become professed Christians. It is not that the Yuquí cling tenaciously to old beliefs and resist Christianity; they simply get what they want out of life without conforming to its demands.

As time went on, my interactions with different members of the band began to change subtly. Monica had been my almost constant companion during my first visit, primarily because the completion of her house required that we spend many hours together. This companionship decreased dramatically during my second visit, although it was Monica who first brought me fire, an act symbolic of our mutual trust. Her house was now located some distance from mine; the brush had grown up, making direct access difficult; and casual meetings were infrequent. Monica spent most of her time with her sons Jaime and Daniel, who were both active and successful hunters. Without a husband and competing with her daughter-in-law for meat, Monica had to be present on a hunt to receive her fair share. Of all the men, Jaime and Daniel went the farthest each day and were gone the longest. Thus I saw Monica only briefly now and then, and the intensity of our former friendship decreased.

Propinquity is a great catalyst, and so it was with my nearest neighbors that I formed my closest alliances. Behind me were Elsa and Joel and their three children, Raquel, Margarita, and Ramón. Next door lived their eldest son, Lucas, married to Florencia. Florencia had an infant son, Marcos, who was a sickly child and received only sporadic attention from his mother, who was young and often bored with the responsibilities of motherhood. Florencia spent a great deal of time with me in my kitchen, sitting in my string hammock with Marcos draped listlessly over her lap. Her young husband ignored her as did her parents-in-law, so Florencia shared her time between my kitchen and Leonarda's. The younger children, ten-year-old Margarita and eight-year-old Ramón, were a delight, laughing and pestering me constantly to teach them Spanish, new songs, or games. Every morning I would cook up a pot of cornmeal mush for breakfast and let them have the leftovers. Soon they began to wake me before dawn to hurry along breakfast. Finally, I worked out a plan with them: They would wait until the sun was right above the papaya tree beside my kitchen (about 6 A.M.), light my fire, and put on the kettle. When the water boiled, they would wake me. I added extra meal to the pot, we all enjoyed mush with sugar and powdered milk each morning, and I avoided the onerous chore of having to start my own fire.

Their mother, Elsa, and I had what I thought was a peculiar relationship, but what in time I realized was quite typical for the Yuquí. She did not see my feeding her children as in any way a favor to her—that was an agreement among Margarita, Ramón, and me. One day we got into an argument about whose papaya trees were growing along the trail between her house and mine. Elsa had at least twenty trees by her house and I had one. The trail was public property from my perspective, but obviously not from hers. To avoid further conflict, I kept my papaya picking to the evening hours when Elsa was safely inside her house. Invariably, she would come by the next morning and see a papaya on my table and interrogate me about its origin. If I could not come up with a satisfactory answer, I was in for a tongue lashing. Then she would go back to her house, find a large, ripe papaya, and offer it to me at an exorbitant price. I was not allowed simply to refuse the offer. After several minutes of haggling, she would take my money and return triumphantly to her house. Once again, she had gotten the better of me.

On the occasion that she and Joel went on an extended hunt, Elsa informed me that I would watch her house to make certain that no one stole anything; in particular, I was to keep a close watch on her papaya trees. As payment, she noted gruffly, I could eat all the papayas I wanted, but only until their return.

In spite of our frequent bickering over one thing or another, usually Elsa's disgruntlement at something I had done or failed to do, she sent me meat and fish when there was an adequate supply for the family. This was not frequently, however, since neither Joel nor his grown son Lucas was often successful in the hunt. Still, it was her recognition that we had an ongoing reciprocal relationship. It was also Elsa who amiably agreed to demonstrate various crafts, such as the weaving of palm mats, and permitted me to photograph her, something many of the Yuquí would avoid if caught at a bad moment.

My status in camp continued to improve as I refused to become the Yuquí's handmaiden and demonstrated that I had many useful skills. I assisted the headman Leonardo in making shelves and a table, and helped Lucas put together a door made from hand-hewn boards he had crafted, and Tomás and I fabricated a storage platform. This required a good bit of ingenuity since the men had only a few bent nails they had found, a few new ones they had bought at the store, and pieces of scrap lumber from missionary packing crates. Often, they did not have enough materials to make what they desired, and we would have to carefully redesign our project so that the supplies we had on hand would suffice. My payment for this type of help, which I learned not to give gratuitously, was usually meat. The Yuquí place the highest value on this commodity and it pained them most to have to give it up.

Part of my research involved the daily weighing of fish and game takes to attempt to obtain a profile of their subsistence activities. When I first began this activity, I received little cooperation from the Yuquí. I would have to gather up the animals or fish myself and weigh them. If the animals were heavy, there was no offer of assistance. I frequently faced the frustrating situation of arriving too late, only to find that what had been caught had already been eaten. I would be given a disinterested reply to my questions about what had been brought back to camp. At times, I dreaded having to make my rounds visiting each house to gather hunting and fishing statistics because of the surly response I often received.

The Yuquí's reluctance to assist with game weighing was ultimately overcome after a trip I made with Francisco Blanco and several of the Indians to Puerto Villarroel, the nearest settlement. Francisco had a large, flat-bottomed barge he had built to take his crops to market. Wanting to borrow the missionaries' outboard motor to power the boat, he offered to take along several of the Yuquí so they could sell some of the previous year's rice crop. I decided to go along both to be able to observe the Yuquí out in the world and to take a short break from the confines of the camp.

Expecting a quiet three-day interlude from camp routine, I took along a little money and a change of clothes, but left behind my sleeping bag and mosquito net. The missionaries had assured me that there was now a hotel in Villarroel where I could stay and that the rooms were screened. I was looking forward to a few days of town life, something cold to drink, and, with luck, perhaps even a movie.

The barge was heavily loaded with bags of rice, plantains, manioc, and papayas to sell in Villarroel. Francisco had brought along his two wives, Concebida and Delsi, their young children, and Oscar. From the Yuquí camp were Leonardo, Lorenzo, Antonia, Tomás, Marta, and several of their small children. We found places to sit on the huge cargo and slowly began our journey down the Chimoré and up the Ichilo River. It was well after dark when we made the last turn around a wide bend to be met by small blinking kerosene lights in the windows of houses along the river. It was a strange sight to see that many people in one place after the solitude of the Chimoré and the Ichilo for so many hours. Francisco tied the barge at a house across the river from the port town where he and the Yuquí would stay with one of his *compadres*. Once the barge was secured, Francisco, Oscar, and I borrowed a canoe and worked our way across the Ichilo toward the lighted streets of Villarroel. Francisco had caught three large fish during our trip that he wanted to sell while still fresh. I found the Hanover Hotel and checked in, telling Francisco and Oscar that I would see them the following morning when they came over with the barge to sell the produce.

Puerto Villarroel was a typical frontier boom town, full of wooden shacks and people out to make their fortune by any means possible. There were bars, stores, a sawmill, the Bolivian Petroleum Company camp, and the Navy base consisting of a few buildings, one or two boats to chase cocaine traffickers, and the Commandant's Office, which was also the local judicial authority. The gravel road from Cochabamba, part of the link with the uncompleted *Carretera Marginal de la Selva* (Marginal Highway of the Jungle) from Santa Cruz, ended at Villarroel and the Ichilo River. The Hanover Hotel, consisting of eight spartan rooms, was owned and run by an older woman from Cochabamba.

Dona María Ruth de Velasco, my host, was a shrewd woman who was making a good living from her hotel in the port town but dreamed of returning to a gentler existence in Cochabamba. She immediately took an interest in me and invited me to share a bottle of the coldest beer I could remember. Ruth was curious about my work and experiences with the Yuquí, but could not understand why anyone would want to study people in so remote a place.

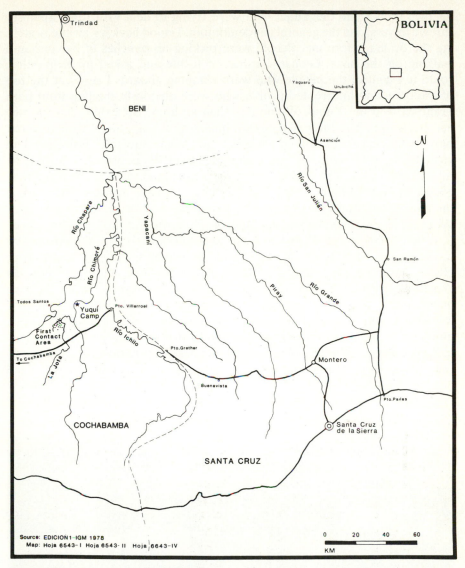

Figure 2. Traditional Yuquí territory

I was beginning to wonder myself why I was bruting it out in a place that was little more than an open swath of clearing in the endless forest. The bright lights, good food, cold beer, and relaxed conversation were in sharp contrast to many of my experiences of the past several weeks.

The next morning Ruth accompanied me down to the quay where Francisco had moored the barge. Evidently he and the Yuquí had just arrived, but word was spreading quickly that a boat had come in with fresh produce and rice. Soon, people began to swarm aboard. Francisco was busy seeing to his own sales while the Yuquí men were trying to deal with rapid Spanish, shrewd buyers, and the general pandemonium. I stood back for awhile, watching the drama before me. People were picking up bunches of bananas and walking off the boat. Leonardo came up to me and asked for help—they could not control the people who were climbing aboard. I stood at the top of the quay and intercepted people who were obviously stealing from both Francisco and the Yuquí. Within less than an hour, everything but the rice had been sold. The three Yuquí men had several bags, some their own but most belonging to the others who had not made the trip. Francisco had virtually his entire crop, 50 bags averaging about 100 pounds each, which he sold to one buyer. The man arrived with a truck and the two spent the next couple of hours weighing each sack, writing down the amount, and loading the rice on the truck. The Yuquí rice, I was told, had been sold to a woman. With everything seemingly under control, I returned to the hotel for lunch.

While I was eating, Francisco came to the door and stood there for a few moments. I invited him to my table and asked him if there was a problem. He answered no, but wondered if I would check some figures for him. He explained that he was about to go down to the rice buyer's store to receive payment and wanted to be certain that he had his totals correct. Francisco was literate, but like many peasants, was inexperienced in dealing with large numbers. I asked Ruth if she had a hand calculator, an item that is now common all over Bolivia. She went to her desk and removed a battery-operated calculator, and Francisco and I set to work figuring out what was owed

Photo 5. The main street of Puerto Villarroel, a typical frontier boom town.

him. We arrived at a total of 322,000 pesos, or about $425, a substantial amount of money. I decided to accompany Francisco down the road to observe the transaction, and the Yuquí men and women joined us. The buyer told Francisco he owed him 316,000 pesos. Francisco looked at me in puzzlement. There was some fast talking on the part of the buyer, and Francisco agreed he would take the money. The Yuquí men were watching all of this very carefully and seemed to understand that there was some discrepancy. At this point, I called Francisco aside and suggested that we go over all of the weights and check our figures with those of the buyer. He agreed. The storekeeper glared at me. One by one we checked our tallies, and then, letting the buyer use his own calculator, we added it all up. It came to 322,000 pesos. Francisco grinned from ear to ear and shook my hand. In stacks of 1000 pesos, all in one hundred peso notes, the money started coming over the counter. The Yuquí gathered around in astonishment. They had never seen so much currency. Francisco and I counted each stack, found that some lacked the full amount, and returned them so the buyer could make up the difference. When we were finished, Francisco put his huge pile of money into a flour sack and we all left.

We were to depart from Villarroel the following day, our third away from camp. By now the Yuquí had spent most of the money they had earned on candy, bread, condensed milk, a box of shotgun shells, and some clothing. They had spent not only their own, but their relatives' share as well. I knew there would be trouble when we got back to the Chimoré. By late afternoon, Francisco was still loading lumber and having the 11 empty fuel drums we had brought along filled with aviation gas for the missionaries. It would be another day before we could leave. I was getting somewhat anxious at the delay since my money was running low and I would now have another night's hotel bill to pay. The Yuquí were settled under a shed roof where they had spent the afternoon out of the sun between visits to the stores. I walked over to find out how their second day in town had been and was met by a highly agitated Lorenzo.

Lorenzo and Leonardo told me that the woman they had sold their rice to still owed them 4000 pesos. I asked them who she was and where she lived, but of course they did not know. Both men were extremely upset and could not understand why this woman, who had promised to return with their money, had failed to do so. I told them that it was probably hopeless, but that I would see what could be done. Back at the hotel I told Ruth what had transpired. With a determined look on her face, she grabbed her parasol and we set out to track down the woman who had the Yuquí's rice. Ruth worded her queries masterfully and seemed to know exactly who to see and in what sequence.

Within the hour we had located the two bags of rice and the woman who had bought them—an itinerant merchant operating a small stall in the market. I confronted her with the problem, and she explained that she had paid the full price: 8000 pesos for four *arrobas* (a measure of 25 pounds) of rice. Since the Yuquí were new at trading, I suspected that Lorenzo had become confused about the measures and the money he was to have received. I returned to tell him I had found the woman, but that she claimed she had given him the correct amount of money. It was then that Lorenzo told me there were six *arrobas* of rice not four. I found Francisco and asked him to meet me at the market with his large spring scale. When we were all present, we weighed the two bags. Lorenzo had been right—there were better than 150 pounds of rice. Francisco began to explain to the woman that she owed the Yuquí another 4000 pesos, but she got angry and shouted him down. By now a crowd had begun to gather in anticipation of a good row. Francisco, however, would not pursue the issue and walked away shrugging his shoulders. I was furious and jumped into the fracas. Soon the woman was nose to nose with me, arguing that in her village of Punata, an *arroba* was not 25 pounds, but 40. I turned to the spectators to ask if they had ever heard anything so ridiculous, and got a shout of support. The woman was beginning to weaken. At this point I let loose with my last but best volley: We would go to the naval Commandant and let him settle the matter. She demurred. The woman then admitted that she did not have the additional 4000 pesos but would give us the rice if we would return her 8000 pesos. While this seemed the best solution, I knew I would have a hard time getting together 8000 pesos since the Yuquí had already spent it. With the remainder of my money and loans from Ruth and Francisco, I paid off the woman and took possession of the rice. We were now faced with the problem of finding another buyer so I could repay the money I had borrowed. But within moments, a man appeared and offered us the 12,000 pesos Lorenzo and Leonardo should have received at the start. By nightfall, the transaction had been completed, the borrowed money had been returned, and the Yuquí had another 4000 pesos to spend. I went to supper feeling that at least we could now return to the Chimoré with our honor intact.

Shortly after dawn the next morning I was down at the river's edge waiting for Francisco to come over to buy last-minute supplies, pick me up, and head back to the Chimoré. As the mist began to clear, I could see movement on the other side of the Ichilo; the Yuquí were preparing to leave. Up and down the high bank they scrambled, loading children and supplies. Then they sat for awhile, apparently waiting for Francisco. I watched them from the shoreline for over two hours, but the barge remained moored in place. After five hours, I decided I would have to find a way across the river to determine the reason for the delay. A man with a small skiff and motor offered to take me over and back for a reasonable fee, so I jumped aboard. Minutes later we pulled up beside the barge where most of the Yuquí were sitting, looking glum. When I asked Leonardo where Francisco was, he pointed up the bank toward the houses above. I was met first by the senior wife, Concebida, and then by Delsi, both worried and angry. They took me around to the back of one of the houses, where Francisco was seated at a small table with three other men. Two of them were asleep on folded arms. Littered around the base of the table I counted 27 empty liter beer bottles. I shook Francisco, and he struggled unsteadily to his feet with a sheepish grin. Oscar was standing

Photo 6. Riverboats tied up at Puerto Villarroel awaiting cargoes.

nearby, obviously not a part of the celebration and cold sober. I motioned Oscar over to the kitchen where we could talk. He agreed with me that the drinking could go on for days, especially now that Francisco had money. Both of the wives, Oscar said, were frightened that he would spend most of their year's income on beer. I also expressed my concern that I was nearly out of money, the Yuquí had none, and there was no way to alert the missionaries to our plight. Then I asked him if he could pilot us back to the Chimoré. Oscar nodded. He had used the outboard before and felt he was capable of operating it. He had also made the trip to Villarroel several times and knew both rivers well enough to make the journey safely. The real problem, he explained, was that in order to leave we had to have a *zarpe*. I had never heard this term before. A *zarpe*, Oscar explained, was a permit from the Commandant's Office to leave port. Without it, the Navy would run us down and detain us. He was certain the *Commandante* would never issue it to us without Francisco, the boat's owner, being present. We approached Francisco and tried to reason with him, at first cajoling and joking; but when he remained steadfast in his intent to continue drinking, we began to threaten. Nothing worked. He became loud and abusive. I told Oscar I would try to get the *zarpe* myself and returned to Villarroel with the boatman.

Once again, Doña Ruth came to my assistance. Her son-in-law was a young lieutenant at the naval station and perhaps he would be able to help us, she explained. Ruth's son-in-law immediately took us to the Commandant's Office, where I outlined the situation. After a number of questions, the Commandant filled out the proper form; I paid the 500-peso fee and contracted the same boatman to take me back across the river. On the way,

I stopped at a kiosk and bought a bottle of beer—I would need something to bait Francisco into the boat. I had to pay the cost of the container as well, which took my last few pesos. One way or another, I knew, we would have to get back on the river.

Once on the other side, I gathered the Yuquí men and Oscar to help me get Francisco into the barge. Fortunately, he had passed out and it would simply be a matter of carrying him on board. But as we lifted Francisco off the ground, he regained consciousness and started yelling and pushing us away. Both Concebida and Delsi tried to talk with him, but he was beyond reason. Then I got out the bottle of beer I had bought, and, like the Pied Piper, I led Francisco down the trail toward the river. The wives, children, Yuquí, and I climbed down the bank into the boat and looked up. Francisco was standing there, rocking back and forth on the brink. We all sat frozen in place wondering if he would pitch head first into the river. To our relief, he stumbled down the bank and into the barge. Once Oscar had the motor started and we were underway, I quietly let the beer slip over the side. This was a risky move, but by now the Yuquí were huddled together looking terrified. Giving Francisco more to drink, I knew, would only increase their anxiety. Unfortunately, Francisco saw the bottle disappear, became enraged, and, grabbing the tiller from Oscar, turned us back around toward Villarroel. We were now on a collision course with a large, steel-hulled barge. The 11 drums of fuel were in the prow of our boat and would take the brunt of the impact. I was sitting on top of them. In panic, I stood up on one of the drums and shouted at Oscar to take control of the tiller. But the younger man was afraid to challenge the powerfully built Francisco. As I came hurtling over the top of cargo and people to confront Francisco, he lost his balance, closed his eyes, and passed out. Oscar caught the tiller and, at the last moment, swung us away from the oncoming boat.

With Francisco slumped in the stern sleeping off his stupor and Oscar skillfully guiding us downstream, I relaxed a bit and turned to chat with the Yuquí. They also seemed to have calmed down now that Francisco was safely asleep and we were on our way home. It was late in the day, however, and both Oscar and I knew we would not reach our destination before dark, requiring us to find a place to tie the barge to pass the night. I had no mosquito net, a dismal prospect I tried to push to the back of my mind.

We were fortunate in reaching the confluence of the Ichilo and Chimoré Rivers before nightfall and were well on our way up the Chimoré before darkness forced us to halt our progress. Oscar selected a place where he knew some colonists had once cleared a small *chaco* and had built a thatched shelter. We tied off the barge, making certain it was secure before going ashore. But Francisco was still asleep, and I was afraid to leave him alone on the boat. It was possible he would awaken, start up the outboard, and leave us stranded. I decided to stay on board with Francisco, as did his two wives and their children while the others went ashore. Concebida found her muslin mosquito net, which we rigged up across the boat, and, after throwing a blanket over Francisco, we all crawled underneath. With three adults and several children under the net, sleep was impossible. While the net afforded us some protection, we had difficulty keeping the insects from crawling in under the edges. The night dragged on. Suddenly the humid stillness was broken by a soft, cool brush of wind. I looked up. Clouds were scudding across the moon. The wind, now from the south, got colder and the sky no longer showed any stars. The rain began to fall, waking Francisco, who by now was quite sober and once again his affable self. He quickly found a sheet of plastic he had brought along to cover his rice, and we huddled under it. The rain poured over us and it got colder. I wondered how Oscar and the Yuquí above were faring in the storm. Wet and shivering, we waited for the dawn so we could get underway. By midmorning we were at the camp, a bedraggled-looking bunch but no worse for wear. The missionaries, by now concerned by our failure to arrive as scheduled, came down to the shoreline to greet us. We were all glad to be back.

The tale of our journey to Villarroel circulated in the camp. Evidently, from the Yuquí perspective, my part in the episode had firmly established me as someone to be reckoned with. I accepted this new status with great relief since it now meant that I was given cooperation and assistance in many aspects of my fieldwork, particularly in weighing game. Even the women were now less prone to testing my limits, except, perhaps, for Elsa. But then, I think I would have missed our frequent sparring. She reminded me that to let up, even for a moment, risked my position of respect in the camp. It had been a hard-won struggle and I was not about to let it slip through my fingers.

2/The People Called "Yuquí"

WHO ARE THE YUQUÍ?

As is true for any people who do not have a written language or a well-preserved oral tradition, the origins of the Yuquí can only be hypothesized. Yet there is strong linguistic and cultural evidence that rather than being native to Bolivia they most likely are relatively recent arrivals from the south. By piecing together explorers' accounts, mission records, and early reports offered by Indians, it would appear that the Yuquí are remnants of a Guaraní migration into Bolivia from northern Paraguay. According to sources such as explorer-ethnographer Alfred Métraux, shortly before European contact a group of Guaraní from the Itatín River region of Paraguay invaded lowland Bolivia, conquered and enslaved the local Chané population, and settled on their lands. These Guaraní-speaking people later became known as the Chiriguanos. Additional expansionist forays into more northern and eastern territories probably gave rise to two more linguistically related groups, the Guarayo and the Sirionó. In the case of the Sirionó, according to a Chiriguano informant whose tale was recounted in 1636, this attempt to conquer new lands failed, resulting in the dispersal of the Chiriguano raiders and their isolation in the forests of the Beni region. As time passed, these once highly organized horticulturalists lost more and more of their cultural traditions. Separated from their relatives to the south, they became nomadic foragers, building simple lean-tos of palm and living off the land. Ultimately, they even lost the knowledge of making fire, depending instead on preserving it. Early settlers named these people "Sirionó," probably derived from the Guaraní word "*siri*," the black palm wood from which the famous Sirionó long bow is constructed.

When Spanish missionaries arrived in lowland Bolivia in the sixteenth century, efforts were made to pacify and make sedentary the frequently hostile Sirionó Indians. As was the custom, bands of foragers were offered gifts of metal tools, cooking utensils, clothing, and food as incentives to take up residence at the missions. Loathing mission discipline and drudgery, the Sirionó often gathered up their prized gifts of axes and knives and disappeared into the forest while their catechists slept.

The Sirionó remained unstudied until the late 1920s, when Norwegian ethnographer Erland Nordenskiold traveled through parts of eastern Bolivia and recorded some of their customs. Alfred Métraux, arriving in the area a few years later, found a group of Sirionó at a place known as Casarabe. Intrigued by their lack of cultural complexity, he recommended further study to a young graduate student at Yale, Allan Holmberg. It was Holmberg who eventually would complete the definitive work on the Sirionó, the well-known ethnography, *Nomads of the Long Bow*. Holmberg confirmed what Métraux had reported: that the Sirionó were among the most technologically simple societies known. In addition to being unable to produce fire, they had no watercraft, no domestic animals (not even the dog), no stone, no ritual specialists, and only a rudimentary cosmology. They lived out their lives as nomads, wandering the forests of lowland Bolivia in search of game and other foods provided by their foraging skills. Today, there are few Sirionó left, most having succumbed to the brutalities of forced acculturation and disease. Those who remain, the largest concentration living at a village site called Ibiato, are now part of the lowland peasantry, combining hunting with farming, and participating in the wider context of Bolivian culture (Stearman 1987).

According to local informants and at least one other researcher (Kelm 1983), the Yuquí most likely are remnants of Sirionó bands that became isolated in the western region of the *oriente* almost three centuries ago. Like the Sirionó, the Yuquí refer to themselves as *Biá*, "people." The origin of the Bolivian term, "Yuquí," is unknown. Until the Yuquí were contacted and better understood, it was assumed that they were, in fact, Sirionó. What little was known about the Yuquí fit known Sirionó patterns.

It is hypothesized that over time and separated from other Sirionó, the Yuquí developed their own language and cultural patterns reflecting adaptation to a different environment. Still, they retained much of Sirionó tradition, such as the typical bow, distinctive arrow construction, nomenclature for plants and animals, patterns of leadership, and kinship terminology. In addition, the Yuquí bear strange notches on the backs of their ears, an inherited trait peculiar only to the Sirionó (Stearman 1984).

In the western reaches of the lowlands, the Yuquí ranged over one of the last great wilderness areas of the Bolivian *oriente*. Although rivers in the region were frequently traveled by Bolivian nationals, the Yuquí learned to avoid detection along these waterways. The ebbs and flows of Bolivian history passed them by: The rubber boom and the Chaco War brought people through their territory along the Ichilo River, but the Yuquí simply retreated farther into the forest. It would not be until the mid-1950s that settlers would earnestly begin eyeing the region for development, bringing to an end the semi-isolation enjoyed by the Yuquí. Although the presence of the Yuquí was suspected as the result of infrequent exploration into the area, their elusiveness, their hostility, and the often apocryphal reports of *mestizo* hunters who encountered them in the forest kept the Yuquí in the realm of supposition. When colonists began to occupy their hunting territories, however, their presence clearly was made known. Increased contact with settlers brought violence and killing on both sides. Suddenly, the Yuquí became a threat to the nation's plans for development, and their lives were forever changed.

CONTACT AND PACIFICATION

In 1955, missionaries from the New Tribes Mission working near the lowland village of Todos Santos received word that a group of settlers had come across a Yuquí camp and staged a sneak attack.[2] The Yuquí men were off hunting at the time, leaving the women and children defenseless before the colonists' assault. In panic, the women and older children fled into the forest, many bleeding from gunshot wounds. No one knew how many had been killed. Several of the younger children were left standing in the camp clearing, rooted in place from fear. Four small Yuquí children were abducted by the settlers and carried off, later to be given to Bolivian families to be raised as servants. The settlers justified the raid as a retaliatory response to the Yuquí's continual pilfering of their crops. The colonists, living a marginal existence to begin with, saw their families' tenuous hold on the land additionally threatened by the Indians.

Several of the missionaries, excited by the prospect of this new opportunity to reach an as yet uncontacted indigenous people, set off in search of the Yuquí. The "contact team," as missionaries term these groups, spent six weeks tracking the Indians through the forest until the trail ended at a large river where they gave up the search. In the meantime, steps taken by mission personnel to recover the four children were unsuccessful. A meeting with the settlers was held, and after a long and frequently volatile debate with the farmers, the missionaries secured an agreement from them to cease hostilities. For the moment at least, the settlers were willing to give the missionaries time to try to make peaceful contact with the Yuquí.

Almost two years passed without further incident but also without contact. Gift trails were cut through areas where the Yuquí were thought to travel. Every few days the trails were checked but the gifts remained untouched. Then on April 17, 1957, news was received that a colonist's wife had been killed by the Indians at La Jota, a small settlement in an isolated sector of the Todos Santos region. Five missionaries set out to try to make contact. Reaching La Jota, they made camp and again began the effort of cutting gift trails and checking them for any sign of the Yuquí. Eventually, some of the gifts (food, knives, blankets, etc.) were taken.

On December 3, however, another colonist was wounded by the Yuquí when he surprised them in his *chaco* (subsistence plot). This time, the settlers were out for blood. Another assembly was called by the missionaries, but the colonists attended grudgingly, wanting to settle the matter quickly with force. Again, the missionaries were able to persuade the settlers to give them more time, pointing out that there might be more than one group of Yuquí and that these others would probably retaliate and kill many people. Several months passed, again without any success at contact.

2. The following history of the Yuquí contact is taken largely from Bruce E. Porterfield's *Commandos for Christ* (1978), and the typescript "A History of the New Tribes Mission Project to Evangelize the Yuquí Indians" (1955–1976). Other details were compiled from interviews with New Tribes missionaries during fieldwork in 1982 and 1983.

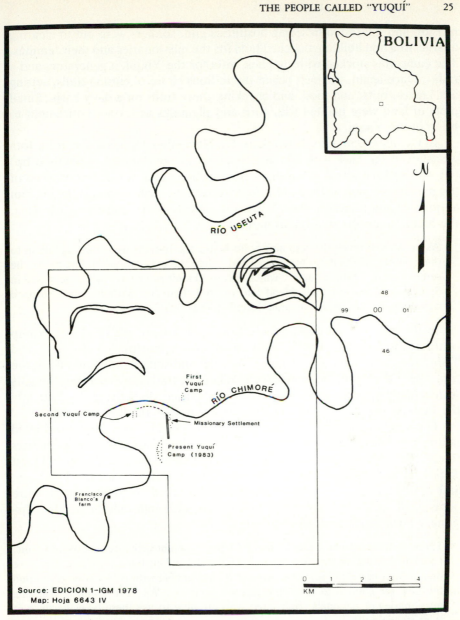

Figure 3. Yuquí camps and lands

In March 1958, another settler was shot by the Yuquí. Although it was not a serious wound, he died a few weeks later from tetanus. This incident occurred near La Jota, where the woman had been killed the previous year. Renewed efforts by the missionaries were made to establish contact with the Yuquí. A new camp was set up at a place called Little Jota, east of the La Jota settlement. With the support of a Bolivian army colonel friendly to the mission and interested in seeing hostilities end, soldiers were put to clearing a large area and building thatched huts for the missionaries and their families. The camp was stocked with supplies, gifts for the Yuquí, a generator, and a radio. Once again, the men began the tedious chore of cutting trails, setting out knives, pots, and food, and checking these trails on a daily basis. Small plots of land were planted with corn and plantains as further enticement to bring in the Yuquí.

In October 1958, gifts were taken. On November 14, a colonist at La Jota was shot in the back with a large "bleeder" arrow (lanceolate bamboo tip) but survived the attack when the arrow hit bone and was deflected. Two of the missionary men walked to La Jota to treat the man's wounds, giving him antibiotics and a tetanus shot. They left separately to return to Little Jota, the first man on the trail reporting that

> As he walked down the trail alone, he heard the Indians whistling, signalling to one another. He realized his danger and yelled the only Sirionó Indian phrase he remembered, "Tatuchu dejé!" which means "Don't run away." Then he yelled in Spanish that he was their friend and offered them his machete. They stopped whistling and Les passed by unmolested. (NTM 1955–1976:4)

In the next several days, gifts left on trails around the missionary camp continued to be taken. Burlap sacks, small knives, mirrors, combs, pots, and T-shirts were tied to poles about six feet tall and staked in the middle of the trail where they could be clearly seen. When the trails were checked, the gifts were gone, but more poles had been cut and placed along the trail—evidently the Indians' message to the missionaries to increase the flow of goods.

The year ended and the new one, 1959, began. The Yuquí continued taking gifts but left none in return, something that disturbed the missionaries since experience in other regions led them to believe that friendship and trust were beginning to develop once there was reciprocation. January, February, and March passed and gifts continued to be taken. Now the Yuquí were occasionally allowing themselves to be seen, although only fleetingly. Missionary Dick Strickler described them:

> These men seem to be around 5 feet 9 inches in height with huge chests and arms. I imagine these are developed from pulling the 7 foot bows they use. We have one of their bows and several arrows and I am unable with all my strength to pull the bow far enough to shoot the arrow effectively. We have found few among missionaries or nationals (Bolivians) who are able to use these bows because of their strong pull.
>
> They wore no clothing at all and were painted with *urucú*. This *urucú* [*Bixa orellana*] is a pod with bright reddish orange seeds, which when mixed with water make a paint with which they cover their bodies. (NTM 1955–1976:5)

On April 2, 1959, the first face-to-face contact occurred. The Yuquí, numbering 17 or 18 men, women, and children, advanced to the edge of the camp clearing. They accepted gifts handed to them by the missionaries. The missionaries attempted to communicate by gestures and began noting down Yuquí words and phrases, although not knowing their meanings. The contact ended late in the afternoon as the Yuquí moved down one of the trails and into the forest, shouting and waving to the missionaries as they left.

Over the next several weeks, the Yuquí became bolder, moving into the clearing to accept gifts. Then the wrestling and choking began. In what appeared to be tests of strength and courage, the Yuquí would leap on a missionary, struggle him to the ground, and then cut off his wind by squeezing on the trachea. In spite of their fear and discomfort, the missionaries did not resist, fighting back enough to make a good show, but always allowing the Yuquí contender to win. One morning, the entire Yuquí band entered the mission encampment and ransacked the houses looking for supplies. Among other things, a 50-pound sack of sugar was taken, but, as Strickler wrote, "There was a spark of generosity in them, however. After they carried off the sugar, they shared some of their wild honey with us" (NTM 1955–1976:7).

By the end of April, the Yuquí were carrying off from the mission settlement whatever they wanted. They were coming on an almost daily basis, staying for six hours or so, demanding gifts, choking the missionaries, and ransacking the camp. Nothing was safe. The missionaries tried hiding their clothes, bedding, cooking utensils, and mosquito nets in the woods, but the Indians would invariably find them and be off into the forest. Nerves frayed and supplies exhausted, the missionaries retreated to Todos Santos, abandoning the camp at Little Jota.

The contact continued, but now the men were working out of Todos

Photo 7. *Early photo of the Yuquí taken during the first years of contact. Note the hair plucked from the women's eyebrows and foreheads, a custom that has now been abandoned. (Photo courtesy of NTM)*

Photo 8. Early photo of the Yuquí. (Photo courtesy of NTM)

Santos, making periodic trips back to the camp at Little Jota to meet the Yuquí. The Indians' aggressive behavior continued. Each contact became more threatening as the Yuquí choked the men, roughed them up, and fired arrows within inches of their heads in what one missionary referred to as the Yuquí's "deadly sense of humor." During this time, the missionaries attempted to teach the Yuquí to plant corn, but having no understanding of agriculture, at first the Indians simply followed behind the sower, digging up the seeds. On another occasion, the missionaries got out hooks and lines to demonstrate how fish could be taken from the river using this technique. The Yuquí, who knew only bow fishing, howled in laughter as the line was tossed into the water. Their ridicule turned to amazement as a fish was quickly hauled ashore, and then another and another, which the Yuquí happily roasted whole over a fire.

It was then decided to build a new camp with an airstrip to fly in men and supplies, shortening the time spent in travel from Todos Santos. With the help of local labor, the landing site was completed and two houses were built, one fitted with walls of flattened fuel drums to act as a strong room. Here, the missionaries would store their supplies and radio equipment, presumably safe from the curiosity of the Yuquí. The strong house would also serve as a fort for the missionaries should events require a hasty retreat.

By November 1959, work was completed and supplies began to arrive by air. At about that time, the missionaries also began finding signs in the forest that the Indians were returning. Later in the month, the Yuquí appeared, accepting gifts of cooking pots and bananas. They circled the camp and the strange metal house, banging on the walls and trying to peer into the dark interior. Then they asked for sugar, but since this had caused so much trouble in the past, the missionaries refused. The headman demanded that the strong room be opened, but again was denied. To focus the Indians' attention on other things, the missionaries proposed a hunt, indicating that there were turkeys nearby. None were found. The Yuquí left camp disgruntled at the unsatisfactory encounter.

During the next several days, the Indians continued to visit the missionary camp, staying for a few hours and then going off to hunt. For a time, they treated the missionaries well, appearing friendlier and being less aggressive. But on December 6, a small group came into camp and began wrestling with the men and choking them, demanding that the strong house be opened. Again, they were denied access.

Two days later a group of about eight Yuquí came out of the forest in an affable mood. They painted the missionaries with red colorant, *urucú*, and plucked hairs from their eyebrows and chests, evidently trying to make the men look more presentable, more like Yuquí. The missionaries were encouraged.

Another two days passed and another small group of Yuquí appeared in the clearing, only now nervous and agitated. They attempted to convey that they had shot three of something, one of these escaping by crawling along the ground. It was later learned by radio that the "somethings" had been Bolivian hunters, two of whom were killed, the third escaping to tell the story.

As the contacts continued, aggression toward the missionaries increased. The Yuquí continued demanding gifts, wrestling with the missionaries, and threatening them with drawn bows. The impenetrable strong house infuriated them. Shortly after Christmas, relations with the Indians began to deteriorate even further, forcing the missionaries to consider giving up the contact, at least for the time being. In January 1960, a missionary was wounded in the hand by one of the Yuquí. It was decided to call an end to the contact before more serious trouble ensued. Eight flights were made in a single day to evacuate the men and their supplies.

Again, the colonists were becoming fearful of the Yuquí and were critical of the missionaries' lack of progress. They wanted to form a "commission" to finish off the Indians. Missionary Les Foster, who had been with the contact team from the beginning, dissuaded the settlers by telling them he would go in alone and try for a friendly contact. Perhaps if he went by himself, he explained, the Yuquí would not be so fearful and aggressive.

On January 14, Foster set out in search of the Yuquí. On his second day out he encountered part of the band. They relieved him of his food and machete, the latter being returned to him so he could help cut trail. After a time, they met up with the rest of the group. But the Indians were not interested in having the missionary remain with them. Rather, they sent him back along the trail, with demands that he return with more gifts. As Foster was leaving, he thought to warn the Indians of the settlers' plan to exterminate the band. Returning to their camp, he indicated to the Yuquí that the colonists with their many guns would be coming in pursuit of them. The Yuquí's response was to scoff at the threat, and Foster was treated to displays of how the settlers would be shot in the eyes with large bleeder arrows.

Foster returned to Todos Santos, intending to renew the contact within a few days. On January 24, however, before he could meet with the Yuquí again, a colonist was shot and killed. On February 15, the settlers went after the Yuquí, reportedly killing one man and an old woman before the group scattered into the forest. In March, the colonists tried again, but were unable to locate the Indians.

In June, several of the contact personnel left Bolivia for a year's leave and the contact effort was suspended. Reports were received that the settlers had killed two more Yuquí in October and that the Yuquí had retaliated with one death in November.

Preparations to renew the contact were not resumed until November 1963. It had now been determined that the team would pull out of the Todos Santos area completely since the colonists' presence only served to aggravate the situation. A fortified river launch was constructed near Todos Santos and then taken down the Chapare River to the Ichilo River, up the Ichilo to the Chimoré River, and then up the Chimoré several kilometers. Having made a large "U" from Todos Santos, the missionaries were now in what they believed was the heart of Yuquí territory. The river boat would serve as a mobile base of operations for the missionaries. It was painted blue with a white strip as were the wrappings of the gifts placed along a nine-kilometer trail leading from the river's edge. This, the missionaries believed, would identify the gifts with the boat. Each day, the men set out in a small skiff to check the trail upriver from where the launch was tied. Months went by with no sign of the Yuquí. The boat would stay for a period of three months and then, after a month's journey back to Todos Santos to replenish supplies, would return to the Chimoré.

In January 1965, returning from the month-long trip to Todos Santos, the missionaries found that gifts had been taken. All along the nine-kilometer track were signs of the Yuquí and that they had remained for some time awaiting the arrival of the missionaries. At the end of the trail, an arrow had been stuck in the ground. Later, the missionaries learned that it was placed there as a gift, not a threat.

More gifts were immediately set out and eventually were taken. This was repeated several times, but still the Yuquí had not shown themselves. Finally, whistling was heard and the entire group could be seen near the river's edge. The headman beckoned for the missionaries to come across. This time the team decided to carry sidearms and left one man with a shotgun on guard in the small boat while the others went ashore. It was hoped that this display of strength would deter the Yuquí from physical aggression. The Indians were upset at seeing the firearms, but let the men proceed. It had also been decided beforehand by the missionaries to keep the initial contact of short duration to avoid any escalation of hostility. This tactic seemed to work, and the meeting proceeded without incident.

The visits continued, at times with violence being threatened by the Yuquí. At one point a missionary drew his pistol and pointed it into the air to stop an episode of escalating aggression. Extremely agitated, the Yuquí backed down but did not force the issue. As time went on, the missionaries were received with greater acceptance. By March 1965, friendly contact had been established, *ten years* after pacification efforts were begun. The Yuquí continued their old way of life, staying near the boat for three or four months, and then going off for a similar period of time to hunt and gather. The missionaries began to build a permanent settlement and airstrip on the opposite side of the river from where the Yuquí were accustomed to camping. The Indians could not swim, and the missionaries were not yet convinced that the Yuquí could be trusted not to kill them.

In 1965, there were 43 Yuquí in the band contacted by the missionaries. In 1975, the group had grown to 57, and in 1983 there were 73 Yuquí. It is unusual for an indigenous group to grow in number during an initial contact period, when native people are so susceptible to disease. In the case of the Yuquí, their population growth can be attributed to the missionaries taking swift action to vaccinate them and provide them with health care. In this regard, being so few worked to the Yuquí's advantage in that every individual's health could be carefully monitored. Still, some died of pneumonia and other Western diseases previously unknown to them. In 1986, a colonist brought chicken pox to the camp and a pregnant Yuquí woman died from complications. Others suffered terribly from the pox, but fortunately survived. To date, there is no venereal disease, tuberculosis, or alcoholism among the

Photo 9. Early photo of the Yuquí. (Photo courtesy of NTM)

Yuquí, diseases that have spelled disaster for so many aboriginal people in the Americas. Yet their small numbers give them very little buffer against these and other threats from the world of the *Abá* that is now, as they are coming to realize, their world as well.

THE CHIMORÉ CAMP

The fear of Yuquí treachery kept the missionaries on the south side of the Chimoré River where they began to build their houses. In the meantime, the Yuquí gradually became sedentary, shortening their hunting trips from months to weeks and finally to day-long jaunts away from their camp on the other side of the river. The lure of trade goods, a constant supply of foodstuffs, and the security offered by living in close proximity to the missionaries ultimately overcame Yuquí nomadism. During this period, the Indians began to experiment with constructing shelters, building crude A-frame type dwellings that were little more than lean-tos. The missionaries showed them how to cultivate plantains as further inducement to remain in the area, resulting in an initial four hectares of *chaco* being cleared and planted near that first stable camp. It is also notable that as structures were built, households began to differentiate themselves, diverging from the traditional camp pattern in which everyone slept and cooked in the same area. These first shelters housed a number of individuals, usually brothers and their wives and children, or parents and their grown offspring and spouses. In April 1972, there were eight structures housing forty-eight people.

Missionary contact with the Yuquí was maintained by crossing the river each day in canoes, ferrying over several of the Indians, and then returning them at night. An early task was to clear and level an airstrip, accomplished by using dynamite and Yuquí labor. By now, a small store had been set up and the Yuquí were being compensated for their work with trade goods. With the airstrip functional, the infrastructure of the camp evolved rapidly since supplies could be shipped directly from Cochabamba in less than an hour as compared with several days or even weeks by land and water.

The decision to move the Yuquí to the missionary side of the river was reached in 1979, but still the Indians were kept at a safe distance from the mission camp. Now, however, the problem was not so much fear of treachery but uneasiness concerning the openness of the Yuquí in carrying out many of their activities. From the missionary perspective, much of this behavior, particularly sexual, was considered immoral and they were reluctant to expose themselves and their children to what they regarded as offensive conduct. As a result, the second camp was laid out upstream about a kilometer from the mission settlement. This camp was designed by the missionaries in a rectangular pattern giving each nuclear family a building space along one of the sides of the trail leading to the airstrip. The missionaries built most of the homes with some help from the Yuquí, but the Indians were not skilled at, or really interested in, this type of endeavor. The roofs of these houses were of tin, not thatch. To have thatched 13 houses simultaneously would have required an enormous amount of palm fronds from trees widely scattered through the forest. Considering the Yuquí's lack of willingness to perform what was for them tedious and unimportant hard labor, the task of gathering enough thatch would have been nearly impossible. A mission supporter in Canada donated the funds necessary to provide the tin roofing, which is still in use today.

This second camp, however, was abandoned in 1982 after several floods threatened the lives of the small children. By this time, the Yuquí were well aware of many of the missionary norms of modesty, including the wearing of clothes and confining sexual activity to private places. In spite of their traditional communal living, the Yuquí, like most foragers, are highly individualistic and adapted quickly to the idea of separate dwellings and the privacy they offered. Today, they are extremely territorial regarding their houses and grounds and do not look kindly on their relatives' intrusions.

When the third camp was built, it, too, was established at a site removed from the mission settlement. But by now, there was little threat to the missionaries from any quarter. Perhaps once discrete living arrangements became the norm, it was easier to continue the old system rather than deal with change. The missionaries are content in their own realm; there is open space and an atmosphere of serenity, and the grounds are orderly, all in sharp contrast to the Yuquí camp at the far end of the airstrip. As nomads, the Yuquí were not concerned with keeping their camp clean because it was simply easier to move on when living conditions became intolerable even by Yuquí standards. Now that they are sedentary, the Yuquí have not suddenly become good housekeepers. As a consequence, their camp is usually filled with decaying animal hides, rotting bananas, discarded fish and animal bone, and filthy clothing that has been abandoned in the dirt until it is noticed and carried to the river to be washed. With the Yuquí's careless attention to cleanliness, it is understandable why the missionaries would prefer to remain apart. Still, it is curious that given the missionaries' desire to attain Yuquí conversion, they have perpetuated a physical situation that makes proselytizing very difficult.

The physical disposition of the missionary settlement is interesting in that whether by design or chance it almost perfectly mirrors the ranking of the camp's members. The most desirable place to live is near the river where it is cooler, there are fewer insects, and it is more visually diverse and appealing. The land on the banks of the Chimoré is occupied by the Porters, the senior couple.[3] Their bungalow-style house is constructed of tongue-in-groove hardwood that has been painted white, presenting a postcard-like setting against the backdrop of the river and forest. Behind the Porter residence is Hank

---

3. At the missionaries' request to remain anonymous, I have given them pseudonyms with the exception of those names that appear in direct quotes from, or reference to, mission documents. While the Mission's preference would have been for me to avoid naming it as well, New Tribes Mission is a public entity and I have cited a number of its publications, making that anonymity impossible.

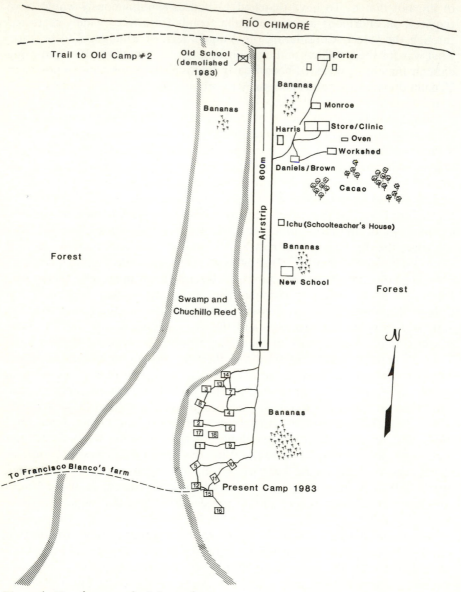

Figure 4. Yuquí camp and mission settlement

Monroe's house. It is much smaller and more rustic in its construction. Monroe's house, the store/clinic, and the schoolteacher's house were built by a team of summer mission volunteers visiting Bolivia. Each of these structures is creosoted board-and-batten with a tin roof. Slightly out of the ranking order is Don Harris' house; as a new arrival he was given the only available space, one of the old, original dwellings built of palm boards and now nearing collapse. At the back of the missionary sector is the large, two-story house that has been home to a number of families that have come and gone through the years. During my first visit, it was inhabited by Mike and Mary Daniels, who during the year I was gone moved to another post. On my second visit, Bill and Jane Brown were living there between Bill's visits to the Vivora River region where he was taking part in the effort to contact one of the remaining bands of forest Yuquí. This house consists of a lower floor of concrete and cement block walls and an upper story of wood. Most interesting is the wrought iron spiral staircase that leads to the second floor. I never entered this house without a sense of wonderment that this huge, heavy object could have been transported to such a remote location. The staircase as well as the other building materials, with the exception of Don's house, were all brought in by boat and airplane. The missionary camp is kept neatly mowed by the Yuquí, who perform this and other caretaking services in exchange for wages that can then be spent at the store.

About halfway down the airstrip is the schoolteacher's house. The family presently residing there is that of Mariano Ichu, a Trinitario "believer" from the Beni who is paid by the mission to teach the Yuquí children. Mariano lives in the small wooden house, a replica of Hank's, with his wife, Leonarda, and several of their preschool-aged children. The remainder of the family stays with Mariano's parents in the Beni, where they attend public school. The placement of the Ichu house again is indicative of the social system operating in the Chimoré camp. When asked why the Ichu house was not built in the missionary area, the missionaries seemed hardpressed for an answer. The house he and his family occupy stands alone between the missionary and Yuquí camps. To a great extent, the Ichus' physical location mirrors their social status as people "in between." Their isolation is often difficult for both Mariano and Leonarda, but they manage to make the best of the situation with the quiet dignity that is so characteristic of the lowland peasantry.

At the far end of the airstrip are the Yuquí. Their houses are laid out in an oval pattern, maintaining a distance of roughly 40 meters between houses. As the missionaries explained, this distance was deemed necessary to keep fighting and sexual transgressions to a minimum. The plan has met with only partial success, however, in that the Yuquí continue to indulge in illicit sexual activity and there is frequent dissention in the camp.

The Yuquí houses are small, measuring about 9 by 12 feet, have the original tin roofs that were transported from the flooded camp, and are enclosed with an array of materials, including palm boards, *chuchillo* reed, and pieces of scrap wood or tin. In 1982 when I first visited the site, the camp area had been recently cleared, leaving relatively open ground with individual houses readily accessible. By my return a year later, much of the undergrowth had again taken hold and the camp was in the midst of tall scrub. Most of the houses had a small cleared area immediately surrounding them, but they were now separated by the encroaching jungle. The several visits we experienced from jaguars and snakes no doubt were encouraged by the excellent cover this growth provided them.

The greatest inconvenience of being so far from the river was the lack of water in the Yuquí camp. A couple of the Yuquí obtained 55-gallon drums and, like the missionaries, capture water off their roofs. These sources, unfortunately, are quickly exhausted and, because they are not universally available, are yet another cause for pilferage and resulting disputes. Thus, the Yuquí trek to the river. Every day they make the almost-two-kilometer round-trip with cans, buckets, and cooking pots to haul water.

A few of the Yuquí, such as the young headman Leonardo, have begun to plant dooryard gardens near their houses in imitation of settlers in the area. By planting close to the house, the Yuquí feel that they can better watch over their cultigens. Still, there are times when the residents are off hunting, at the river, or in the missionary area, leaving their untended gardens prey to the quick hands of a neighbor. In response to this thievery, several Yuquí have erected small fences, no doubt also having borrowed this idea from colonists who fence off domestic animals. The Yuquí fences, however, are little more than a few crossed sticks, their presence more symbolic than functional. The fences come and go, or change location over time, indicators of the present condition of social relationships in the group.

Linking each domain of the Chimoré camp—consisting of the missionaries' houses, those of the Yuquí, the schoolteacher's home, and the school—is a web of small footpaths. Generations of walking single file through the forest have not been altered by the sudden openness of an airstrip and settlement. The trails are narrow and the Yuquí faithfully follow them, heads lowered to mark the cadence of the feet moving immediately in front. Up and down the airstrip, back and forth from Indian camp to missionary settlement, into the forest and out again they move in a single line. Much has changed in the lives of the Yuquí, but then much has not.

3 / Adaptation

THE PHYSICAL ENVIRONMENT

The area that is home to the Yuquí stretches along the Ichilo River near the base of the Andes. Here, a band of dense forest grows, nurtured by moisture that, finding itself trapped against the eastern slopes of the mountains, falls at a rate of 3000–5000 mm. (about 180 inches) a year. From the air, the rain forest presents an impenetrable canopy of hazy green where any activity taking place on the ground is totally screened from view. Even the smoke from small Yuquí cooking fires is dispersed by the heavy foliage and high humidity before it becomes visible from above. A random glimpse into the realm of the forest is provided by meandering rivers that snake across the land, moving north to their final destination, the Amazon. Most often they flow in a small, serene ribbon with wide beaches that provide gathering places for a multitude of fowl. At other times they become raging torrents carrying the huge volume of storm water emptying from the mountains to the west, churning brown with silt and pushing immense log jams downstream with the force of a freight train.

During the majority of the year, the climate of the *oriente* is warm and humid with temperatures at times reaching well into the 90s. But with the "dry" season months of June, July, and August come the cold Antarctic winds. These cold fronts, called *surazos*, or southers, may drive the temperature down into the 40s and, occasionally, even close to freezing. Combined with the high humidity of the region, the cold not merely is uncomfortable but becomes a fearsome opponent in the bone-chilling battle to keep warm with any means at hand.

The season of *surazos* does, however, bring some respite from the otherwise continuous onslaught of insects. The Ichilo River region, like so many similar tropical areas, is inhabited by numerous varieties of biting, annoying insects: mosquitos, deerflies (black and yellow), and the ubiquitous *ejene*, the miniscule fly that can pass through mosquito netting. Added to these pests are the greater threats of poisonous snakes, stinging ants capable of paralyzing an adult or killing a small child, stingrays in rivers, and carnivores such as jaguars and pumas. But just as Americans must learn to survive in freeway traffic, manipulate mechanical and electrical appliances, and avoid becoming targets of criminal acts, the Yuquí too must learn to manage risk in their own

37

environment. While the city and the forest in many respects may be less than ideal human habitats, they nonetheless provide the necessities of life. Whether one world is inherently more dangerous than the other is only a matter of perspective.

The forests of the Ichilo River region harbor many of the same flora and fauna found in other parts of the Amazon Basin. Among plants, probably the most universally useful is the palm in its multitude of varieties. Most have an edible fruit that can be consumed raw or cooked; the leaves provide shelter, mats, and baskets; at least two species of palm (*Bactris spp.*) are used to make bows, arrow points, and other implements. The Yuquí also harvest the heart of the palm, an always abundant source of nourishment, particularly when meat or other foods may be scarce.

In addition to the palm, the Yuquí utilize other edible plants of the forest, gathering over 50 varieties of tubers and fruits. Unlike many other forest nomads, however, they have little knowledge of herbal remedies, probably having lost this lore long ago along with the ability to make fire. Their primary medicinal plants, which also have some ritual significance, are two colorants; *urucú* (*Bixa orellana*), a red dye, and *dijá* (*Genipa americana L.*), a blue-black dye. Both are used to ward off evil and illness as well as to treat wounds and body aches. Another plant that provides both fruit and a useful fiber is a fig-like tree called *imbai* in Yuquí and is a member of the Cecropia family. This tree, when stripped of its bark (a no mean feat given that its hollow center is always inhabited by thousands of small but ferocious red ants), produces a coarse, hemp-like fiber.

An important by-product of the forest flora is honey. The Yuquí value honey to such a degree that they have 16 named varieties in their language. Even today, with the availability of refined sugar, the Yuquí will go to great lengths to collect wild honey from the hollow trees scattered throughout the forest. On several honey expeditions I attended, for example, the Yuquí males in our group expended tremendous amounts of energy cutting down trees in excess of two feet in diameter with only the suspicion that they might contain honey.

While forest plants provide for many of the needs of the Yuquí particularly in terms of diet, the one food recognized by all as vital to life itself is meat. The preferred varieties of meat come from the larger species of animals or those that herd together, thereby offering a potentially large catch. The tapir is a prized game animal because of its great size (averaging 150 kilos). But for sheer quantity of meat, the Yuquí depend on the white-lipped peccaries, or "troop pigs" (*puerco de tropa* in Spanish), that root in the forest in herds that at times exceed 200 animals. Other important sources of meat include capybaras, agoutis, armadillos, monkeys, anteaters, sloths, collared peccaries (smaller than the white-lipped variety and normally found singly or in small numbers), deer, pacas, tortoises, and hundreds of species of birds.

All of these animals, including fish, were hunted with bow and arrow prior to contact. Like the Sirionó, the Yuquí fashioned a black palm bow almost eight feet in length. Arrows of equal length were made from reed, black palm, and bamboo. Their construction will be discussed later in this chapter. Also like the Sirionó, the Yuquí used only two types of arrows: a bamboo lanceolate point for large game and a black palm barbed point for smaller animals. It was not until prolonged contact with outsiders that the Yuquí began to fish in earnest and learned to use a hook and line. Before that, moving out into the open along rivers was considered too dangerous. Fish were shot with arrows now and then when they became trapped in oxbow lakes, or, as was more frequently the case, were simply scooped up in crudely but quickly made baskets as the water evaporated from shallow ponds.

The wilderness that is the Yuquí homeland has great variety in its composition, belying the sameness of the landscape viewed from the air. Near rivers, much of the terrain is low and swampy, giving refuge to those animals whose habitat is wet: caimans, capybaras, and marsh rats. Other areas are higher and drier, attracting such game as deer and white-lipped and collared peccaries. Although the Yuquí became more and more fearful of exposing themselves to Bolivian nationals travelling on the larger, navigable rivers of their hunting territory, they continued to hunt as they do today along the beaches, where hundreds of birds frequently gather to preen and mate.

The forest itself is often remarkably clear underneath, permitting fast travel along relatively straight trails under the canopy of trees. Although not offering much opportunity for animals to feed on low growth, the huge trees frequently bear edible fruits that attract numerous species of game around their trunks. Other areas of the forest, those where trees have fallen or a stream has cut through, are choked with underbrush. Typically, the growth here is like the proverbial briar patch, its thorny vines, sticky tendrils, and serrated razor grass leaving even the hardy Yuquí hunters torn and bleeding after pursuing game into its interior.

In spite of the variety the forest offers, there are still few dependable landmarks. A tree can fall, a river changes course, and that which was familiar now seems unknown. There are miles of forest with little differentiation, where the trees form such a perfect cover that it is difficult to see the sun. As well as the Yuquí knew their old territory, they also knew the danger of getting lost, of becoming separated from the band. Even today, with a much smaller range to forage, they continue to mark their trails by breaking the tips of foliage as they pass along. It is an old habit that is hard to change.

During the last 30 years, the large wilderness areas that give life to the nomads have dramatically decreased. Settlers began moving into the regions north and south of the Yuquí homeland following the 1952 revolution in a vise-like push that forced the Indians into a smaller and smaller range. The revolution and the agarian reform laws following a year later, in 1953, radically altered the old social order of Bolivia. Large landholdings were expropriated and debt peonage was abolished. The tin mining industry was nationalized. The reforms also created new dilemmas: In the mountainous interior of Bolivia where over 80 percent of the population was located, farmland was at a premium; in the heavily settled intermontane valleys, peasants promised land found there was not enough to go around; and in the mining sector, strong labor unions increased the labor rolls, which, along with poor management practices and price fluctuations, soon had the mines operating at a loss. Like many other South American nations with a large wilderness area in the Amazon Basin, Bolivia turned to the *oriente* as a solution to its many social and economic problems. Additionally, Bolivia had a long history of regionalism that frequently threatened national integration. The *oriente* had been settled during colonial times as the result of Spanish explorations from Paraguay. Over the centuries, a small, fiercely independent population of lowlanders developed, isolated from national governmental centers by the immense geographical barrier of the Andes Mountains. Lack of communication networks between the highlands and lowlands strengthened the factionalism that historically divided the nation. On several occasions, lowlanders attempted secession from the rest of Bolivia, believing themselves to have stronger ties with Paraguay and Argentina. Thus, one of the goals of the revolutionary government was to put an end to the separatism of the *oriente*. By encouraging large numbers of highland people to move to the lowlands, the government believed that the problems of scarcity of land, underemployment, mine featherbedding, low agricultural production, and separatist movements would all be resolved. In the end, none of these goals was achieved to the degree anticipated; but the wilderness was opened for colonization and the indigenous populations there, including the Yuquí, began experiencing pressure on their foraging territories.

This pressure became intense in the 1960s, when Bolivia received monetary aid from several international sources to underwrite three major colonization zones: the Alto Beni, the Chapare, and the Yapacaní. The Chapare colony, located north of the Yuquí, brought settlers from the Cochabamba Valley. To the south, the Yapacaní colony attracted settlers from all areas of Bolivia, who entered the region through the lowland gateway, the city of Santa Cruz. It was not long before both of these settlements began extending their boundaries north and south into the "vacant" lands inhabited by the Yuquí.

Recently, the missionaries at the Chimoré camp instituted proceedings with the Agrarian Reform office in Cochabamba to allocate 7800 hectares (about 17,000 acres) of land to the Yuquí. At mission expense, a surveyor and *Juez Agrario* (Land Judge) were flown to the camp. The Yuquí were taught to use a compass and, over a period of several months, cut boundary trails around the property. The titling process is difficult and will require constant effort if it is to be completed, however. Bolivia has a very poor record of ceding titles to those without wealth and political patronage.

My data indicate that for the present, the Yuquí population is small enough for their land to continue providing animal protein in adequate amounts. If their numbers continue to increase, greater stresses will be placed on game resources as colonists tighten the circle. In many ways, the Yuquí are caught in a no-win situation: If their population fails to grow significantly, it is unlikely that they will survive as a cultural entity; if it does, they will find it increasingly difficult to continue their traditional existence based on hunting and gathering.

TECHNOLOGY

As a nomadic people, the Yuquí were greatly limited in the amount of material goods they could acquire. Unlike mounted nomads such as the South American Gauchos and the Plains Indians of North America with their horses, everything the Yuquí owned had to be carried, principally by the women. Yuquí men went largely unencumbered, enabling them to be constantly ready to hunt or protect the band as it moved through the forest. The need to be instantly mobile to avoid hostile contact with Bolivian settlers, hunters, and loggers no doubt further reduced the burdens the Yuquí were willing to carry. For in addition to household items, most adult women had young children that had to be hastily picked up at the first sign of danger. Thus, with the pressures of threats from the outside world, constant movement, and a diminishing population, Yuquí material culture was reduced to the bare minimum for survival. Much of their technology was expendable: items that could be quickly made and then discarded as the group moved on.

It is also evident that over time many skills were simply forgotten from lack of practice or need. The Yuquí preserved and carried their fire but could not make it. Neither did they build structures in which to pass the night or to protect themselves from the elements. As Yuquí material culture diminished, so did the less tangible aspects of their tradition, leaving them with only traces of those cultural embellishments that are normally a part of the human experience. From one vantage point, the Yuquí represent one of the least complex levels of technology among living people; but from another, they demonstrate the remarkable adaptability of the human species under the most adverse conditions.

Weapons

As noted previously, the staple food of the Yuquí diet is meat. All other foods are considered of secondary importance, and a Yuquí feels that hunger is imminent if meat is not available. The primary means of capturing animal protein in the past was with the bow and arrow, although burrowing animals could be dug out of their holes and clubbed with any available stick. Still, it was the bow and arrow that dominated Yuquí existence. Although only men used the weapons, women helped in their construction by making the various thicknesses of twine necessary for bindings and bowstrings.

The unusually large size of the Yuquí bow and arrow remains a mystery given that contiguous groups such as the Yuracaré use much smaller weaponry. The almost-eight-foot-long bow and equally long arrows frequently appear ill-suited to the forest environment of the Yuquí. The extreme length makes movement somewhat awkward, and a hunter may be forced at times to drop his bundle of arrows in pursuit of game. In trying to determine possible explanations for the length of Yuquí weaponry, several seem feasible. Greater accuracy is gained by having longer projectiles, but it is doubtful that this

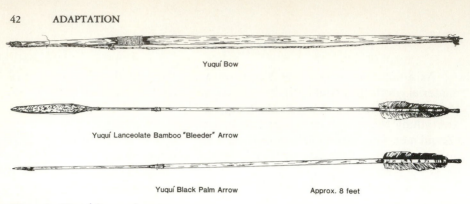

Yuquí Bow

Yuquí Lanceolate Bamboo "Bleeder" Arrow

Yuquí Black Palm Arrow   Approx. 8 feet

Figure 5. Yuquí bow and arrows

alone would offset the disadvantage of carrying an eight-foot arrow through the forest. Another explanation relates to killing efficiency. Many animals are not hit in a vital spot and so death comes not as the result of arrow penetration but from bleeding. Having a long, heavy arrow means that the wound will bleed more and the animal will be impeded in its flight. The latter function would be extremely useful in game retrieval. Finally, there exists the possibility that the size of the Yuquí bow and arrow has no adaptive advantage whatsoever and is simply a vestige of their earlier culture in the more open areas of the Paraguayan region.

The Yuquí bow and upper shaft of the arrows are made from black palm, a practice typical throughout the Amazon Basin. Black palm is an extremely hard, dense wood that also has great tensile strength, making it ideal not only for the arrow shaft and point, but also for the bow, which requires flexibility. In precontact days, a fallen palm was first split into slats by using a wedge, and then the slat selected for a bow was shaped into its oval forms by scraping it with an animal canine or incisor. The Yuquí used the incisor from an agouti or paca; they secured the tooth to a wood or bone handle. The ends of the bow were tapered to a point, but no "hip" was carved to hold the string. The bow then was finished by smoothing the surface with a piece of shell, a common item in the lowlands where land snails are plentiful. Today, this work is accomplished with steel tools: axes, machetes, and knives.

Fabricating the bowstring is the women's task. It, like many other Yuquí items, is made from the fiber of *imbai* bark. Three heavy strands are twisted together forming a cord approximately five-sixteenths of an inch thick. The bow string is held in place by a hip formed by wrapping untwined *imbai* strands around each end of the bow. Characteristic of both the Yuquí and the Sirionó bow is the additional length of bowstring coiled around the lower end about one-third of the way up the shaft. Should the bowstring break, this extra length can be quickly unwrapped and the bow is once again serviceable.

While making a bow is a relatively uncomplicated task that can be accomplished quickly, especially now that metal tools are available for the shaping, arrow making requires greater skill, precision, and patience. As previously noted, the Yuquí make use of only two types of arrow points: the barbed, black palm point and the large, bamboo lanceolate "bleeder" arrow. Other than the differences in the points, both arrows are constructed identically.

The main arrow shaft, which makes up most of the arrow's length, is the flower staff from the river reed, *chuchillo*. The flower staff, which looks very much like a pampas grass flower, is straight, lightweight, and strong. These are harvested periodically and gathered into bundles to cure and dry by the open fire. Once cured to a dark honey color, the straightest staffs are selected for arrow shafts.

Any large bird's wing feathers are used to fletch the arrow, although by far the most colorful and striking feathers are those that come from the macaw parrot. The spine of the feather is removed carefully, and the feather is split into halves. Each half is then "glued" to the shaft using warm beeswax (the black wax made by a stingless bee is the preferred variety since it dries to a resin-like hardness). Once in place, the feathers are secured with a hair-like palm fiber and then another coat of wax is applied. The end of the arrow is wrapped with a coil of finely twined *imbai*, a knocking plug is carved from soft wood, coated with wax, and pushed inside the shaft.

To prepare the barbed-type point, an 18-inch strip of black palm is scraped until it is round and the tips are sharpened. A separate barb is carved from a small piece of palm, wrapped in place with *imbai* near one pointed end, and then coated with beeswax. The other end of the palm shaft is coated with wax and then forced into the main shaft, which has been previously wrapped with *imbai* string to prevent splitting.

The bamboo "bleeder" arrow is made in a similar manner except that the palm shaft is shorter and a piece of bamboo, almost a foot long and three to four inches wide, is fastened to it as a point. The bamboo tip and sides are honed to razor sharpness, completing the process.

Although bows and arrows are seldom used for hunting today except by some of the older men, the Yuquí continue to manufacture them for the tourist market. A set consisting of a bow and two arrows marketed in Bolivia's urban areas by the missionaries will bring about US $15–20, a significant amount of cash income for the Yuquí. It is interesting that although the Yuquí understand that these weapons will never be used for hunting, they take great care in their manufacture. When Guillermo offered to make a set for me so that I could photograph the process, he spent time selecting only the best of his *chuchillo* staffs and constantly checked the arrows throughout the procedure for trueness. Even the shorter black palm shaft was heated over a fire several times and then bent across Guillermo's head to achieve the straightness required for an arrow that will shoot properly.

The money earned from making bows and arrows frequently may be applied toward the purchase of a firearm. Fearing settlers' guns for years, the Yuquí nonetheless were eager to learn to use this new weapon. Owning a gun now has become a status symbol as well, and those men who are interested in achieving greater recognition attempt to purchase more than one. Most of these weapons, usually 16 gauge shotguns or .22 rifles, are supplied by the

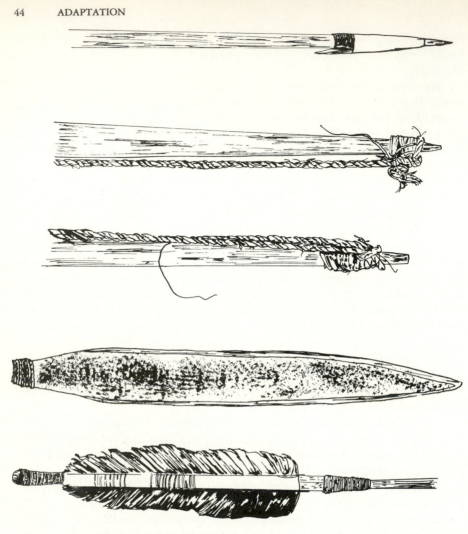

Figure 6. Details of Yuquí bow and arrows

missionaries, who, through other contacts, are able to locate used weapons in good condition that the Yuquí can reasonably afford to buy. Each Yuquí acquiring a firearm for the first time is taught by the missionaries how to use it and must demonstrate his proficiency and knowledge of safety procedures before receiving the weapon. In spite of the magnitude of the technological leap from bow and arrow to firearms, the younger Yuquí men made the change easily. The shotgun is carried with the same aplomb as a bow, creating an image of man and weapon as uniquely one.

Having a gun greatly increases hunting efficiency (Hames 1979), but it also has contributed to the depletion of game in the areas near camp. Firearms present an additional problem in that shells must be purchased, creating a dependency on the outside world for subsistence. Still, guns are now a necessary part of survival for the Yuquí both as a means to provide meat as well as a symbol of safe conduct in the world of the *Abá*. A man carrying a gun in the forest is immediately recognized as being "civilized."

Stringmaking

Yuquí women are makers of string. It was string that enabled men to hunt and it was string that defined the boundaries of Yuquí society. Next to the bow and arrow, which provided food, hammocks and baby slings represented the comfort and identity that were so important to group and individual existence. It was these three items, then, that were the essence of Yuquí technology. All else was transitory, made and then discarded.

Stringmaking begins by stripping the tough, fibrous bark from the *imbai* tree, a task performed by both men and women. As noted earlier, these trees are infested with red ants so the gathering of bark is a painful chore. The outer bark must then be peeled off, leaving coarse strips of leather-like cortex. This is chewed, shredded, and soaked until a bundle of thin fibers remains. Once sun-dried, the women twine the fibers into cord by rolling them across

Photo 10. Guillermo holds his completed set of bow and arrows. The store/clinic stands in the background.

Photo 11. Elsa stripping imbai *bark to prepare for stringmaking.*

their bare thighs. It is the making of string itself, rather than its incorporation into a finished product, that is so time-consuming. But because it is a mechanical act learned from early childhood and carried out almost without thought, women will sit and chat or tend meat on the fire, all the while rolling *imbai* into string.

When the New Tribes missionaries first contacted the Yuquí, the women were seen wearing what was presumed to be a garment. Actually, it was a baby sling, worn over one shoulder and across the body, giving it a sarong-like appearance. As women continued having children, they added to the sling, repairing places and widening it as well. Over time, the sling became larger and larger, holding a child comfortably to free the woman's arms for other tasks.

A baby sling was manufactured by continuously wrapping *imbai* string around the knees while the woman was sitting on the ground. As the woman spread her knees wider, the sling became larger in circumference. When the desired width was reached, several cross-strings were tied through the wrappings to hold each in place. The new sling was stiff and scratchy at first, but quickly became soft and pliable as animal fat and body secretions were worked into the fibers. Nowadays, Yuquí women prefer to use cotton cloth rather than *imbai* for baby slings or have abandoned them altogether.

Needing money and aware of my interest in the "old ways," Carolina agreed to make a sling so that I could record the process. Carolina put her hands on my shoulders to judge the size of the sling and then sat down and began to wrap her knees with one long continuous length of twine. About halfway along, she let out an angry grunt and unwrapped it all to begin once again. The problem? She felt she had misjudged my broad shoulders and the sling would not fit properly. I attempted to convey to her that I simply wanted the sling for demonstration purposes and that I had no intention of bearing any more children. But like Guillermo, she insisted that the product be serviceable and so remade the sling to her own satisfaction.

Another major application of string in the past and still in use today is in the manufacture of hammocks. The Yuquí hammock is similar to many of those made by other Amazonian people. Unlike many groups, however, who use the softer tree cotton fiber for twine, the Yuquí use *imbai*. Hammock cord is heavier in gauge than that used in baby slings but not as heavy as bowstring. Again, it is the twining of the string that occupies several weeks, while the actual making of the hammock takes less than a day. Once the cord has been prepared, two stout posts are cut and set upright in the ground. Then the twine is wrapped continuously around the posts until the desired width is reached. Another string is woven through the center to hold the individual cords in place, similar to fabricating a sling. Thick *imbai* rope is passed through the looped ends, tied, and the hammock is removed from the poles ready for use.

Hammocks are repaired frequently and may even be widened on occasion, but they are seldom replaced entirely. Today, the Yuquí sleep at night on palm board platforms, using blankets and mosquito nets provided by the mission. Contrary to commonly held notions that people such as the Yuquí become oblivious to biting insects and are able to ignore them, the mosquito

Photo 12. Making a string hammock.

net has become a most prized possession. Before contact, the Yuquí hung their hammocks over a small fire and slept in the protection of smoke. When nets were offered, they were quickly accepted as a superior method of avoiding the swarms of mosquitoes that appear at dusk. I was made aware of the value of the mosquito net to the Yuquí prior to dawn one morning at the Chimoré camp when I heard a strange sound in front of my house and got up to investigate. It was Manuel, a man in his 40s, sitting on my porch crying. He was distraught. I thought perhaps someone had died during the night. He told me that his net had gotten too close to his kerosene wick lamp and that a large hole had been burned in the side.

In spite of having sleeping platforms now, the Yuquí continue to use their hammocks as napping, resting, and social places. Men, for example, have not given up the tradition of returning from the hunt and promptly retiring to the hammock while someone else cleans their game. Hammocks are usually hung near the cooking fire as they were in the past when the hammock and fire signified the personal space of the nuclear family. In this manner, food can be easily reached from the hammock since eating is a normal part of socializing.

While among the Yuquí, I had no furniture other than what I could provide from local materials. I hung the hammock Elsa had made for me near my cooking fire and quickly realized the advantage of having a place to sit and rest that was near my source of food. It took me little time to adopt the Yuquí pattern of lying in my hammock while I ate. After a while, I learned that I could also do much of my cooking from the hammock as well. Accustomed to a much larger, wider, and more tightly woven Guarayo hammock (not native to them, however; the Franciscans taught Guarayo women to weave on an upright loom), I found the Yuquí hammock quite uncomfortable. The heavy cotton Guarayo hammock has a tight weave that supports the body well and is thick enough to keep mosquitoes from biting through the bottom. The Yuquí string hammock, on the other hand, offers no such protection, the reason why it was so quickly abandoned for nighttime sleeping when mosquito nets became available. The strings also must be periodically rearranged as they begin to place pressure on different parts of the body.

In the past, both a man and a woman slept in a single hammock, heads at opposite ends, with the youngest child in the middle. Since the Yuquí hammock is by no means commodious, sleeping in this arrangement was warm and intimate but not extremely restful. Then too, the fire had to be tended, children nursed, and an ear kept alert for the sound of an approaching jaguar or other dangers. The Yuquí slept in snatches and depended on periods during the day when they could sleep without such concerns. The camp now is usually quiet at night as people sleep under their nets and with few of the fears of the past.

During the precontact era, it is unlikely that the women spent as much time in stringmaking as they do now. Once the baby sling and hammock were made, they would need only occasional repair or alteration. Bow and arrow making also was not an ongoing activity and required the production of string

Photo 13. Julia works on a handbag, using imbai *cord to make the macramé article.*

only occasionally. Now the women have another use for their string and they also have more time in which to prepare it. Life at the mission camp is more secure but also less challenging. Women do not accompany their husbands on the hunt as frequently as they used to in the past. There is a stable supply of food in the form of store products and so inactivity is greater. This free time is spent in chatting or cooking and eating, but it is also spent in making string into macramé items that are sold in the cities along with the men's bows and arrows. For many of the women, this is a primary source of outside income and provides them with mirrors, cloth, soap, thread, needles, hair clips, combs, and other commodities. Family finances are a common area of contention as men and women vie for the small amount of ready cash for their individual needs. Women typically keep household money in a jar or can that they carry with them constantly to avoid theft; but as the custodians of the family bank account, they are often less than generous in handing out the money to their husbands.

Basketry

Insofar as basketwork goes, the Yuquí do not stand among the ranks of the most proficient or versatile. Their baskets are rudimentary at best and have little aesthetic appeal. Like virtually everything else in their lives as nomads, baskets and other objects woven of palm had a strictly utilitarian value, and were used until they wore out or were simply discarded as the group moved to another camp.

Actually, Yuquí basketry is more a form of mat making, consisting of folding a palm mat to form a basket-like container. A standard double her-ringbone weave, used throughout the Amazon, is employed in all their work. The center stalk of the palm, any number of varieties of which are used, is selected for most articles manufactured by the Yuquí. This center is the new growth and as such is pliable and has an almost velvet-like feel. The color, a soft yellow, is also pleasing to the eye. In precontact years, this young stalk could be broken out of the palm crown or cut with the teeth. Today, it is cut cleanly with a machete or knife.

The most commonly made articles are the *jinoquio*, which is a palm back-pack carried with a tumpline of vine, and the *iruu*, an envelope-type basket made in differing sizes to store food, household articles, or arrow-making supplies. The *jinoquio* is usually made on the spot, when something needs to be carried back to camp, and may consist of the larger, coarser palm leaves as well as the center stalk. This is a hastily made rectangular container fre-quently crudely woven and characterized by open spaces and stray leaves protruding from the sides. It is finished by braiding the edges. The *jinoquio* seldom lasts very long. It may come apart even before camp is reached; it is repaired with vines and then discarded after it has been unloaded.

The *iruu* is a palm mat that is folded in half and then braided together to enclose the remaining two sides to form a container. These are better made than the *jinoquio*, will be kept for a longer period, but ultimately are ex-pendable. This basic basket shape is also used to catch mudfish by scooping them up from shallow ponds. The Yuquí call these baskets *jirayruu*, literally "fish basket" (jira = spiny fish; iruu = basket). The fish, which are quite small, are then packed into a *jinoquio* that has been lined with leaves to keep them from slipping through the holes, and carried back to camp.

Other Technology

One afternoon Leonarda, a few of the Yuquí women, and I were talking about trying to make some pottery. Julia said that she knew where to find clay, and the next day she and several others arrived with a few large chunks. We mixed the clay with water and began to try our hand at pottery making. Leonarda and I had both made pottery previously and so were able to fashion a few objects. None of the Yuquí women with us, however, demonstrated any knowledge of this craft, leading me to believe that it was unknown to them. But then one of the women said, "Let's go get Ángela, she will know

Photos 14a, 14b. With son Ramon sharing her hammock, Elsa weaves a palm mat inside their house. The smoke from the cook fire can be seen in the background.

how." Ángela, perhaps in her late 70s, is the oldest living Yuquí. She is also quite blind now, and had to be led to us by one of the women. When she was settled on the grass beside us, I handed her a ball of clay, which she immediately began to work, a small smile appearing on her face. In her clipped, high-pitched voice she told about a dream she had recently. In her dream, she said, she was once again holding clay, something she had not done for many years. Her gnarled fingers made a few crude coils and she began to fashion a small pot. After a while, she gave up the effort, but it was obvious that at one time she had been able to make pottery. Later, I learned that when the group fissioned from the parent band many years ago, the women who "knew" how to make pottery remained behind. This was an interesting incident, since it is indicative of how quickly a form of technology can be lost. As I have previously noted, the Yuquí are most likely a people who have experienced deculturation, or the loss of culture, as the result of their isolation and diminishing population. No doubt the increase in hostile encounters with Bolivians in recent years has contributed to an even greater acceleration of culture loss as more people were killed and the group was forced to move frequently to escape detection. Then too, once contact was made with the missionaries and trade articles were available, such things as clay pots would be quickly given up in favor of aluminum utensils and dishes.

In a similar fashion, the Yuquí lost the technology to produce fire. This phenomenon is relatively rare, given that fire is so essential to human adaptation. Yet, at the time of contact, the Yuquí, like their Sirionó cohorts, had no means of making fire and depended instead on preserving it. The loss of fire, an infrequent occurrence because great care was always taken to ensure that live coals were available, meant not only the inconvenience of not having light, heat, and protection, but also the real threat of hunger. The Yuquí will not eat raw meat or, for that matter, meat showing any sign of being under-cooked. Thus, losing fire meant that the band would have to subsist on fruits, tubers, and palm heart until fire could be secured. Lightning strikes would be a convenient source if found, but more likely the group would have to raid a farm to replenish its fire. This was dangerous from the perspective not only of being killed outright, but of carrying disease back to camp, where it would spread among the others.

It is interesting that even with the availability of matches and kerosene, many of the Yuquí continue to tend their fires through the night. There is always fire in camp, and if one needs it, a burning brand can be gotten from a neighbor. It is also common, as it no doubt was in the past, for women to carry fire along when they accompany the men on a hunt. In this way if the hunt is successful, some of the meat, particularly the organs, can be consumed immediately. Also, if a great deal of game is captured a long distance from camp, a hunter may prefer to remain in the forest to smoke the meat over a *quietá*, a triangular- or rectangular-shaped grill made of green sticks. Once the meat is cooked and dry, it can be more easily transported back to the settlement. There is another motive for this, however, and that is to avoid sharing a large portion of the meat with one's relatives. Rarely will a man stay in the forest alone; rather, he will have his wife with him or will return to get her after he has made his kill. The time away from camp with an abundance of meat becomes a private interlude for the couple, that is, if the news of a kill can be kept secret. More likely, others will accompany him back to where the game is to share in the feast or to help carry it home. When men hunt without their wives, they prefer to carry matches in order to have both hands free.

Prior to contact, the Yuquí built actual structures only for the dead. These were called "corpse houses" (*jirisue tai*) and consisted of forming large palm fronds into a "teepee" over the dead. Recently, in the contacts with the forest Yuquí in the Vívora River area, it was reported by the missionaries that the corpse house used by this group was of a somewhat different style. The Vívora band tied a cross-piece between two trees and stacked palm against it. This is particularly noteworthy in that it corresponds exactly to the type of structure built by the Sirionó as a dwelling place, further corroborating the theory that the Sirionó and Yuquí once formed a single group. It is also significant that while the Yuquí gave up shelters for themselves, they continued to honor their dead by providing them with a "roof" (*tai*).

In the heavy rain forest of the Ichilo region where the overhead canopy is dense, building a palm shelter becomes somewhat redundant. Then too, with the group being pressed to move on, the chore of erecting a structure every few nights would rapidly become tedious. During rain or cold weather, palm would be placed over individual hammocks to provide additional protection. Even now, with adequate shelter, the Yuquí are seldom daunted by poor weather. Many of the men will leave for the hunt in pouring rain, returning hours later cold and soaking wet. It is also common to see several people sitting in the missionary area during a steady drizzle, resting under the trees by a smoky fire cooking fish or eating fruit. Getting rained on is simply a minor inconvenience.

In addition to cutting a few palm fronds during inclement weather, in the past the Yuquí required that women "go behind leaves" following childbirth and during menstruation. This "menstrual hut," known as a *queesa* (the word also means "nest"), also could not be classified as an actual structure since it consisted only of a few fronds placed butt-end in the ground to form a screen.

This, then, completes the Yuquí inventory of traditional technology, with perhaps the exception of bamboo slivers used as cutting implements and a hastily made container for honey (see Figure 7). As technologies go, it is one of the least elaborate known. Yet the Yuquí survived; and had those at the Chimoré camp been left unmolested, no doubt they would have continued to exploit their environment in ways adequate to meet their needs. But with their limited technology and confrontation with the modern world, the Yuquí were quick to adopt the conveniences offered by outsiders bearing more sophisticated knowledge. Clothing, cooking pots, knives, machetes, axes, matches, and firearms, along with a myriad of other items, are now necessities of Yuquí existence. The seduction is complete, making it unlikely that the

Figure 7. Palm flower sheath container (normally used for honey)

Yuquí could ever return to a simpler way of life. It is this dependence more than anything else that ties them to the mission and makes them so vulnerable to the forces that control their lives but remain beyond their comprehension. Now, many traditional technologies such as making bows and arrows and baby slings are important only as anachronisms, the items to be sold to tourists and visiting anthropologists.

HUNTING AND FISHING

When I first began living among lowland Bolivian peasants, I thought it very unsportsmanlike of them to hunt with lights and bait. However, I soon learned that for the peasants, the purpose of hunting was not sport but to secure meat for their families. Thus, they would build a *chapapa*, a platform in a tree that was dropping fruit, and there the hunters would wait in the dark, ready with guns and flashlights as soon as game could be heard eating at the base of the tree. Lowland hunters were also not above leaving salt in likely places, returning a few days later to capture some animal habituated to the baiting site.

Except for using lights now and then to hunt at night, the Yuquí have continued their old pattern of walking the forest in search of game. They do not set bait, build platforms, or use snares of any type, including modern steel spring traps for animals whose hides have commercial value. Considering that the Yuquí travel so much of the *monte* (forest) barefoot, steel traps would do them no great service.

Most hunting takes place from early morning until dusk, when men will go out alone or in groups of two or three. Women as well may accompany hunters and are skilled in tracking, calling animals (particularly monkeys), and helping to carry game back to camp. When a large group of white-lipped peccaries is sighted (usually heard and smelled first), a hunter will return to gather all the available men in camp and together they will kill as many animals as possible. For days afterward, meat will smoke on *quietá*s and people will be seen carrying large pieces around with them to eat at their leisure. When there is meat in camp, the Yuquí eat constantly until it is gone. In fact, they have been known to make themselves sick with vomiting and diarrhea from overindulgence. Having meat also means that men may remain in camp for several days before going out again in search of game.

With the availability of flashlights, the Yuquí venture forth at night more often now than in the past, particularly if there is a full moon to help light the way. Some animals are known to be more active in the early hours of the morning before daybreak. Small groups of hunters, at times accompanied by wives and children, will leave camp at two or three in the morning knowing that if they are successful in finding game, it will be daylight by the time they return.

The Yuquí begin a hunt by deciding on what direction to take from camp. Many strategies may operate in arriving at this decision, including having had a previous successful hunt along that particular route or the knowledge that the area has not been hunted recently. Sometimes an animal will be seen during a hunt but not taken, and the hunter is hopeful that it will be there

Photo 15. A group of Yuquí rest in the forest during a hunting trip.

on a return hunt. Since hunting is often combined with other activities such as gathering wild fruits or collecting honey, knowledge of the availability of these resources also will influence the hunter's direction.

Trails used for hunting radiate out from camp in all directions, becoming less visible as the distance from camp increases. The Yuquí will tend to follow these trails, since they are familiar routes and offer the course of least resistance. Once an animal is sighted or heard, the hunter will take off through the forest in pursuit. It is at this point that the hunt becomes exciting and dangerous since hunters are virtually oblivious to the barriers they may encounter as they track their prey. Once shot, if the animal does not die immediately, it will usually seek the most difficult cover, forcing the hunter into even more dense underbrush or marsh to retrieve his animal. Those species that can defend themselves will take this opportunity to turn on their two-legged enemy, gashing a limb with a tusk or leaving a bite that quickly becomes infected.

Once the animal has been retrieved, a hunter may choose to place it in a tree while he pursues other game. If it is a large animal and the likelihood of getting more game that day seems dim, he will simply tie a vine through its mouth and around the hindquarters, sling it over his shoulders, and return to camp.

In years past, the Yuquí went on long hunts of several days, travelling 20 or 30 kilometers from the Chimoré camp. These hunts are becoming less frequent now as the Yuquí enjoy the comforts of their houses and the amenities of a sedentary life, and are also encouraged to remain in camp in order for their children to attend school. While I was with the Yuquí, only one family, that of Joel and Elsa, my closest neighbors, left camp for more than a day. They were gone for five days; but from all accounts, they were never more than one day's walk from the settlement. It is interesting that this was the family that suffered most from meat shortages. It was their hope that by moving away from the overhunted camp area, they would be more successful in capturing game. A collared peccary was taken during this trip, but this one animal alone did not fulfill the family's expectations of plentiful meat. They returned somewhat disheartened and tired from the trek.

While the Yuquí enjoy the advantages of a settled existence, it has also meant that game has become increasingly scarce. For example, the men complain that monkeys are now much harder to find unless the hunter ventures far from the camp. It was also true that those hunters who had access to canoes and therefore were able to cross the river, where hunting was less frequent, tended to have the higher totals in kilos of game taken (see table 1) during my 56 days of observation (October through December).

As game has become more scarce, the Yuquí have had to increase their dependence on fishing to supply animal protein. Lacking a more elaborate technology and fearing being spotted in open places, in the past the Yuquí limited their fishing to small ponds on a seasonal basis. At least according to their own perception, fishing was a relatively unimportant subsistence activity.

Photo 16. Manuel with a peccary he has brought back from a hunting trip. He skinned and gutted the animal in the forest before tying vines around its head and midsection to carry it back to camp.

Thus, their society developed a strong emphasis on hunting, and all that was valued was linked ultimately to the provision of meat. Since the Yuquí regard the hunt and hunting ability so highly, it came as a surprise to learn that 57% of Yuquí animal protein is now provided by fish (see table 2). From a statistical standpoint at least, the Yuquí are no longer "hunters" in the strict sense of the term. It was also notable that two of the men, Lorenzo and Jonatán, did no hunting whatsoever during the study period. This has a number of interesting implications. The Yuquí men were, of course, aware that I was keeping some type of count of their hunting and fishing activities. Thus it would be naive to think that this did not influence their behavior to some extent. (Some of the men eventually began to question me about how much game their neighbors had captured for the day. I tried to avoid any direct response to these questions, to reduce the possibility of open competition among the hunters.) Since hunting remains a high prestige activity, it would be expected that during the time of my survey at least, there would be a tendency for men to hunt more frequently and fish less often in order to achieve parity with their peers. That this did not happen in two cases is curious, and perhaps it is indicative of the changes that are occurring in Yuquí concepts of prestige. The two men who fished only were both *saya*, or "ruling caste" (this will be discussed in Chapter 4). Therefore, it could be maintained that they had little

TABLE 1   RELATIONSHIP BETWEEN HUNTING ACROSS THE
RIVER AND POTENTIAL HUNTING SUCCESS

Rank by Total Game Captured	Number of Hunts Across River	Number of Hunts Across River as a % of Total Number of Hunts	Kilos of Game Captured Across River as a % of Total Kilos of Game Captured
1. Jaime	8	38	73
2. Leonardo	7	50	54
3. Humberto	2	15	40
4. Daniel	6	37	87
5. Alejandro*	3	37	67
6. Joel	2	18	40
7. Jorge	2	22	67
8. Timoteo	2	18	25
9. Tomás	1	12	27
10. Lucas	2	11	65
11. Guillermo†	1	10	6
12. Victor	1	20	64
13. Manuel	2	33	55
14. Benjamin	0	0	0
15. Jonatán‡	—	—	—
16. Lorenzo‡	—	—	—

* Alejandro's 150-kilo tapir has not been included here; it was a jackpot kill on the camp side of the river.

† Guillermo captures tortoises and armadillos on the camp side of the river. This type of game is often not sought by the better hunters since it is easy to capture and, therefore, of low prestige.

‡ Did not hunt.

to risk in the first place. But given the traditional importance placed on hunting no matter what one's status might be and the fact that the men knew that they were being monitored, the deviation from expected patterns is significant. Even those men who were poor hunters and spent most of their time fishing, like Guillermo, tried their hand at hunting now and then, if only to avoid scorn. With this in mind, it is also noteworthy that Humberto, an ex-slave and socially isolated at the time of my research, was one of those who hunted most frequently. While I did not document his behavior during those periods when I was not taking game counts, I have the suspicion that he was hunting far more often than usual, leading me to believe that he was trying to use my data gathering as a means to improve his status within the band. He also had the highest rate of success, pointing to the fact that by simply going out more frequently, a hunter will increase his chance of encountering game, and, if he is reasonably competent, will bring it in. It should also be mentioned, however, that Humberto ranked only fourth in total number of kilos of animal protein captured, outperformed by two other hunters and, more importantly, by Lorenzo, one of the two men who chose only to fish during this 56-day period (see table 3). What this indicates is that while Humberto went out

TABLE 2 RANKING OF YUQUÍ BY GAME AND FISH TAKES

GAME TAKES		FISH TAKES	
Name	Kilos	Name	Kilos
1. Alejandro	226.00*	1. Lorenzo	279.60
2. Jaime	185.50	2. Guillermo	199.25
3. Leonardo	152.50	3. Jonatán	198.00
4. Humberto	144.75	4. Benjamin	128.00
5. Daniel	78.00	5. Tomás	123.80
6. Joel	74.50	6. Humberto	120.50
7. Jorge	59.50	7. Daniel	119.50
8. Timoteo	51.00	8. Lucas	107.50
9. Tomás	51.00	9. Jaime	101.00
10. Lucas	46.00	10. Alejandro	53.75
11. Guillermo	45.75	11. Victor	38.25
12. Victor	29.50	12. Joel	34.25
13. Manuel	14.50	13. Manuel	28.50
14. Benjamin	10.50	14. Jorge	23.00
15. Jonatán	0.00	15. Leonardo	8.50
16. Lorenzo	0.00	16. Timoteo	1.50
Total	1,169.00	Total	1,564.90

Total fish and game captured = 2,733.90 kilos.
  game as % of total taken = 43
  fish as % of total taken = 57

* Includes 150-kilo tapir.

TABLE 3 RANKING OF YUQUÍ
FISH AND GAME TAKES BY WEIGHT

Name	Kilos
1. Jaime	286.50
2. Alejandro	279.75*
3. Lorenzo	279.60
4. Humberto	265.25
5. Guillermo	245.00
6. Jonatán	198.00
7. Daniel	197.50
8. Tomás	174.80
9. Leonardo	161.00
10. Lucas	153.50
11. Benjamin	138.50
12. Joel	108.75
13. Jorge	82.50
14. Victor	67.75
15. Timoteo	52.50
16. Manuel	43.00

* Includes 150-Kilo tapir.

TABLE 4   FISHING AND HUNTING SUCCESS RATE BY TRIP

Name	# Trips Out	# Trips Successful	Rate%
1. Humberto	31	29	93%
2. Benjamin	12	11	91%
3. Jonatán	27	24	88%
4. Guillermo	37	31	83%
4. Victor	12	10	83%
5. Daniel	34	28	82%
5. Lorenzo	23	19	82%
6. Lucas	29	23	79%
7. Leonardo	18	14	77%
8. Alejandro	30	23	76%
9. Manuel	12	9	75%
9. Tomás	20	15	75%
10. Jaime	30	22	73%
11. Jorge	11	8	72%
12. Timoteo	11	7	63%
13. Joel	21	12	57%

more often and was usually successful (93% of the time), he brought back less in total weight than those men who went out less often (see table 4). Much of this can be explained by the fact that he always hunted alone and did not have access to a canoe, and was therefore restricted to hunting on the camp side of the river.

Fishing with a hook and line is a new technology, taught to the Yuquí by the missionaries. Of late, a net was acquired and it is Lorenzo who has learned how to use it most effectively. Lorenzo also purchased a small outboard motor with the money he made from selling fish to the mission pilot, who flies it out to Cochabamba. The outboard enables Lorenzo and the two younger men who most frequently accompany him, Jonatán (who like Lorenzo chose only to fish) and Tomás (who engaged in some sporadic hunting when he could borrow a gun, usually mine), to fish farther afield and to cover more area in a single day of fishing. It is notable that Lorenzo sold[4] the greatest amount of fish and game (98+ kilos) of anyone, including those men who hunted as well as fished, giving him the single highest cash income derived from foraging activities. Lorenzo, Jonatán, and Tomás, the three men who elected to fish, ranked one, two, and three in terms of total kilos of fish and game sold (see table 5), but it should be noted that what they sold was *fish*, not game. While perhaps Tomás chose to fish only because he had no firearm of his own, Lorenzo and Jonatán, who both had guns, obviously had determined that the best returns no longer came from hunting but from fishing; more important, they were willing to challenge traditional values of prestige to pursue this activity.

4. Fish and game were sold to the missionaries for their own consumption and to the missionary pilot who took primarily fish to Cochabamba where it was distributed among mission personnel and other clientele.

Photo 17. A young Yuquí cleans and fillets a catfish, one of many varieties of large catfish found in the Chimoré River. This fish is being prepared for sale to a mission pilot. Normally, the fish are cooked whole over the fire or cut into large pieces.

While Lorenzo, Jonatán, the ex-slave Guillermo, and perhaps Tomás selected fishing as a preferred subsistence strategy, the other men persisted in their efforts to secure animal protein by hunting. Alejandro with 226 kilos of game taken in the 56-day period ranked number one, although 150 kilos of his total came from one animal, a tapir. If we exclude this animal, he would rank only fifth in a field of 16 hunters. Discounting the two men who did not hunt at all, the ex-slave Benjamin ranked last in game captures, bringing in only 10.5 kilos of meat during the two-month study period. Part of Benjamin's lack of success as a hunter can be attributed to his having lost his .22 in the river when a canoe overturned. At that time, he did not know how to use a shotgun, but shortly before I left, he demonstrated his ability to use one to the satisfaction of the missionaries. It might be surmised that if he is able to obtain a firearm or borrow one frequently (quite unlikely given that the owner will want to use it as well), Benjamin will increase his success as a hunter. Like his brother Guillermo, he is a good fisherman, and ranked fourth among the men in this activity. He also has the highest number of hours logged working for the missionaries, and, of all the Yuquí, seems to enjoy it most. Benjamin worked 138 hours during the 56-day period during which I tabulated his activities, as compared with the next highest man at 36 hours. As a wage laborer and fisherman, Benjamin does well by his family, although he is isolated somewhat because of his excessive attachment to the missionaries. This isolation is increased because he is an ex-slave who con-

TABLE 5   FISH AND GAME EXCHANGE

Name	Kilos Captured (Sold)		Kilos Given (to Number of Individuals)	Kilos Received (from Number of Individuals)	Total Consumed
1. Jaime	286.50	(4.00)	57.50 (7)	0.00 (0)	225.00
2. Daniel	197.50	(0.00)	20.75 (8)	8.00 (2)	184.75
3. Benjamin*	138.50	(10.00)	18.50 (4)	25.75 (5)	135.75
4. Timoteo*	52.50	(0.50)	3.00 (2)	88.75 (11)	137.75
5. Jorge	82.50	(1.00)	15.50 (3)	7.50 (2)	73.50
6. Jonatán	198.00	(50.50)	19.00 (3)	0.00 (0)	128.50
7. Lucas	153.50	(16.50)	51.00 (7)	5.00 (1)	91.00
8. Joel*	108.75	(8.50)	25.75 (8)	3.00 (1)	77.50
9. Guillermo*	245.00	(23.00)	50.50 (8)	5.00 (1)	176.50
10. Leonardo	161.00	(0.50)	57.00 (7)	77.00 (12)	180.50
11. Manuel	43.00	(0.00)	4.00 (4)	78.75 (7)	117.75
12. Victor	67.75	(10.00)	5.75 (4)	86.00 (9)	138.00
13. Alejandro	279.75†	(3.00)	60.50 (6)	25.25 (4)	241.50
14. Lorenzo	279.60	(98.25)	59.50 (10)	15.00 (2)	136.85
15. Humberto*	265.25	(0.00)	98.00 (7)	9.25 (2)	176.50
16. Tomás	174.80	(74.80)	10.50 (3)	27.50 (5)	117.00
Totals	2,733.90	(300.55 sold)	556.75	461.75	2,338.35

Total kilos consumed = 2,433.35.
  (Unaccounted for = 95.00 kilos—probably given to Carolina and Ester, a female household)
  * Ex-slaves.
  † Includes 150-kilo tapir.

tinues to perform menial tasks, while his brothers and other ex-slaves do no more than other men in need of cash. In addition, he is married to Rebeca, a young woman who reportedly was struck by lightning and is partially paralyzed. Her handicap makes her the brunt of jokes, and she is unable to perform the same activities as other women.

While hunting and fishing activities that make use of technologies such as hook and line, nets, poison, firearms, or bows may be "flashier" and therefore more noteworthy from the perspective of the observer, I also found that a good deal of fish and game are taken simply by clubbing or killing the animal with a machete. It must be remembered that with the use of firearms, the Yuquí must purchase ammunition, a limiting factor in deciding what to shoot and what to take using other means. Many animals are slow moving or can be found in burrows. Armadillos, for example, are found under the ground, and after digging with a stick or machete, the Yuquí club them or cut the neck with a blade. There is something uninvolved about seeing an animal shot with a gun from a distance, almost as if death had come from some unknown force of nature. Witnessing an animal being clubbed to death is a much more personal experience and one that I found distressing at times. But on those days when meat was scarce, I discovered that my squeamishness was short-lived as I anticipated a nice fat little armadillo roasting over the fire.

Tortoises are another animal that is captured and then bludgeoned. They are relatively plentiful and, on those days when a hunter is not successful, become a last resort so that he does not return home empty-handed. They were also the favorite catch of the poorer hunters, typically ex-slaves, or the older men who were not up to daily treks in the forest. The advantage of the tortoise is that it is the Yuquí's only storable meat. Several tortoises can be tied with vines and then hung from a post in the house, or in some cases can be tied to a leash and allowed to roam the corner of the sleeping area. Some attempt may be made to feed them as if they were pets (they take ripe plantains quite readily), but ultimately they will be slaughtered.

This same approach is used with fish both in oxbow lakes and after the river has flooded. The Chimoré River has periods of severe flooding, when the waters may rise up over the banks and flow through low areas. The water becomes opaque with silt and is choked with trees and brush that have been swept off eroded banks. When the flood waters recede, large ponds remain in the sandy river banks, trapping numerous fish that can be easily clubbed or killed with a machete. This is a favorite activity of the women and children since there is no danger of drowning and the fish are already beginning to become sluggish from lack of oxygen and the rapidly heating water. The fish

Photo 18. Although he took along a shotgun, Timoteo failed to shoot any game. Instead, he brings home a large tortoise, which will be kept alive until the family decides to kill and eat it. In his left hand, Timoteo holds a piece of cooked meat someone has given him.

Photo 19. *Joel and Elsa admire a good catch of fish while daughter Margarita selects a fish to smoke over the fire.*

are simply hacked at, often unseen, as blades cut indiscriminately through the water.

When fish are plentiful, a few of the Yuquí inevitably will build a fire near the river and begin cooking their catch as soon as it is brought in. After several days of this, I became tired of a constant diet of fish, wishing that the men would go on a hunt. When I questioned the Yuquí whether they as well were tiring of the steady diet of fish, they just laughed and made fun of me. On other occasions, however, I found that the wives of those men who primarily fished did complain of the lack of meat in their houses and, to break the monotony of their diets, would trade their fish with those neighbors who hunted.

The Yuquí also fish in the oxbow lakes that are scattered throughout their territory. Here, the water is stagnant and fish are more easily caught. The older men continue to bow fish in these ponds, waiting for a telltale ripple as a fish surfaces briefly and then shooting it midbody. I always felt very much in awe of the Yuquí and their ability to see these small signs of fish. No matter how hard I tried to spot a ripple, I was always a few seconds late in making my identification. At the moment I caught the movement, an arrow had already pierced the water. Some of the men continue to fish in these small lakes by using *chimbó* vine (a type of barbasco). The vine is cut into lengths of about 18 inches and tied in a bundle with a liana. After wading into the water, the men begin beating on the bundle with sticks, shredding the pieces of vine. A white sap is released, turning black as it mixes with the pond water. As the poison spreads, some of the fish begin to seek the surface where they can be scooped up or clubbed. Others move to one end of the pond in an attempt to escape the flow of poison, only to be captured by the women who wade in with sticks or old arrow points used as short spears, or who simply pick up the stunned fish with their hands.

Anthropologists have frequently mentioned the importance of redistribution among foraging peoples, focusing on the tradition of reciprocity in providing for relatively equal distribution of resources. I found this concept of egalitarian behavior to be somewhat more complex among the Yuquí, and at times simply not the case.

During precontact years, the Yuquí all shared a single camp, and anyone returning from a successful hunt was immediately surrounded by his kinspeople and expected to share the catch. Theoretically, everyone still has equal access to fish and game since no request will be denied. But with separate houses now, a man may return to his home with fish or game before anyone notices; and once inside the seclusion of his own grounds, there is greater reluctance to share his take. Since much of my research involved keeping track of fish and game captured by the Yuquí, I always tried to be present when a hunter returned with his catch. If I waited too long, it was likely to be consumed before I had a chance to weigh it. What I did not realize at first was that my presence while the meat was being dressed was a signal to the Yuquí that I expected some for myself. Hence, I was not welcomed at the fire and frequently was met with indifference or even hostility. A portion was always offered, but I would refuse, not feeling comfortable about taking part of the family's meal without having some stake in it. This reaction was typically

Photo 20. Two Yuquí men prepare chimbó *vine to poison fish in a small pond. The vine is beaten, releasing the sap into the water. The fish collect in the shallow end of the pond and are picked up by hand or speared using old arrow points.*

TABLE 6   ANIMAL PROTEIN CONSUMPTION (FISH AND GAME)

Name	Total Consumption (56 Days) in Kilos*	Family Size†	Total Average Consumption per Person in Kilos	Average Consumption per Day/Person in Kilos	Usable Portion Consumed per Day/Person (65% of Live Weight) in Grams	Animal Protein Consumed per Day/Person in Grams‡
1. Jaime	225.00	6	68.29	1.21	780	156
2. Daniel	184.75	(Shares meat with Jaime)				
3. Benjamin	135.75	3	45.25	.80	520	104
4. Timoteo	137.75	4 (1)	34.43	.61	390	78
5. Jorge	73.50	8 (1)	25.25	.45	290	58
6. Jonatán	128.50	(Member of Jorge's household)				
7. Lucas	91.00	(Shares meat with Joel)				
8. Joel	77.50	7 (1)	24.07	.42	270	54
9. Guillermo	176.50	6 (1)	29.41	.52	330	66
10. Leonardo	180.50	4 (1)	45.12	.80	520	104
11. Manuel	117.75	4 (1)	29.43	.52	330	66
12. Victor	138.00	5	27.60	.49	310	62
13. Alejandro	241.50	5	48.30	.86	550	110
14. Lorenzo	136.85	3 (1)	45.61	.81	520	104
15. Humberto	176.50	4 (1)	44.12	.78	500	100
16. Tomás	117.00	2 (2)	58.50	1.04	670	134
Totals	2,338.35	61 (10)				

Average grams animal protein consumed per day/person = 88.40 (computed on base figures).
   (Adjusted to game consumption only = 38.01)
   (Adjusted to fish consumption only = 50.39)
 * Carolina and Ester's consumption unknown.
 † ( ) = Children under 2 years of age. They are excluded from calculations.
 ‡ Protein per 100g edible portion of fish or game is 20g (Leung and Flores 1961).

met with puzzlement, since it is incomprehensible to the Yuquí to refuse any offering of food. Once the people realized that I did not expect a share of the day's take, some of the indifference displayed at my untimely arrival abated. However, it was not until I began doing favors for individuals and had established myself as someone of worth that I felt comfortable accepting meat. But once I did, I had entered into the system of exchange involving debts and obligations. Meat was now offered without grudge and I gladly accepted it. The Yuquí were always concerned by the small amounts I took (usually about a half pound) and would often inquire if I was *"erasi"* (sick). What to me was an adequate supply of game for at least two meals was considered a mere snack by the Yuquí.

    In computing grams of animal (both fish and game) protein consumed by the Yuquí, as a group they compare favorably with other Amazonians. (See table 6.) Chagnon (1983), for example, in comparing eleven observations of eight groups, lists an average protein consumption per adult of 88.8 grams per day. Adult Yuquí consume an average of 88.40 grams per day, but it should also be noted that if it were not for fishing, Yuquí animal protein intake of 38.01 grams per day would fall far below other averages.

The existence of present-day unequal exchange among the Yuquí is particularly evident if we examine the individual rates of protein consumption. They range from a high of 156 grams per day to a low of 54 grams per day, a significant difference in access to this important nutritional element. While it may be simply coincidence, the family that had the lowest per capita consumption of animal protein also suffered most frequently from internal strife and debilitating illness, further reducing their hunting opportunities. This was Joel's family, also the only one to go on a long hunt in an effort to secure more game by moving away from the overhunted camp area. The high rate of protein intake by some Yuquí also corroborates other findings that indicate that native peoples do not have self-imposed limits on the amount of game they take, or, as Clad (1984) comments, to *automatically* ascribe resource management skills to indigenous populations "buttresses the fallacy of the 'noble savage,' a uniquely European concept." The Yuquí persist in hunting far beyond what nutritionists have established as "reasonable" subsistence needs (about 55 grams per day) and consume meat in enormous amounts simply because they like the taste of it. However, it is important to note that they also are subject to "feast or famine" situations, experiencing periods of several days when no meat whatsoever is captured and therefore also suffering hunger. When game is encountered in large quantities in a "windfall" hunt, the Yuquí will kill all they can, feasting on the meat continually until it is consumed.

Underscoring the importance of meat in the Yuquí diet from a cultural if not nutritional perspective is the fact they they have two verbs to express hunger: *toria i*, to be hungry, and *eyibasi*, to be meat hungry. They also will consistently complain of hunger if meat is not available in large quantities. Their perception of meat scarcity would seem to be based not so much on absolute quantities but on relative amounts and inconsistent availability. Thus, on those days when the hunt has been "poor" (a couple of monkeys instead of a white-lipped peccary), the Yuquí perceive themselves as "suffering." Part of this reaction no doubt derives from the psychological insecurities inherent in depending on natural fauna for meat and the anxieties that build when game becomes intermittently scarce. From the Yuquí perspective, happiness is 18 peccaries or a 150-kilo tapir roasting on a fire. (For more on the debate on ecological determinism in protein consumption, see Johnson 1982; Sponsel 1986.)

GATHERING

One morning just before the sun was up over the horizon, several Yuquí came by my house to invite me to go on a honey-collecting expedition. This was the first of many such trips, although it was by far the most interesting since we would be going after the aggressive Africanized ("killer") honey bee. Actually, I did not know this at the outset; had I known, I probably would have found a convenient excuse not to join the party. My first indication and warning that this would be an unusual honey-gathering trip was the amount of extra clothing people were carrying along to cover themselves.

As is customary, the bee tree had been sighted by one of the men while hunting several days earlier. This is common practice among the Yuquí, both men and women, while they are out in the forest engaged in other activities. It is unusual to go specifically after honey without some prior knowledge that a tree has become home to a colony of bees, and I observed no occasion when someone simply grabbed an axe and began to wander through the forest in hopes of finding a convenient tree.

Thus, our group of five headed off into the woods in a direction known to all but me. In typical Yuquí fashion, we traveled single file down a known trail that gradually became less and less visible as a human concourse. Arriving at the edge of a small oxbow lake, the women promptly began to gather up firewood and started a fire with the brand that we had brought along. In the meantime, the men had gone farther down the trail encircling the pond to get a better look at our quarry. I followed Monica's daughter Cristina to see what we would be going after. The tree was immense, probably a good three feet in diameter and stretching to the top of the forest canopy. Hanging from a limb about 40 feet up was a large nest. I had never seen an external hive before since most bees prefer to protect their hives in the security of a tree bole. Africanized bees, I had once read, will build a colony in the open, a fact that apparently contributes to their aggressiveness. Seeing that the bees were uncontained in any way made me even more reluctant to participate in the project.

Cristina and I returned to the fire where the men had now gathered as well. Dried palm fronds were collected from the floor of the forest and placed near the fire. Then the men returned to the tree and began cutting at the base. Each axe blow sent vibrations up through the trunk and the bees responded by swarming around the nest and increasing the pitch of their buzzing. Convinced that this episode was going to lead to stung hands and faces or worse, I found a safe hiding place among a stand of broad-leafed plants and got down on my stomach. Cristina joined me, looking a little embarrassed at my surprised glance in her direction. We were at a safe distance but could still watch the entire scene unfolding in front of us.

When the men were at a point where only a few more blows would fell the tree, the women returned to the fire, gathered up the palm fronds and set one of them ablaze. They then returned to the tree while the men finished the job. As soon as the tree hit the ground, the remainder of the fronds were set on fire and people covered their heads with the extra clothing they had brought along. Waving burning palm, the group rushed into the cloud of furious bees. With fire and smoke they drove off the bees, the sound and smell of burning insects thick in the air. The honeycomb was quickly chopped up into pieces and placed into the cooking pots we had brought for that purpose. I could tell by all the slapping and swatting that people were getting stung and I felt no guilt at having chosen only to watch. Cristina seemed to share in my response. The honey was returned to the fire where we all sat down and began to eat, pulling off chunks of comb and dipping out the honey running into the bottom of the pot by using our fingers. I pulled off a chunk of comb and carefully began to remove the bee larvae that were interspersed among the cells filled with honey and pollen. Julia remarked that I was throwing away the best part, the "milk." I tried a few of the larvae, finding them more like blackboard chalk than milk, and decided that I would pass on this delicacy to my companions. Later, I reflected on this new development. The Yuquí, unlike many Amazonian foraging societies, will not eat insects or grubs. Since roasted or fried palm grubs are a favorite treat of many people in the Bolivian lowlands, including many of the *mestizos*, I was surprised when I learned that the Yuquí will not eat them. I could only conclude that in the Yuquí taxonomy, bee larvae are for some reason not categorized as either grubs or insects, but are indeed "milk" and therefore do not violate the Yuquí's dietary law that to be eaten something must have wings or feet (which also, consequently, excludes snakes).

Although the Yuquí today have access to refined sugar, they continue to pursue honey with remarkable zeal. It is also likely that they may actually consume greater amounts of honey now than they did in precontact days because of the availability of axes. In the past, honey located high up in a tree would have been difficult if not impossible to obtain. Now, the tree can be quickly felled and the honey extracted. The importance of honey in the Yuquí diet should not be underestimated given its abundance, the frequency with which it is consumed, and the fact that the Yuquí eat not only the honey but the larvae and pollen as well. The Yuquí are also capable of eating prodigious amounts of honey, and it is not uncommon to see an adult consume two pounds in a single sitting.

For the Yuquí, the forest is also a storehouse of fruits, tubers, and fiber. All useful plants are given names; in a period of just a few days of collecting specimens of these plants for me, the Yuquí provided a list of 95. This is especially significant given that the collecting was done within a radius of only about a kilometer from the camp and the fact that the Yuquí have a very poor inventory of medicinal plants. Thus, the great majority were items that were considered either edible or useful in providing some element of Yuquí technology.

Palm fruits are probably the most consistently available and prolific fruits gathered by the Yuquí. Palm heart (in the southern United States called "swamp cabbage") is another important item in the diet, although it is considered a "starvation" food because when meat was scarce in the past, the Yuquí were forced to fill up on this item. It is abundant in the forest and can be eaten raw or cooked, tasting a little like soft celery or cooked artichoke hearts. Since it is not a highly starchy food, however, it must be eaten in large amounts to satisfy hunger. Today, bananas and manioc have largely replaced palm heart as filler foods. Extracting palm heart involves a fair amount of effort, requiring that the palm be destroyed in the process of cutting

Photos 21a, 21b. Julia and Guillermo go out to take the honey from a tree Guillermo has spotted a few days earlier. First, Guillermo checks the tree to see if bees are still coming in and out of a small hole up in the trunk, indicating there is fresh honey present. While Julia waits, Guillermo prepares to start cutting down the tree. Once the tree is felled, the honey and beeswax are removed from the tree in large chunks. On the way back to camp, Guillermo takes a side trip to the river to catch some fish for dinner.

out the soft core from which new growth springs. On the other hand, bananas produce prolifically and simply have to be picked and peeled.

While the axe has proved a distinct advantage in the collection of honey and causes little environmental damage since the trees that contain this food harbor bees only because of disease in the tree's core, it is decidedly harmful in fruit collection. In the past, fruit was picked by climbing trees. Now they are commonly felled, destroying the source of the fruit. Some varieties, of course, grow quickly and if seedlings are present, will be replaced within just a few years. Others, however, require years of growth to reach maturity, and their destruction leads to the impoverishment of the Yuquí's supply of wild foods.

Gathering is a task that is typically viewed in many societies as primarily a woman's chore. Among the Yuquí, however, gathering is done by both men and women depending on the demands made on the time of each and the particular circumstances involved. Women, for example, will commonly gather *imbai* bark since it is they who will make the string and fabricate it into hammocks and baby slings. Nonetheless, if a woman is occupied with other chores and there is an available male, he will be prevailed upon to carry out this task. Fruits and tubers may also be gathered by both sexes if the male spouse or a son is unoccupied or would simply like to participate in the excursion. Gathering, like hunting, is seen by both men and women as an opportunity to have time alone together for sex, and for this reason children or other potential companions may be left behind.

Gathering is also an activity that is carried on while in the forest hunting or walking to a fishing hole. It is important to note that all of these activities—hunting, fishing, and gathering—while treated here as analytically separate, are not necessarily so in the minds of the Yuquí. Any excursion into the forest, for whatever reason, will take advantage of opportunities for food getting as they arise. If honey is encountered, for example, the hunt may be interrupted while it is extracted, assuming, of course, that members of the party have brought along an axe. If not, they will return the following day for it. Honey expeditions are particularly joyful and frequently involve several people. The person who first sighted the tree or hole where the bees are is the honey's "owner" and will organize the trip. If the honey is a good distance from camp, this will be a day-long excursion and additional food will be carried along, making a picnic of the event. While women and children sit and eat honey and roast plantains and manioc, the men will wander off periodically to look for game, and, if fortunate, the group will return home with both honey and meat.

FARMING

The Yuquí are an anomaly in today's world, for they represent a way of life that has all but disappeared. They are true foragers—people who do not farm. Many people of the Amazon who continue to hunt and gather while

Photos 22a, 22b. Not all honey hunts are successful. After Lucas fells a tree and cuts open the trunk to get at the hive, Loida discovers they have come up empty. There is very little honey in the hole.

also planting crops have been erroneously classified as foragers. In discussing this phenomenon with regard to the Yanomamö, Napoleon Chagnon writes (1983:59): "Although the Yanomamö may spend as much time 'hunting' as they do gardening, the bulk of their food comes from cultivated plants. The Yanomamö were persistently described by early visitors to the region as 'hunters and gatherers.' " The Yuquí, on the other hand, are what Steward and Faron (1959) termed "marginal foot nomads," groups that inhabited the fringes of the Amazon Basin, particularly the western reaches, where the Yuquí are found.

It is certain that at some point in their history, as part of a larger, more complex society, the Yuquí did indeed farm. If not, it would be difficult to explain the persistence of words in their language, which mesh perfectly with other Tupí-Guaraní groups who are farmers, for crops that they have no knowledge of producing. This is simply another strong indication that the Yuquí became full-time foragers as a last-ditch attempt to survive under conditions of extreme stress.

As greater numbers of colonists moved into the Ichilo region, it was not only the propinquity of strangers in Yuquí territory that ultimately led to hostile encounters, but the temptation of cultivated food. Had the Yuquí been willing to do so, they conceivably could have secluded themselves for a few years longer without significant discovery. They are astute at hiding under the cover of the forest and can remain undetected from all but the most experienced woodsmen. But the pleasures of consuming plantains, manioc, and corn were simply too much to resist. They became petty thieves, pilfering from the fields of the colonists, whose margin of risk was so small that they could not afford to allow the Indians to continue their activities. It was this that ultimately led them into a sedentary existence, for the missionaries were able to capitalize on the Yuquí's desire for both continued access to cultivated crops as well as the safety the mission offered from the retaliation of the settlers.

Swidden Horticulture

Before beginning a discussion of the Yuquí and their recent attempts to learn to farm, it is important to spend a few moments looking at farming technology in the Amazon in general. In this manner, the Yuquí and their shift in subsistence patterns can be understood in a wider context.

"Swidden" is an old English term rescued from obscurity by anthropologists and others to denote slash-and-burn methods of land clearing. "Horticulture" is another term used by anthropologists to describe farming that involves primarily the use of hand tools and human labor. Swidden horticulture is probably one of the earliest forms of growing crops and is still practiced by traditional peoples in much of the tropical and subtropical world.

Although it is common for proponents of modern agricultural practices to malign swidden technology as primitive, unproductive, and harmful to the environment, under traditional conditions it is probably the most adaptive and environmentally sound farming system yet devised for tropical areas like the Amazon Basin. There are two major conditions, however, that must be met for the system to function properly: low-density population and long fallows.

For many years people believed that the Amazon was an area of tremendous agricultural potential. After all, it was reasoned, if the Amazon could grow all those trees, it should be able to produce huge harvests of cereals and other "useful" plants. What eventually was learned, ironically, was that all that richness was tied up in the forest—the forest was feeding itself. It was the tremendous biomass, the living matter, that fell to the ground and created the fragile, shallow soils below that permitted the trees to grow and thrive. For this reason, many of the larger tropical trees have "buttresses" to support their huge mass. In a temperate climate like that of the United States with its fertile and deep soils, trees establish a long tap root to support their aboveground weight. In the tropics, trees must extend shallow root systems to take advantage of available nutrients near the surface. To counter this lack of underground support, buttresses extend from the flanks of the tree to add stability. Still, it is not uncommon in the Amazon forest to hear trees falling every so often. They simply topple over from too much mass or improper growth that affects their equilibrium.

Swidden horticulture involves the cutting, sun-drying, and then burning of an area to be cultivated. Because the surrounding forest is usually quite damp and humid, the fire is normally contained in the cut-over area. The ash that is deposited adds additional nutrients to the soil, and because the area was originally covered with climax forest, the problem of weeds is reduced. The land is commonly farmed for two to three years and then abandoned to return to its original forest cover. Ideally, the forest should be left untouched for at least 50 years, allowing the renovation process of leaf and limb litter to restore the soil to its original fertility.

Thus, this type of farming demands that cropping areas be continually shifted to allow for the regeneration cycle. It is therefore land extensive, requiring that a large area of land be available to each family in order to keep the cycle functioning. It is when too many people begin to pressure the system that the destruction occurs. The land is cleared in huge tracts, making forest regeneration difficult since many species of tree seeds cannot reach the interior of these areas. The two generations needed to allow the forest to recover are now replaced by short fallows of only a few years, or in some cases no fallows at all. Grasses frequently invade large areas of cleared land, interrupting the cycle indefinitely. In many cases, grass is purposely planted in an attempt to extend the usefulness of the land by converting it to pasture and introducing cattle. In the latter instance, it has been found that the compounding problems of soil infertility and compaction force out even the ranchers after a few years, leaving behind a devastation that will take hundreds of years to recover (Parsons 1976). It is for these reasons that many individuals alarmed about the imminent demise of the great tropical forests are looking to native systems as perhaps better models for the Amazonian environment than much of Western technology.

The Yuquí are learning some of these traditional farming practices from indigenous peasants like Francisco Blanco and other lowland frontiersmen. Unfortunately, they are also being introduced to a national marketing system that inspires continually expanding land use patterns to produce cash crops. As the frontier reaches out to incorporate Yuquí territory in the process of colonization, the Yuquí forest reserves will become threatened by settlers with insatiable appetites for cultivable land. It is under these conditions that a real threat to Yuquí subsistence will be apparent.

Yuquí Horticulture

Once the Yuquí were permanently settled, the missionaries, with Yuquí assistance, planted a four-hectare stand of plantains, manioc, corn, and rice near the first campsite on the far side of the river. During these first few years of contact, the Yuquí showed little interest in following up on the original four hectares. They were content with the plantains, which continued to bear adequate supplies of fruit; the food brought in by the mission plane and sold at the store; and, of course, what they were able to forage from the region. The missionaries did not press the Yuquí about farming, no doubt concerned that if too many demands were made, the people would become disgruntled and leave.

When Francisco Blanco moved into the area to clear a homestead upstream about three kilometers from the Chimoré camp, a new epoch in Yuquí experience began. Francisco was their first encounter with a Bolivian national on an extended basis. Francisco's opportunistic motives for settling where he did deserve some comment, however. Like many indigenous peasants, Francisco learned that the world can be a very difficult place and it is best to make good allies. Thus, he moved in quite literally next door in order to be able to prevail on the mission and its many material advantages for support. It is also likely that he sized up the situation with the Yuquí long before he moved to the Chimoré, recognizing a very convenient source of labor. That the missionaries not only put up with Francisco and his various transgressions but continue to provide him with assistance is also an interesting study in mission philosophy. Francisco is a "saved" Christian, sends his children to the New Tribes school in Todos Santos (where he learned of the new camp at the Chimoré), and so is considered to be part of the mission "family." The missionaries bemoan his two wives, his periodic backsliding when he drinks, his verbal and physical abuse of the Yuquí, and other such digressions from mission teaching. When the missionaries confront him, Francisco invariably repents his errant ways and is welcomed back into the fold.

For the Yuquí, visiting the Blanco farm is an experience in learning about what indigenous peasants do to survive, how they live, and what they value. The missionary settlement is so far removed from the Yuquí realm that there is little that they can relate to in terms of their own lives and expectations. It is Francisco Blanco's farm with its *chuchillo* buildings and thatched roofs, chickens, pigs, and garden plots that has become a model for living in the minds of many of the Yuquí. From time to time, several of the men will work for Francisco and in this way have gradually learned something about farming. Francisco, however, never ceases to complain about the Yuquí's lack of commitment to working at a steady pace or finishing an assigned task. In short, from Francisco's perspective, they are incredibly poor excuses for farmers.

In 1983, during my preliminary visit to the Yuquí camp, the missionaries decided that it was time for the Yuquí to learn to farm in earnest. This was the first such attempt since the original four-hectare *chaco* was planted across the river in the mid-1970s.

The mandate to farm was accompanied by the news that the store would no longer supply ammunition, rice, or other carbohydrates. This was intended as an incentive to get the Yuquí into the fields. As might be imagined, this edict was met with no small amount of grumbling. The women in particular were not enthusiastic about the prospect of going into the fields and found every excuse to avoid it. Finally, a few men wandered into the forest at the end of the airstrip and began to haphazardly and unenthusiastically clear underbrush. The rice *chaco* was not off to a propitious start. Since this was my first experience with the Yuquí, I watched all of this unfold with growing interest. The senior missionary couple was gone on "furlough" in the United States, leaving behind the recently arrived Daniels to cope with the Yuquí and their rice. One evening I ventured to suggest that perhaps the Yuquí could use some guidance in clearing their *chaco*. It was decided that the missionaries would approach Francisco Blanco and Mariano Ichu, the schoolteacher, to see if they would act as advisors in the first major effort to produce a crop for both consumption as well as sale. Unfortunately, I did not remain long enough to witness the progress of this field, but received periodic updates from the Daniels and was able to reconstruct a great deal of the episode on my return a year later. Evidently, Francisco and Mariano decided that the Yuquí were capable of farming six hectares given the number of able-bodied workers in the group. Unfortunately, they did not take into consideration the problem that the Yuquí were inexperienced and, even worse, unwilling farmers. The felling dragged on and on, pushing the process into the beginning of the rainy season. The burn was adequate, but both Mariano and Francisco later claimed that the Yuquí had come close to "failure." The planting was erratic, with too many or too few seeds to a hole and uneven spacing. The Yuquí did not weed early enough, often enough, or properly, and so lost productivity.

The harvest was carried out by everyone—men, women, and children. The Daniels' replacements, the Browns, kept a log of who picked what, and when some of the rice was later sold, each individual received his or her share of the sale. Even children demanded that they be given their part. A trip was made to Puerto Villarroel with Bill Brown, who monitored the rice sale. The profits were exhausted in a matter of hours on bread, candy, condensed milk,

Photo 23. Attempts to reclear the six-hectare chaco *were largely unsuccessful. Weeds and a flood eventually caused most of the crop to fail.*

and other sundries. Mariano taught each family to make a *pilua*, a square container fashioned from flattened palm boards and raised off the ground to keep the grain they would use for seed and food. The average *pilua* was about a cubic meter in size, storing a more than adequate amount of rice for each family. When I returned a year later, this rice was largely untouched because no one had the skill or stamina to hull it on a consistent basis. Using a chain saw, Mariano had roughed out several *tacúes*, wooden mortars made from large logs, but only two of these were eventually completed by the Yuquí. Thus, the Yuquí were surrounded by rice but either had little interest or lacked the tools to convert it into an edible form. When I made the trip with them to Puerto Villarroel in 1984, it was this still uneaten rice that was offered for sale.

That same year an attempt was made to try to *carpir* (weed) the old *chaco* to be used again for another crop. Had Mariano or Francisco been at the task, they probably would have succeeded in clearing most of the weeds away so that the area could be replanted. But for inexperienced farmers, this is a most difficult chore since weeds have already gained a foothold and one must work quickly and efficiently to keep ahead of the regrowth. The Yuquí, of course, were not up to the challenge. There was disagreement among the men about who was working and who was avoiding work by hunting. The missionaries once again stopped selling ammunition, which forced a few of the men into the fields. Still, the weeding process was slow and intermittent, ultimately culminating in less than a hectare being planted. This crop fared poorly from lack of attention like the first, but it did not have the advantage of being planted in virgin soil and was soon overcome by regrowth. Then, in February 1985, a flood finished off most of what the weeds had not choked out. It was meager harvest and many of the older men lost heart with the entire process.

In spite of their generally poor results and lack of initiative with large *chacos*, over the years the Yuquí have attempted small, individual dooryard plots with growing success. In the beginning, the numbers and varieties of plants were small, and to someone like Francisco, who with the help of his family cultivates several hectares of land simultaneously, these first efforts verged on the pathetic. One afternoon during my first visit, Benjamin insisted that I come look at his "garden." It consisted of a volunteer tomato plant, two onions given to him by one of the missionary women, and a few stalks of rice. I remember that my initial reaction was amusement; but seeing the earnest expectation on Benjamin's face, I congratulated him on his fine effort. These early attempts were in many ways experiments that in the privacy of the house drew little derision from neighbors. The few plants could be watched carefully, weeded, and even watered when the weather turned dry. The following year, Benjamin's garden had grown in size, resembling something more on the order of a cultivated field with manioc, corn, and other cultigens that had been planted. There was also a citrus seedling that had been carefully fenced off with *chuchillo*. I noted that several of the other Yuquí houses were also now surrounded by gardens, some in better condition than others, but all producing food. Comments about farming were frequently framed in terms of what Francisco had around his house and how things were supposed to look.

Over time, the Yuquí no doubt will develop the expertise necessary to become adequate farmers, passing on this knowledge to their children. Still, if the Sirionó experience is an example of what may lie ahead for the Yuquí, farming will never take the place of hunting as long as there is game. After more than 50 years of growing crops on cleared land, the Sirionó remain unenthusiastic farmers who still would rather be in the forest gathering fruit or hunting peccary. It must be remembered, however, that the Sirionó live in an area of large ranch holdings and open grasslands, a situation that has generated little pressure on land resources and game densities. The Yuquí will not have this advantage, unfortunately. Their lands lie close to population centers and are being circumscribed by the inevitable push of settlers.

4/Social Relations

When the missionaries made peaceful contact with the Yuquí and ultimately convinced them to settle permanently at the Chimoré River camp, there were only 43 people in the band. It is hard to imagine one's entire universe of human interaction encompassing only 43 individuals, most of whom are children. From Yuquí accounts, the Chimoré band separated from another approximately 50 years earlier and never encountered this group again. Thus, we are discussing a people who for at least two generations had no social contacts other than those with their own close relatives. There were no annual "tribal" gatherings, no special occasions set aside for courtship and marriage, no intricate maneuverings by families to establish alliances among neighbors, no feasts, no large ritual events. Forty-three people were living out their lives in complete isolation from others of their own kind as nomads in the wilderness. Knowing this, it is easy to understand why the Yuquí occupied an almost mythical place among native peoples of the Bolivian Amazon for so long. No one knew exactly who they were or even if they actually existed as a people. There were no villages or other cultural signposts to mark their presence. They simply appeared suddenly and then just as mysteriously were swallowed up again by the forest. When questioned about other Yuquí that might be present but as yet uncontacted, the Chimoré Yuquí demonstrated little interest. They feared even their own as potential enemies.

During those years preceding contact, the Yuquí considered themselves the only true humans existing. They called themselves *Biá*, "people," while all others were either enemies or spirits. During the initial years of contact, the Yuquí thought the missionaries, and all whites for that matter, were dead Yuquí—spirits returning to molest the living. The strange paleness of the outsiders' skins gave credence to this belief. It was not until several Yuquí had been taken to Bolivian cities for medical treatment that they were forced to reevaluate this concept. The presence of thousands of *Abá*, "others," obviously not dead, put an end to the traditional Yuquí view of how the world was structured.

Among most human groups, social relationships cover a broad matrix of individuals, including consanguineal kin ("blood" relatives), affinal kin ("in-laws"), neighbors, age mates, and other relatives and friends separated in terms of both geographical as well as social distance. Typically, any person can activate relationships and deactivate others when convenient or necessary.

There are always ways to temporarily escape the stresses of intensive social contact by visiting someone in a distant camp or village. For the Yuquí, none of these options existed. All of their social relationships were with close relatives. Thus, every person in the Yuquí universe was someone known since birth and seen virtually every day since. This created an intensity of interaction seldom encountered, except perhaps in situations where people have been forced to live with a closed group as the result of incarceration or institutionalization. Thus it is not simple metaphor to speak of the Yuquí at the Chimoré as a "family." The band is indeed a single kindred where even "in-laws" are not outsiders but members of one's own consanguineal kin group. Tensions predictably are frequent as evidenced by the amount of bickering and at times physical aggression mounted against one another. It is in this context, then, that all social relationships are structured.

Among most people who are foragers, the organization of society is egalitarian. This means that resources are available to everyone in relatively equal amounts. Thus there is very little social differentiation or specialization. It is not until access to resources becomes unequal that we see the evolution of social ranking and, ultimately, class structures. Foragers organize their society primarily along the lines of sex and age. Tasks are assigned according to these two fundamental categories. Leadership is fluid and consensual. There are no hereditary leaders with power to coerce or accumulate resources beyond what others may have. The fact that the Yuquí are foragers but also demonstrate certain characteristics common to agriculturalists is yet another indicator that they were once part of a much more complex society. Perhaps the strangest anomaly in their social organization is the existence of hereditary slavery.

SLAVERY

Slavery is an institution that normally is associated with the development of agriculture and the need these societies have to continually expand their resource bases. In order to accommodate growing demands for greater wealth to satisfy emerging social classes, early agriculturalists participated in territorial conquests. It was important to increase not only their land supply, but also the labor to work it. Thus, the taking of slaves became a frequent outcome of war. In addition to providing agricultural labor, slaves were also able to perform many of the menial tasks necessary to survival, thereby freeing their masters from the drudgery of daily existence. In trying to reconstruct Yuquí history, it is known that the Guaraní invaded Bolivia prior to the arrival of Europeans and were on several occasions successful in subduing and enslaving local populations. Slavery among the Guaraní was institutionalized, and those who were slaves passed on this condition to their descendants. All the evidence points to the Yuquí as remnants of these early Guaraní invaders, most likely raiding parties that became isolated in the forests to the north of the areas of more concentrated settlements. Over time, they experienced deculturation, losing much of their cultural heritage as it became necessary to remain mobile and live off the land. But while many elements of their culture may have been lost, others were not. Slavery, evidently, was one of these. A custom as complex as institutionalized slavery among a group of less than 50 individuals is difficult to imagine, yet it did exist.

Sometime in the 1930s, judging by the probable ages of those who recount the tale, the band presently living at the Chimoré camp split off from its parent group. The reason given for this move involves a dispute over a woman. According to the Chimoré Yuquí, the headman, Eriyogüe, "wanted all the women for himself," angering his younger brothers. As a result of this altercation, the next eldest brother, Equitá, took his wife Taineguatsi and their small children to another part of the forest. Accompanying them was Equitá's younger brother, Pa (Eracuyá), their two sisters, Biguachi and Tiasorá, and four slaves and their children. Once this group left the main band, they never crossed paths again. Many of the Yuquí believe that the original group may have been wiped out in a skirmish with Bolivian nationals. The fissioning of the large group is interesting in that it poses several questions. Had the original group not disappeared, would the two eventually have settled their differences and rejoined? Or was the fissioning part of a larger process that was simply expressed in terms of this particular incident, the argument over a woman? The original band may have reached an optimal size given the availability of resources. Once these resources were stressed because of the growing population, it is likely that tensions increased as food supplies diminished. Given that the Yuquí grew no crops whatsoever, the optimal band size would necessarily be quite small. While the fissioning may have been expressed in social terms, it is likely that environmental limitations may have actually triggered the move. There is the additional factor of danger from the occasional Bolivian hunter, logger, or frontiersman during this period. Although pioneer settlement had not yet become a real threat to the Yuquí, these encounters did occur. While living in the lowland village of San Carlos, located on the periphery of Yuquí territory, I frequently heard accounts by Bolivian peasants of sightings of people whose description matched that of the Yuquí. These stories often were laced with vivid descriptions of close calls or actual shootings involving both frontiersmen and Yuquí victims. This real threat to Yuquí security in the forest, albeit infrequent, would no doubt have influence over the size of the band. As foraging groups grew larger, they not only put stress on resource availability but also endangered the group in terms of greater visibility. The larger the group, the more easily it could be located and then tracked. Hence, it is probable that both of these factors may have contributed to the group's fissioning more than 50 years ago.

The size of the Yuquí band that fissioned from the original group can only be estimated since all but one of the Yuquí who were present at the time are now dead. The sole survivor is Taineguatsi (Ángela), Equitá's widow, whose memory fades as she grows more infirm. It is probable, however, that the group numbered only about 12–14 people. What this ultimately meant was that "*saya*," the Yuquí term for upper caste, were forced to marry "*enem-*

baco," slaves, in order to have mates. Thus, Equitá's sister Biguachi married the slave Juamia. Their six children, three males and three females, were all considered slaves. Benjamin, Guillermo, and Timoteo were the three boys. Equitá's other sister, Tiasorá, married the slave Elbaradú, and had as offspring the slaves Eribaira (Joel) and Tiasudn. Pa, the younger brother of Equitá, eventually married Erecuatá, another slave, but their children were considered *saya* and not *enembaco*. Thus it is evident that the male line was dominant, and those offspring born to female *saya* married to slaves were slaves. This is a strong indication of patrilineality, or the tracing of descent through the male line. The inheritance of leadership through the male line, to be discussed in a later section, also is indicative that the Yuquí, or at least their predecessors, were a society based on patrilineal rules of descent.

The lot of the Yuquí slave was what might be expected of anyone considered the property of another. Slaves were expected to help track game and then carry it back to camp; but they were rarely permitted to hunt. This helps to explain the poor hunting records of Joel, Timoteo, Benjamin, and, until recently, Humberto, who seems to be interested in developing his hunting skills in an attempt to improve his status. But then, Humberto was never a willing slave and was known to frequently disobey his master Yabia (Victor). Slaves were also responsible for gathering firewood in the evenings and tending the fires all night. While others slept in hammocks, most slaves were relegated to the ground, unless someone took pity and let them use an old hammock or share one with a child. If it rained, they would have to get up to gather palm fronds to cover the hammocks of their masters. They were given leftover food to eat and were noticeably thinner than the *saya*. During the early years of contact, the slave Joel was seen carrying a pot of putrid meat around with him so that no one else would take it. When asked if it would make him sick, he responded that as long as he kept cooking it, it would not harm him.

Slaves were also used to prevent the spirits of the dead from returning to take one of the living with them. The Yuquí believed that the dead were lonesome in the spirit world and therefore would seek to take a companion along on their journey. To prevent having to sacrifice a highly valued individual, it was common practice to kill a slave at the death of a member of the group. Ta, the headman Equitá's daughter, died in childbirth. Her slave Equiachi was then killed by Equitá to accompany his daughter into the afterworld. When the population diminished to the point that even slaves became valuable as potential marriage partners, the Yuquí would go in search of a Bolivian colonist. Thus, Victor later explained that he had killed the colonist woman at La Jota in 1957 to appease the spirit of Abariquí, his brother and Monica's first husband. The group initially wanted to kill Monica (Eracuyasi) because no one else was "available" at the time and they could justify the act because Monica's mother had been a slave. (This is an interesting case in that Monica's father was *saya*, so Monica was not considered a slave. However, it is obvious that in the need to find someone to appease a dead person's spirit, such technicalities might be overlooked. As the widow of the dead man, she would also be a logical choice.) But a shortage of women saved Monica from death. The headman's other son, Tibaquité, wanted her for a mate and had his way.

Contact with the missionaries brought many changes to Yuquí social organization, especially in the realm of slavery. No single factor is responsible for the disappearance of slavery but rather a combination of events that worked to alter this pattern. When I questioned the missionaries about their possible involvement in the slavery issue, I was assured that they had not interfered. In fact, they were quite honest that they had not sought to abolish the institution since slavery is condoned in the Old Testament; their concern was that slaves obey their masters as the Bible requires. While the missionaries did not openly work against Yuquí slavery, the disruption brought about by mission life nonetheless had its effect. When the old headman, Equitá, died within a few years of contact, there was no immediate replacement for him. One of Equitá's remaining two sons probably would have been selected as headman, but the social disorganization was such that succession was difficult. Then too, neither man had acquired the new skills that leadership now required, particularly the proficient use of a firearm. In the meantime, the missionaries were grooming their own leader, Leonardo, a much younger man who was deemed more suitable for the task ahead and who, it was hoped, would lead his people into Christianity.

With Equitá gone and uncertainty reigning over the camp, the former slaves saw their opportunity for freedom. It was now more common to refuse to perform certain activities and there was less chance of reprisal. At the same time, people had begun to differentiate their living arrangements into nuclear family households that were characterized by separate dwelling places. Slaves as well built their own houses and now the break was almost complete. On the surface slavery is gone. With careful observation, however, the status of ex-slaves is apparent in many ways, and some of the old linkages between master and slave are activated on occasion. For example, Timoteo, a notoriously poor hunter, will often accompany several of the *saya* hunters to carry back their kill or will appear at their houses when game is brought in. While the hunter rests, Timoteo dresses the game, performing a typical task of a slave, but in return now receives a fair share of the catch. It is also Benjamin and Timoteo, the two ex-slave brothers, who most frequently are found at the other end of camp working for the missionaries. *Saya* will do this as well now, but there is always a reluctance to show too much eagerness or deference. Old Abadn (Carolina), who must depend on her *saya* sons and married daughters to provide food for her and her unmarried daughter Ester, is a regular employee in the house of the senior couple, the Porters. The Porters provide Carolina with food in addition to the small salary she receives. But Helen Porter notes that she must often play out a charade with Carolina in which Helen comments to no one in particular that she is in terrible need of help and has no idea how she will get all her work done without someone to assist her. At that, Carolina brusquely reminds her that she is there and perhaps could be persuaded to work.

It is noteworthy that the image of the slave as someone who performs labor for another and as someone to be scorned is still strong among the Yuquí. Even today, the Yuquí insult another by saying that he or she will be "so-and-so's slave." When one of the women would get angry at me about something, I would be told that I would be the missionaries' slave. Evidently, this was but another way of recognizing the stratification between missionaries who are *Abá* (as am I) and the very status-conscious Yuquí, who regard themselves, albeit grudgingly, as subordinate to whites because of the huge differences in technology and knowledge of the wider universe. Thus, to insult me by telling me that I would be a Yuquí's slave was not potent enough—I would be the slave of another white.

LEADERSHIP AND PRESTIGE

At the time of contact, Equitá was the Chimoré band's headman. The term for headman in Yuquí, *Papa*[5], was not only his title but also signified his relationship to the rest of the group. *Papa* is how a wife addresses a husband and children address their father. The Sirionó use the term *Ererecua*, "first born," to refer to their leaders; but they also address their leaders as *Paba* (the voiced /b/ is used in Sirionó as opposed to the unvoiced /p/ common to Yuquí). The use of this particular term is not coincidental. Band membership among both the Sirionó and the Yuquí was based on being related to the headman, who in a broad sense was "father" or "husband" to virtually every member of the group. As bands became smaller, this became even more apparent. Thus, if we look at Equitá's group, we find that everyone of his generation is related to each other at least by marriage. When we get to the next generation, everyone is related by blood. In a very literal sense, then, Equitá was the *Papa*, the father of his band.

Like the Sirionó, leadership among the Yuquí is hereditary but not necessarily limited to the present leader's first-born son. That the Sirionó continue to use the term "*Ererecua*" to designate their leaders is reminiscent of an earlier period when in a more complex society primogeniture no doubt was the rule. What is noteworthy about Yuquí and Sirionó leadership patterns are the adaptations that have occurred as the result of their becoming foragers. Without the built-in safeguards present in a large sedentary society, a small mobile group could not afford poor leadership. Thus, primogeniture in a pure sense gave way to selective leadership that would better meet the needs of

5. The Yuquí and Sirionó terms of address for father or headman seem remarkably similar to the Spanish word for father, *papá*. In all languages these coincidences occur from time to time. For example, the word for "yes" in both Sirionó and Yuquí is "*ai*." Until I became accustomed to hearing this word in its own context, I felt as if I were a character in *Treasure Island* who, along with Long John Silver, would respond to a question with "Aye, matey." To assume, however, that the Yuquí word for "yes" is an English borrowing defies logic. On the other hand, it is not inconceivable that *papa/paba* may be Spanish borrowings. There is strong evidence (Stearman 1984) that both the Sirionó and Yuquí had intermittent contacts with Spanish Jesuit and Franciscan missionaries in the seventeenth century.

the band. Ideally, the preference of the Sirionó and the Yuquí is to select the eldest son of the present leader as the next headman. But if for some reason this individual is deemed unworthy, a second or third son may be chosen, or even a nephew or other relative who can trace his line to the present leader. Among modern-day Sirionó, the potential *Ererecua* has to prove only that he is of a "chiefly line," and can trace his lineage through either the mother's or father's side. It should be noted, however, that the Sirionó still consider a direct male line the superior choice and will accept more tenuous claims to *Ererecua* status only if necessary to successfully elect a leader.

In another curious meshing of foraging and agriculturally based social patterns, the Yuquí and Sirionó headmen may attain their positions as the result of birthright, yet they do not enjoy the absolute authority that is often linked to hereditary leadership. The relative power of a headman is manifest in his ability to settle disputes, but this authority is primarily consensual. This implies that he is a leader only as long as people are willing to follow. The ability of headmen to maintain the trust and acceptance of their constituents is based in large part on prestige gained through skill, particularly hunting. One leader can be replaced by another who poaches power through the provision of meat, which brings him respect and inevitably greater access to women, assuming, of course, he has a legitimate hereditary claim to leadership.

When Equitá died, his place as leader normally would have been taken by one of his sons. Monica's second husband, Tibaquité, one of Equitá's sons, was the strongest contender for the leadership position. But Tibaquité was killed in a strange incident involving one of the Yuquí who had been stolen as a child by settlers and raised as a servant. Hearing of the pacification of the band at the Chimoré, the estranged Yuquí arrived one day in search of his past. Suffering from the severe emotional disturbances brought on by his kidnapping and subsequent marginalization, and then rejected by the Yuquí who no longer recognized his place among them, the young man retaliated by killing Tibaquité. The shock of this episode coupled with the disruption caused by contact left a widening gap in Yuquí leadership. The remaining sons, Victor and Jorge, were not considered headman material by the Yuquí or the missionaries. The missionaries were quick to assess the situation and moved to fill the void with Leonardo, a young man of their choosing, who was beginning to demonstrate leadership qualities. As the old headman's grandson, Leonardo could make a legitimate claim to Equitá's position.

Leonardo still has not attained the complete acceptance of his people as the legitimate headman, however. Several factors have contributed to the Yuquí's unwillingness to recognize his position. Just as social disruption freed slaves from subservience to their masters, many of those who were dominated by Equitá see the perpetuation of traditional leadership patterns as contrary to their hopes for greater freedom and independence. By rejecting Leonardo, they are rejecting the old system that hardly worked to their advantage. Leonardo is also the missionaries' choice, not necessarily the Yuquí's. The

Yuquí are a proud, aggressive people, and while their relations with the missionaries are generally positive, they also resent their virtually complete dependence on the missionaries. The missionaries' selection and support of Leonardo as headman is yet another reminder of who really controls the camp. Finally, his relative youth (he is in his mid-30s) works against Leonardo's acceptance as headman.

Coming from a highly patriarchal mission tradition, the New Tribes missionaries are training Leonardo to pattern his leadership in a similar style. Thwarting this to some degree is the decision-making authority exercised by women, a common situation among foragers. Senior women do not hesitate to make their views known. They still control the distribution of meat once it has arrived at their doorstep, an important sign of their power in camp. In spite of the missionaries' attempts to redefine the role of the female to achieve greater compatibility with fundamentalist beliefs, Yuquí women refuse to be dominated by the men, including Leonardo.

In an attempt to expand Leonardo's authority, efforts are being made by the missionaries to include him in such activities as the settling of disputes. Still, the Yuquí normally seek out a missionary as a mediator, signalling their incomplete acceptance of Leonardo as headman. To date, much of Leonardo's role as nominal headman is limited to his participation in the late afternoon prayer sessions presided over by one of the male missionaries.

Some of the resentment directed toward Leonardo also has to do with his demands for a share of game from members of the band. When Equitá was headman and the group lived together in a single camp, one of his rewards as *Papa* was the first share of the day's take. It would be normal for Leonardo to expect the same, but since he is not yet fully recognized as a legitimate leader, there is reluctance to give meat to him or his immediate family. By requiring people to surrender meat, Leonardo, at least in his own mind, validates his claim to leadership. Nonetheless, many Yuquí believe that it is only the latent power of the missionaries that enables Leonardo to coerce them into giving up part of their kill.

Since Leonardo's house is centrally located, most hunters must pass through his yard on their way home. It is typical for Leonardo or, more commonly, his wife Loida to be strategically stationed in front of the house to intercept passersby and exact a tribute before the game is otherwise disposed of. It is this act that particularly infuriates the women since it deprives them of their traditional right to distribute game. If a man returns to his house with part of the kill obviously missing, he will suffer a tongue lashing from his wife. One man, an ex-slave who is frequently called upon to share his catch, told me that he purposely takes a circuitous route so as to avoid having to give up a portion of his kill and suffer the wrath of his spouse. The news of game in camp travels fast, however, and Loida is quick to send sister Lydia or daughter Andrea to ask for a portion of the catch. The fact that Loida is obese does not help the situation. Many of the people point to her size as an indication of their having to give up meat to support her huge appetite. It is noteworthy that although Leonardo is a good hunter, placing third in game takes and therefore not in need of meat as is someone like Timoteo, he ranked fourth in amount of meat received, for a total of 77 kilos. He also received meat from the greatest number of individuals, 12, also lending support to subjective claims that "everyone" is required to give meat to Leonardo's family.

Although there is often disgruntlement over Leonardo's attempt to assume a position of authority over the band as a whole, there is little doubt that he will eventually succeed. By having daily access to the missionaries he is becoming acculturated much faster than the other adult men, a tremendous advantage in dealing with a rapidly changing lifestyle. Not only does Leonardo have the backing of the missionaries in his bid for leadership, but he also has access to their knowledge and tutelage. Leonardo has now made several trips to Santa Cruz, Cochabamba, and Puerto Villarroel, and while perhaps not yet an old hand like Francisco at dealing with Bolivian nationals, he is far more experienced than anyone else. His knowledge of Spanish is also increasing, placing Leonardo in the important position of becoming a cultural broker for his people. His road to authority is often a difficult one in that he must straddle two often contradictory worlds. Leonardo's traditional expectations of leadership responsibilities and rewards are based on a social environment that no longer exists, but it is the only model he knows. At the same time, Leonardo must adapt to a situation that he, in common with the other Yuquí, cannot as yet fully comprehend.

THE YUQUÍ LIFE CYCLE

Interwoven with the Yuquí's concern with such issues as leadership, prestige, masters, and slaves are the sequences of events that structure other social relationships: birth, childhood, puberty, courtship, marriage, old age, and death. Each of these adds special dimensions to Yuquí life in both dictating and describing the Yuquí as a distinct cultural entity.

Pregnancy and Birth

Among the Yuquí, conception is understood as being the result of sexual intercourse. However, according to Yuquí belief, it is also possible for the spirit of someone or something to "jump" on a woman and impregnate her. Thus, Abadn (Carolina) was given her name ([Abá + dn] = little white) because her mother saw a Bolivian national at about the time Carolina was conceived and claimed his spirit jumped onto her. The Yuquí also maintain that intercourse only "plants the seed" of the child. It is repeated intercourse that permits it to grow. Thus, the Yuquí believe that while one man may conceive the child, others may help to "develop" it. If a woman fails to become pregnant, it is considered to be the man's fault, unless she has iogüe rusudn, "fat thighs." Such women, it is said, are not easily made pregnant. If pregnancy does not occur after a normal interval of time, a man will seek out another male to have intercourse with his wife and, he hopes, impregnate her.

Even today, women say they learn they are pregnant through a dream. In precontact times, when a woman was certain that she was in fact pregnant, the hair from her forehead was freshly plucked with the help of a female relative or friend. This was done by rubbing ash on the fingers to create a good gripping surface. During pregnancy, the woman, her husband, and her father were all expected to observe a number of taboos to ensure the safe birth of the child. These taboos reflected Yuquí attitudes about their universe, and those of similar people like the Sirionó, whose lives were inextricably linked with the natural environment. The Yuquí were part of the forest they inhabited and as such considered themselves subject to the same forces that they believed influenced the plants and animals around them. But as *Biá*, people, they could attempt to manipulate nature by avoiding its obvious traps and pitfalls or by performing acts of magic. Thus, women were not to eat "twin" fruits, since this would encourage the birth of twins, one of which most certainly would fail to survive. They were not to eat deer head, since deer have runny noses and this would bring forth a child with similar problems. Likewise, neither she nor her husband and father were to tie knots, and she could not make twine since this might cause the umbilical cord to wrap around the child's neck and strangle it. The husband and father could not feather arrows, rub beeswax on arrows, or gather *chuchillo* staffs and season them. It was assumed that the condition of the woman weakened them as well and so would affect the efficacy of their weapons. The pregnant woman and her husband and father were to avoid hearing loud noises (gunshots), smelling bad things, or in any way jeopardizing the tranquility of the child growing within. Clubfeet, for example, called *antajisa* (anteater foot), were blamed on the mother not having exercised proper caution and falling in the forest.

Also, prior to contact, when a woman went into labor, her husband was informed, she was removed from the band and taken to a place five to ten minutes' walk from the main group. She would be accompanied by women who were experienced in childbirth. A small area was cleared, a fire was built, and the pregnant woman was allowed to rest in a sitting position with her back against a small tree. The attendants warmed their hands over the fire and began to rub the laboring woman's abdomen. During each contraction, the woman grasped the tree behind her head for support. As the moment of birth approached, the woman assumed a squatting position and the child dropped to the ground. The fall on the soft forest floor was usually enough to cause it to gulp its first breath and break into a cry. The cord was cut with a piece of bamboo and the placenta was disposed of in the forest. A newborn child was considered dangerous to everyone but the mother until it could hold up its head. Thus, no one could touch it and only women would tend the mother, who was now "behind leaves" in the *queesa*. Much of this was linked to the fact that after childbirth a woman would bleed in a manner similar to menstruation and therefore was believed to threaten the health of the entire band. Among many cultures, particularly those that have a tradition of male dominance, menstrual blood is treated as polluting and dangerous, and women are separated from society during menses. A newborn has been contaminated by this blood and is also more likely to succumb to disease or birth defects during these first few weeks of life. The baby was therefore regarded as not yet belonging fully to the world but lay somewhere between the spirit domain and that of the living. Old men, however, no longer at great risk in terms of their procreative and hunting abilities, were often the first to pay a formal visit to the newborn.

The Yuquí father was subject to a limited couvade and post-partum sexual taboo during the time that the child's neck was strengthening, or about three months. He could not hunt for his wife nor for younger men, including his own sons, thus protecting them from possible harm. The woman could receive meat from her father or older brother. The couvade, separating the husband from his wife and newborn child and limiting the access of others to them as well, is an interesting custom that has been demonstrated to have practical as well as ideological significance. During the first weeks of life, newborns and their mothers are most susceptible to infectious disease. By isolating mother and child in the forest and restricting visitation through a series of social and dietary taboos, the incidence of contact with others is greatly reduced. As a consequence, exposure to infectious disease is also controlled.

Although many of the beliefs and practices outlined above have been abandoned or are observed minimally, there are still certain prejudices that come into play when a child is born. If it is a girl, not much is said about the sex. In fact, if comments to this effect are made, a swift rebuke will follow. In years past, girl babies were frequently killed because they were unwanted—they could not provide meat for the group. It is also desirable that the child have light skin, or be "amachi." Where this preference may have originated is unknown.

Today, childbirth takes place in the small clinic at the Chimoré camp, and Yuquí women are attended by both their female relatives and missionary women. With the availability of air transport, if a severe problem arises and the weather cooperates, a plane will be called in to take the woman to a hospital in Cochabamba (flying time is 35 minutes). The missionaries, who must pay for these flights, willingly provide transportation in the case of a medical emergency. Loida, the wife of the young headman, Leonardo, probably would have died during the delivery of her first child if she had not had access to modern medical resources. Both of her children were delivered by cesarean section in a Cochabamba hospital.

Abortion and Infanticide

Both abortion and infanticide were commonly practiced among the Yuquí. The first pregnancy was almost always aborted since this child was considered weak. Abortion was accomplished by having the woman's husband or mother kneel on her abdomen until she expelled the fetus. This was termed "breaking the child" (tacó siquio). If it was not successful the first time, the process would be repeated. A woman still nursing a child or who for some other reason did not want to give birth would use the same method to terminate her pregnancy. When women were angry at their husbands, they might kill their children, particularly boys, in retaliation. Thus, when Victor rejected his first wife Quenesí for Justina, the former strangled their three-year-old son to get even. If a woman wanted to get back at her husband for some transgression such as adultery, she would hold her legs together when the child was being born, causing stillbirth. In the case of a nursing child who lost its mother, sacrificing the infant to appease the mother's spirit as well as to resolve the problem of finding someone to care for the baby was common. For example, when Equitá's sister, Tiasurá, died, she had a nursing infant. Equitá dashed the baby against a tree so that it could accompany its mother into the afterworld. In addition, girls who were very young, 11 or 12 years old, were not permitted to keep a child and it would be destroyed. Not only were they deemed too young for motherhood, but they had no husband to provide for them and the child.

It would appear that abortion and infanticide are no longer practiced to the degree they were in the past, or perhaps the Yuquí are simply less open in discussing these issues. Both abortion and infanticide are difficult to document, since it is easy to attribute the loss of a child to so many other factors. There have been a few highly "suspicious" incidents, however, when a perfectly healthy infant died suddenly due to unknown causes. In these cases, it was generally known that the mother, father, or grandparents were not pleased either with the birth of the child or with its sex. Pregnancy outside of marriage was something always considered undesirable and is particularly so now because of missionary presence, and parental displeasure may result in abuse or neglect of an infant by its young mother. There is also the problem of group support for the mother, who relies on the goodwill of others to help in the care of her infant. In Florencia's case, she found motherhood stressful and bothersome, particularly since her husband, Lucas, as well as his parents, Joel and Elsa, were not particularly supportive. Neither Joel nor Lucas was often successful hunting during my stay, and it was this extended family that received the least animal protein of the group. Florencia's mother-in-law, Elsa, treated the girl harshly, forcing Florencia to seek refuge in Leonarda's or my kitchen. Florencia, whose mother Ta is dead, had no real ally to turn to for recourse. The baby Marcos at times seemed on the verge of death, thin and sickly since birth and receiving only minimal care from his beleaguered mother. That he survived his mother's neglect is a testament to the infant's will to live.

Infanticide, particularly in the form of purposeful neglect, is not uncommon to human society, including our own. It seems to be particularly prevalent, however, among those peoples where environmental stresses are great and resources are limited. In short, it is a means of controlling population growth to ensure the survival of the group. Popular myth notwithstanding, people like the Yuquí seldom have secret, magic potions they take to prevent conception. Thus, to avoid adding unwanted children, they are limited to either abortion or infanticide. Since the methods of abortion used are invariably dangerous to the mother, infanticide is usually the necessary choice. Although it may be difficult for members of our society to comprehend this dilemma, an adult female capable of bearing more children must be valued over a newborn whose chances at achieving maturity are, at this point, less than even.

Infanticide also typically takes a selective form: Females more often succumb than males. Marvin Harris has discussed this phenomenon in several contexts (Harris 1974, 1977; Divale & Harris 1976), pointing to multiple causes rooted in what he terms the "male supremacy complex." In the case of the Yuquí, male supremacy cannot be denied, but it is linked to the food quest rather than warfare. Since the Yuquí traditionally depended on game for the large majority of their diet, and males provided this commodity, it is not difficult to understand why male children were preferred and, to a great extent, still are.

It is also the number of females, not males, that determines the rate of population growth. Thus, if a population is to be controlled, it is a reasonable assumption that efforts will be made to reduce the number of females. This is best accomplished through infanticide, after the child has been born and the sex can been determined.

The Yuquí practice of aborting the first pregnancy is an interesting issue. It could be argued that it is counterproductive to the survival of the group, given that the fetus is destroyed without regard to sex and that the mother is placed at very high risk. Perhaps the best explanation is that it may be a response to the unusual stress that this society has experienced. Most foraging peoples live in a dynamic equilibrium with nature that requires constant monitoring of available resources and resulting population adjustments. This would be true for the Yuquí as well; but added to this was the problem that the Yuquí were a hunted people, in continual fear of detection and forced to move almost constantly to avoid being killed. The smaller the group, the more mobile it would be and the less likely to be seen. It is conceivable, then, that in these circumstances, "extreme" measures to curb population growth would become commonplace. In this context, many of their practices, including the aborting of first pregnancies, the execution of slaves or others to accompany the dead, and the killing of children out of spite or anger, can be better comprehended.

Childhood and Puberty

Children were named at birth, usually after an animal that the father killed while his spouse was pregnant. If the child had some particular unusual physical characteristic, this might be chosen as a name. Susana, who has rather large, protruding eyes, was called *yeyú detsá* (fish eye). On occasion, a child would be given the name of a deceased relative, particularly if he or she was thought to resemble that person. Although pronouncing the name of a dead Yuquí is forbidden since it might invoke that person's spirit, it is also believed that reincarnation occurs. The physical similarity of a child to a deceased relative is an indication that the spirit of that individual has entered the infant and is therefore incarnate. Hence, it becomes proper to use that person's name once again. Although every individual had a given name, in the years before contact these were seldom used. Teknonymy, or referring to individuals in terms of their relationship to their children, was one form of address among the Yuquí. The missionaries were corrected when they addressed the old headman as *Papa* or *Papaquitá* (a contraction of Papa Equitá) since he was "not their father." Instead, they were told, he should be addressed as *Yabierú* [Yabia + eru], Yabia's father, a more polite and correct form. It was also common to refer to someone as older brother, younger brother, mother-in-law, and so on, rather than use a given name. Since the Yuquí "know" everyone, there is no word in their language for name and no way to express the phrase, "What is your name?" Nowadays, Spanish names are the rule, and these are what people use when addressing each other or referring to another. Children no longer are given animal names; but among nuclear family members, old terminology such as *yaqui* (son) or *papa* (husband, father) continues be the norm.

Children grow up with very little formal care or training. They are expected to learn by watching adults and to become self-sufficient at a very early age. They are often left alone to fend for themselves while the parents go off on a hunt. Young children, particularly those who are still nursing, are shown considerable affection. Once another baby is born, however, the older child is rebuffed and expected to take his or her place with the other siblings. Older children are ignored much of the time, unless, of course, they do something to catch a parent's attention, such as failing to perform an assigned task. The punishment is swift and forceful: a slap across the face, a pole over the back, or something thrown at the offender.

Sexual experimentation begins quite early among both males and females, and it is not uncommon for brothers and sisters to engage in sexual intercourse while young. This is considered wrong, but the penalty if caught is not severe. The offending siblings are usually forbidden to warm themselves by the fire for a time, a form of social isolation since the fire is the center of all group activity. In addition to prohibiting sexual relations between brothers and sisters, the Yuquí consider it incest (*erua*) to have sex with the following individuals:

1. One's children
2. One's mother's children (sex with one's father's children is permitted if they have a different mother)
3. One's parents
4. One's female sex partner's child if one had sex with the woman while she was pregnant with this child

Although the missionaries continue to discourage premarital sex, a young girl will begin having intercourse prior to the onset of menses. According to Yuquí belief, it is only by having intercourse with a man or a number of men that she is able to achieve sexual maturity, or to *yecuaquiú* (to be sexually active, to be able to bear children). The men who have intercourse with a prepubescent female are usually close male relatives, father's or mother's brothers in particular. She may also have already paired with a young man who is, or will become, her husband. In this case, it is he who is said to have caused the young woman to *yecuaquiú*.

Prior to contact, when menstruation first occurred, the girl's forehead was plucked and she was painted with *dijá*, a blue-black fruit dye that covered most of her upper body. If she had already paired with a young man, he also would be painted with *dijá* juice. It was believed that this would encourage the growth of pubic hair for both the male and female. The woman would then stay "behind leaves" for the duration of the menstrual period and on through the next, when she was allowed to return to the camp. Leonardo and Loida went through this ceremony together and became spouses. Julia, however, had no partner for the ceremony but was pledged to Guraquiate (Humberto). It was said that he had caused her to *yecuaquiú* but she refused to marry him. Guraquiate was too dark-skinned (he was also a slave, but the only available partners at the time were all slaves) so she remained behind leaves for several months to avoid having to be with him. When she finally emerged, she was pregnant. The pregnancy was terminated by her mother, Carolina. Eventually, Julia married Guillermo, a slave too, but one who was *amachi*, light-skinned.

Marriage

Selection of a mate may be highly individualized, with young men and women meeting surreptitiously in the woods until their companionship is generally known and accepted. On the other hand, parents and other family members can also have significant influence in the selection of a mate. As we saw with Julia, the choice of Humberto as her husband was not to her liking and she simply avoided marrying him by staying behind leaves. When I first began building my house at the Chimoré, Jonatán, an older adolescent, would come by and talk about some of the marriageable young women. He always tried to be circumspect with his questions, but it was obvious that he was interested in my opinion and particularly if I thought his choice, Raquel, was a good one. He seemed genuinely delighted when I told him he had made an excellent decision. Within a short time, he and Raquel were a regular item in camp, and Jonatán began to build a house for their impending marriage. Now, the wedding ceremony is conducted by one of the missionaries and follows Christian tradition. In the past, the prospective groom would approach his fiancee's mother and give her enough *imbai* to make a hammock. If she accepted, the marriage was considered arranged. Once the hammock was ready for use (an interesting means of leverage, since the bride's mother could take as long as she wished to complete the hammock while keeping the young man busy providing her with meat and other gifts), the couple simply began sharing it in the presence of the band. The hammock was a symbol of the marital union and the establishment of a separate household.

It is probable that the Yuquí, like the Sirionó, were at one time polygynous, with a man having more than one wife. Among the Sirionó, the ability of a man to "grab off" more than one woman at a time was a frequent source of dispute in any band, and in several cases resulted in the group splitting over these disagreements. This, of course, has its parallel among the Yuquí, and, according to them, explains the origin of the Chimoré band.

At the time of contact, the Yuquí did not practice polygyny. Monogamy may have come about as the result of both the earlier dispute over a woman that "caused" the fissioning as well as the unusually small number of adults in the remaining band. Although the Yuquí do not conform to mission expectations in terms of refraining from sex outside of marriage, the rule of monogamy has not been difficult to encourage. It is interesting that the Yuquí evidently understood that in order to maintain group cohesion, suddenly necessary given their isolation in the forest, there would have to be greater equality in the accessibility of mates. Sexual access by senior males to younger females, however, was never a problem. There was an expectation that these men would assist a young woman to achieve sexual maturity, *yecuaquiú*, as part of their role as close male relatives. It was also not unknown for a woman, too tired to meet her spouse's request for sex, to ask another woman to take her place.

Adultery

Certainly by our own standards as well as those of many other societies, the Yuquí enjoy a great deal of latitude in terms of their sexual behavior. Nonetheless, even with such apparent freedom in sexual activity, the most common disputes arise, paradoxically, over infidelity or illicit sex. It therefore must be observed that adultery (*yerequió*) or other forms of unacceptable sexual conduct are not a matter of rule but of context. Thus, a woman who asks another to perform surrogate sexual service has sanctioned the act. If the husband were to seek out sexual gratification from another female without the consent of his wife, that is an entirely different matter. Arguments about illicit sexual activity on the part of both males and females are frequent and often based solely on rumor. It is a favorite means of retribution after a dispute to accuse one's enemy of illicit sexual activity, whether true or not. The camp was thrown into an uproar when one of the unmarried girls, angry at Mariano Ichu, publicly accused him of having sex with her in the forest. After several meetings with parents and relatives who initially wanted the man expelled from camp, Mariano's innocence was finally established. Under pressure from the entire band, the accuser finally admitted she had made up the story. This revelation and the resulting humiliation later led to a "swear" or curse the girl muttered to Mariano's wife, Leonarda. Having recently lost two children to an epidemic in her hometown, Leonarda responded with tears when she was told by the girl, "All of the rest of your children will die like those did!"

Adultery, always carried out in the woods away from camp, is the constant worry of everyone. Since actual discovery of the offending couple is rare due to the virtually unlimited number of meeting places that may be used, suspicions and doubts run rampant. Women who in the past were confined to the *queesa* during menstruation were sexually unavailable to their husbands and at the same time were restricted from keeping an eye on them. At these times there was particular concern that adultery would occur. If a woman suspected unfaithfulness or was informed of this by relatives, the husband would suffer a verbal barrage and perhaps not have the company of his wife in the hammock for several days while she slept elsewhere. This abandonment of the marital hammock brought embarrassment to the male as well as discomfort from the cool, humid nights. A woman accused of adultery was often struck with a bow or a burning brand from the fire. Then she might be denied access to the hammock, increasing her humiliation. Ultimately, however, these incidents would blow over and once again the family would settle back into its normal routine.

Sexual prowess is very much a part of the Yuquí male image, and while women enjoy the danger and diversity of an illicit sexual affair, it is men who take greatest pride in their exploits. On the other hand, too much sex is seen as debilitating. It is believed that gray hair will result from too many affairs, particularly if they are with older women.

Divorce

Although unfaithfulness will lead to fights, some of which escalate rapidly to include other relatives who immediately take sides, this alone is seldom reason for divorce unless it becomes a constant pattern. In the past, the greatest cause for divorce was not alienation of affection *per se*, but failure to furnish ample supplies of meat. If a man consistently gave meat to another woman in exchange for sex or failed to provide adequately for his wife, she would leave him. A woman disgruntled with her husband as a provider would attempt to establish a relationship with another man who could give her more satisfying quantities of meat (Holmberg 1969). If he were unattached, this meant that she would eventually be invited into his hammock. The spurned husband would have to decide whether she was worth fighting for. If the man already had a wife, widespread dissention would occur as the camp began to draw lines of support. Nowadays, there is greater stability among married couples, no doubt because there is a more secure supply of food (provided by the mission at the store) and animal protein (through the addition of river fishing to subsistence activities) as well as missionary efforts to discourage illicit sexual activity.

Divorce, like marriage, was not accompanied by any significant ritual event but rather was simply a group recognition that a marital union had dissolved. This dissolution, again like marriage, centered around the conjugal hammock.

Once a man or woman abandoned his or her spouse's hammock to take up residence in another, everyone knew that the marriage had terminated and a new had begun. In spite of the apparent simplicity of this action, it can be assumed that divorce was neither common nor effected without turmoil, as is true in any small society. Given that there are so few Yuquí, even today it is impossible for any activity to occur outside the general knowledge of everyone. Thus, the period of estrangement between a man and woman can be one of extreme stress for the entire band as family members are forced to take sides with the litigants.

Only two divorces are known to have occurred within the Chimoré band since contact. They are both interesting cases in that they underscore the pressure that women exert on men to provide meat (Siskind 1973a, 1973b) and their willingness to leave a man who does not. The first case involved Alicia, who was married to Timoteo. Alicia is the daughter of the headman, Equitá, and therefore *saya*, upper caste. Timoteo is a slave. Thus, from Alicia's perspective, the marriage was not an ideal one from the start. What ultimately led to Alicia's abandonment of Timoteo, however, was his lack of skill as a hunter. Timoteo ranked second to last in total number of kilos of fish and game taken and absolute last in hunting success (this is the number of hunting trips divided by the number of times meat was secured). Had Manuel not been sick for several days, thus reducing his fish and game takes to put him in last place, Timoteo would have enjoyed this honor. While I was busy making quantitative measurements of animal protein brought into camp and noting which hunter caught what, I kept an open mind regarding relative hunting abilities. I was relying solely on empirical data to arrive at any conclusions. Months later, when I sat down to sort out my many observations, I was both surprised and amused to discover that the Yuquí had been right all along—Timoteo was indeed the group's least successful hunter. I was tempted here to write "worst" instead of "least successful," but Timoteo has such an ingratiating personality, something quite rare among Yuquí men, that it is difficult to be critical of the man. His engaging personality notwithstanding, Alicia soon left Timoteo when a younger man and better hunter was available. She took up with Alejandro, her sister's son, and eventually moved into his hammock. Alejandro ranks as the band's second best hunter following Jaime.[6]

The second case of divorce involved Victor, his first wife Quenesí, and Justina. In the complicated and interwoven relationships so typical of the Yuquí, Victor was married to Quenesí, the daughter of the slave, Juamia, who was married to Justina, Victor's sister's daughter. Justina remained married to Juamia until his death. In spite of his slave status and an injury suffered from a tree fall, Juamia was a good provider. In today's parlance, Juamia knew how to "hustle," hunting the slower, burrowing animals, collecting

6. For a while, Timoteo had two dogs, given to him by one of the missionaries. These animals helped him track game, and Timoteo began bringing in larger amounts of meat. During this time, however, he was envied, not admired for his success. When the dogs both died, Timoteo returned to being a poor hunter.

honey to trade for meat, and dressing game for the other men to receive part of the catch. When Juamia died, Justina set her sights on Victor, no doubt abetted by her mother and his sister, Carolina. As the daughter of the slave Juamia by his previous wife Biguaachi, Quenesí was considered to be of slave status along with her brothers Timoteo, Guillermo, and Benjamin. Justina, a *saya*, was therefore able to simply "take" Victor away from her. Quenesí never stood a chance. She died within a short time of Victor's abandonment, after having strangled their three-year-old son in retaliation. At the time, this was Victor's only male offspring, making the killing of the child a particularly effective form of vengeance.

Even today, with the availability of a diversity of food items, the provision of meat significantly influences relationships between Yuquí men and women. Much of the pertinent anthropological literature tends to focus on hunting as the "incentive to gain access to women" (Siskind 1973b:234) and the numerous variations on this theme of exchanging meat for sex. In most cases, it is the male who must compete for women who, through mechanisms such as polygyny, female infanticide, or rules of morality inhibiting sexual access, become a scarce commodity (Holmberg 1969; Maybury-Lewis 1967; Siskind 1973a; and others). In dealing with the Yuquí, one must consider the problem from the female perspective as well. Contrary to Lee and DeVore's statement regarding hunters who "depend for most of their subsistence on sources other than meat, mainly vegetable foods" (1968:7), the Yuquí grew no crops and gathering was conducted as an activity supplemental to hunting. Therefore, at least according to the Yuquí, women did not, as is usually the case, "provide the bulk of the food supply" (Siskind 1973b:234). Like Inuit (Eskimo) women, they were largely dependent on men for their survival. This placed them in the situation of having to use sex as a means to acquire meat. Modern feminist writers point to the fact that this rule applies to any situation where women do not contribute significantly to the subsistence base. Thus, middle-class women in American society whose sole hope for survival was to marry well and live off their husband's income became "sex objects" (Margolis 1984).

It is also apparent that although the Yuquí practiced methods of infanticide that selected against females, they also killed males as well; and additional numbers would be killed, frequently men, in skirmishes with settlers. There is no indication, at least in terms of modern Yuquí history, that men far outnumbered women. At present, there are actually more women than men: 38 females and 35 males. Therefore, there is some question as to who competes for whom. Ultimately, however, the stability of a relationship, particularly marriage, will depend on the man's ability to provide the woman with adequate supplies of meat. If he fails to do this, she will become an easy target for seduction, or will seek meat, and affection, elsewhere.

Old Age

For any nomadic group, growing old is a difficult period since mobility is so crucial to survival. Many stories have been told of how the Inuit put old people out on the ice to perish once their ability to travel and perform useful chores had ended. In actuality, many older people made this choice themselves or remained both mobile and useful until the day of their death. It is those few cases of abandonment that draw attention to what, from the Westerner's perspective, seems callous and inhumane treatment. In his description of the Sirionó, Allan Holmberg also described the abandonment of not only the elderly, but the infirm as well:

> When a person becomes too ill or infirm to follow the fortunes of the band, he is abandoned to shift for himself. Since this was the fate of a sick Indian whom I knew, the details of her case will best serve to illustrate the treatment accorded the aged in Sirionó society. The case in question occurred while I was wandering with the Indians near Yaguarú, Guarayos. The band decided to make a move in the direction of the Río Blanco. While they were making preparations for the journey, my attention was called to a middle-aged woman who was lying sick in her hammock, too sick to speak. I inquired of the chief what they planned to do with her. He referred me to her husband, who told me that she would be left to die because she was too ill to walk and because she was going to die anyway. Departure was scheduled for the following morning. I was on hand to observe the event. The entire band walked out of the camp without so much as a farewell to the dying woman. (1969:225–226)

It would be inappropriate to comment on whether people like the Inuit, Sirionó, or Yuquí experience emotions such as sadness at having to leave a family member behind. Nomadic groups are well aware of the realities of their life and that the survival of the many must often outweigh concern for the individual. The need for constant movement to obtain food or to make it difficult for enemies to pinpoint a campsite must be considered as primary factors in decisions to leave behind those unable to keep up. These instances were relatively rare, however, since a lingering death was uncommon. Foragers like the Yuquí were more likely to die suddenly from accidents, or within a short period of time from snakebite, childbirth, illness, or infection whose advance was rapid. In addition, older people who were unable to hunt and gather enough food to keep up their strength would decline quickly, since their care and feeding was not likely to be taken over by other band members on a regular basis. In one regard, the inability of the infirm to provide for themselves would place undue stress on those younger people who had greater need of nourishment. In another, once infirmity set in, to continue to feed these individuals would simply prolong their life unnecessarily.

In the past, elderly Yuquí women (but not men) were subject to a number of food taboos. They were forbidden from eating otter and catfish. The origin of this belief is unknown, but given that otters were relatively scarce as game animals and that the Yuquí rarely went near the larger rivers where catfish were plentiful, these taboos were more symbolic than real. Of greater consequence to elderly women was the taboo that while behind leaves ("elderly" by Yuquí standards often meant a woman in her middle to late 40s who was still menstruating), a woman could not receive meat killed by a younger man since this was viewed as contaminating and dangerous. Thus, as a woman grew older, fewer and fewer men were able to provide her with meat during the time she was in the *queesa*. With the Yuquí dependency on meat as the major dietary mainstay, for an older woman to go without it meant that she was effectively deprived of food. This alone was likely to hasten her demise.

Ángela (Taineguatsi), Equitá's widow, is the oldest Yuquí. Judging by the generations that follow her, she most likely is now in her late 70s, an unheard of age in precontact times. It is certain that if the band had remained uncontacted, she would have died long ago. Not only is she quite feeble, but she is also blind. It has been largely through the attention of the missionaries and Leonarda that Ángela has managed to survive as long as she has. Her offspring, following the old traditions, see no particular benefit in keeping her alive since she no longer is a productive member of the band. The missionaries, however, encourage them to care for her and keep her fed. This has become the duty of her two eldest sons, Victor and Jorge, who take turns housing and feeding Ángela. On several occasions she has fallen seriously ill and had to be carried in the wheelbarrow up the airstrip to the clinic. To everyone's amazement, Ángela survived each time to return to the camp. At one point she was so ill that her close relatives were on the verge of digging a grave in anticipation of her death. When chicken pox struck the group, a much younger woman succumbed from the epidemic, but Ángela again escaped.

Part of Ángela's longevity can be attributed to her unflagging and crafty efforts to secure food in spite of the unwillingness of her relatives to provide it. She spends a great deal of time in Leonarda's kitchen, where she not only is protected from the elements and warmed by the fire, but is likely to receive food. Leonarda, brought up in a different tradition, is often angered by the Yuquí's neglect of the old woman and makes certain that she is fed. Ángela will also ascertain which of the band has meat, often simply going on her sense of smell as a clue. Finding someone to lead her to the site, she will drop in on the unsuspecting household precisely at the moment that the family is ready to eat. In order to free themselves from Ángela's demands for more food, one of the members of the household will locate another relative with food prepared and lead her there. I fell into this trap late one afternoon when I happened to visit a house where Ángela had taken up temporary residence. Seeing the opportunity to move her elsewhere, the occupants prevailed upon me to take her to her son Jorge's house. With me leading the old woman by the hand, we began to move down the trail at a snail's pace. Since the camp at the end of the airstrip was relatively new, there was a maze of felled trees we had to work our way around and over. Getting Ángela over these obstacles proved extremely difficult and time-consuming, and soon I began to lose the light of day. I now understood why everyone smiled when I agreed to escort Ángela to her next place of residence. Finally, I decided it would probably be easier simply to carry her. She seemed so frail in her shapeless dress and was so advanced in age, I expected her to be hardly more than a sack of dry bones. Little did I realize that while Ángela might be old and blind, she was well-fed and solid as a rock. I positioned her on a log and then put her arms

Photo 24. Angela, the oldest Yuquí. Like the hair of some of the other older women who plucked their foreheads for many years, hers has grown back white.

around my neck. Since the Yuquí often carry their children in this manner, she immediately understood what I wanted and swung herself onto my back. I nearly collapsed under the weight. Staggering down the trail in the murky dusk, I tripped over a tree root and went sprawling, trying to buffer Ángela from the fall. I hit the ground first with Ángela resting heavily on my side. She railed at me in her high-pitched voice but climbed right back on. We arrived at the house amidst the amused chatter of her son Jorge, his wife Rosa, and all their children.

Death

While I was working as a Peace Corps volunteer in the lowland village of San Carlos, at the end of each day I looked forward to an evening spent in the retelling of old tales about the lives and experiences of the community's residents. These stories were full of the bizarre and supernatural to such an extent that it was often difficult for me to sort out truth from fiction. Many such tales involved a rather infamous old *patrón*, a man named Pontiano Chávez, who prior to the 1952 revolution was one of the most powerful landlords in the region. He was reputed to have had 46 children by 19 different women, a claim I was prone to accept since so many individuals in San Carlos carried the Chávez surname.

San Carlos is located in what was once the territory of the Yuquí and Sirionó, only ten kilometers from the old *reducción* of Buena Vista, where numbers of Sirionó and possibly Yuquí were brought to learn the ways of mission life. Well into the 1950s, these forest people were still being contacted peacefully or otherwise, and older people still talk of the encountering of *"Chori"* (the local term for the Sirionó and Yuquí) in areas close to the village. Many people told me that Pontiano Chávez had taken a *Chori* woman, probably a captive, as a companion. She lived with him for a number of years and bore him several children before her death. The villagers considered her wild and strange but an entirely appropriate mate for the also wild and strange Pontiano, who, among other eccentricities, named many of his children according to his own whim, defying both religious and local convention. Two of his sons were given the names of Inca kings, Atahuallpa and Huascar. Then there were his daughters, América and Europa. Thus, when I was told that he kept the *Chori* woman's skull in a box under his bed it struck me as both consistent with his other exploits but also bizarre enough to be quite improbable. By then I had heard so many stories about the Chávez family that I was ready to discount many of them as apocryphal. Twenty years later, having learned more about the ways of the Sirionó and Yuquí, I am not so willing to dismiss the possibility that Pontiano might have honored his mate in a way that was important to her. For in addition to learning about the mysterious skull under the bed, I was also told that it was painted red with *urucú*.

As nomads, the Sirionó and Yuquí devised a means of keeping alive the memory of their deceased that did not involve burial. Cemeteries are artifacts of the sedentary, people who can set aside a place for the dead that can be visited and cared for. Thus, in San Carlos on the eve of All Souls' Day, November 1, the villagers would turn out to clean the cemetery and then stand vigil all night with food and candles as offerings to the dead. The Yuquí had to move on and could afford no such luxury. They wrapped the corpse in three long mats of palm interwoven to form a burial basket called *teicua biasu* (*teicua* is a flat mat; *biasu* means "for *Biá*," people, or Yuquí), and then placed it on a small platform covered with a "teepee" of palm fronds, the "corpse house" (*jirisue tai*). By being wrapped in palm, the body was allowed to decompose with less likelihood of the bones being scattered about by predators. The Yuquí would return to this place from time to time to check on the cadaver and place the old *teicua biasu* inside a new one. Finally, when ants and beetles had stripped the corpse clean, the skull and perhaps a few other bones were removed, painted with *urucú*, the red colorant (in this context called *"seso"*), and placed in a basket. These remains would then be carried by a close relative and kept under the hammock at night. The skull housed the spirit of the deceased, which could be called upon for protection against other malevolent spirits of the dead (*Yirogüe*) in times of need. After several years, the bones would begin to disintegrate and would finally be abandoned, the duty of honoring the memory of the dead having been fulfilled by the living.

The preservation of the bones of the dead was limited to adults of high status. The elderly, slaves, and children would be wrapped in the *teicua biasu*;

but once left in the forest, their bones were seldom recovered. No doubt the Yuquí's fear of the spirits of the dead and their relative power over the living paralleled Yuquí perception of these individuals' importance while alive.

The death of Pa, the headman's brother, occurred shortly after the Yuquí had settled at the Chimoré. The following account, excerpted from the mission's file, relates the Yuquí's reaction:

> Prior to his death, Pa's wife [Carolina] did not go around him much. Their daughter said it was because he took meat from her. At the first sign of his death, his wife and second eldest daughter began chanting the *jirase*, the same chant used over sick people. Almost immediately, Pa's daughter-in-law ran to the river and threw away his cooking pots. Later they threw away a spoon and a can that belonged to him. Then his daughter Pachi [Elsa] put his head in her lap and chanted over him. The wife and daughter chanted over him while others joined in from time to time. This continued until dark, throughout the night and until the next day. As different ones came into the camp, they would squat beside the body, chant for a while, and then go on about their business. The immediate family stayed near the body. Later, his wife and brother broke his arrows. Pa's wife and children and brother began a fast to show their grief.
>
> Two of Pa's sons saw to it that palm leaves (*jinoa*) were gathered to weave the burial basket, the *teicua biasu*. The body was placed inside and covered with pieces of cloth [an innovation from contact when cloth was available from the mission]. Small children had their hair cut to protect them from the dead man's spirit. The body was surrounded with other belongings including the man's hammock, knives, and bows. A teepee about 12 feet high was then placed around the corpse. It was said that the *jirase* was sung to protect the living from the dead man's spirit but also to call the *Yirogüe* (spirits of the ancestors) to come and sit down with them. (NTM n.d.)

Death for any human group is traumatic; but it is particularly so when the group is as small as that of the Yuquí. Death signifies that something has gone awry, something is amiss; otherwise the natural sequence of life would not have been interrupted. From the Yuquí's perspective, death is caused by illness or misfortune brought about by the spirits of the dead, which occupy an ambivalent place in the Yuquí world: They can both help and harm the living. It is believed, for example, that those who die will be sad and lonely in the afterworld and so will seek to take one of the living with them. Fearing the unpredictability of the spirit world, the Yuquí would select an individual to accompany the dead before the decision was made for them. Commonly, these would be infants, children, or slaves. When convenient, a Bolivian national would be killed, thus sparing the group from taking one of its own.

Like many other peoples, the Yuquí link life with breath and believe that the life force escapes through the mouth. Thus, when the headman's daughter, Ta, lay dying in childbirth, several of the women blew softly on her. In her last moments, Ta's saliva was scooped from her mouth by Rosa and Alicia, who placed it in their own, a last attempt to prevent Ta's spirit from leaving her body and flying free.

Today, the Yuquí bury their dead, covering the fully clothed corpse with banana leaves, a custom learned from the missionaries. Although they no longer speak of the spirit world, the Yuquí have clung to many beliefs concerning the dead. Graves are not marked and are never recalled. It is also forbidden to mention the names of those who have died, except in the most oblique manner. For this reason it was very difficult for me to find out much about past relatives or their experiences. Now and then I could get Julia, Helen Porter's informant, to talk about her forbears but only if she was alone with me in my house. She would speak in hushed whispers, and I always felt that we were doing something terribly shameful. I was aware of the taboo against speaking the names of the dead, but like any custom unexperienced, it was something I did not fully comprehend until I inadvertently violated it.

When I first visited the Yuquí in 1982 and was just beginning to learn names and faces, I had difficulty differentiating two young women, Marina and Rebeca (their mothers were sisters, Ta and Alicia). Between my first and second visit, the missionaries informed me that Marina had died of snakebite. One afternoon during my return visit a year later, I was sitting with a group of the women at the gathering place near the store/clinic. Looking at Rebeca, I mistakenly addressed her as Marina. Instantly, I knew that I had misspoken, but I was unprepared for the group's reaction. There was shocked silence. Mouths fell open and then several of the women turned their backs to me. Rebeca began to cry. Old Carolina began to scream at me in the high-pitched staccato the Yuquí use when they are angry or emotionally upset. Tears were running down her face. Julia stood up and stared at me. Angry, she spit out the words, "Why! Why! Why did you say that?" I told her that I had confused the two women before, that the name just came out, that it was a mistake. The explanation sounded feeble, and I could feel myself beginning to cry with everyone else. I put my head down between my legs in shame. My tears and obvious remorse seemed to calm down the women. Julia softened her voice and told me that she knew that it was not done in harm, that sometimes they as well did the same thing. Rebeca stopped crying and wiped away her tears. It was a terrible experience and one that still makes me extremely uncomfortable when I reflect on it. But it was also an episode that contributed to my growing understanding of the Yuquí world view. While the missionaries' teachings have attempted to erase many of the old beliefs, those concerning death and all of its ramifications still remain strong. The mention of the name of Marina not only reminded the Yuquí of someone greatly missed, but it also called forth that individual's spirit, made it present again and therefore a threat. Without realizing it, I had managed to pronounce what in many respects was tantamount to a curse not only on Rebeca but on the entire group. It was only my obvious pain that convinced the women that it was done unintentionally and saved me from becoming a social outcast. In the days that followed, I realized that in addition to what I had learned about the Yuquí from this experience, I had gained an additional measure of social acceptance as well. I, an *Abá*, had been knocked down to size, made to suffer the same humiliation meted out to their own when transgressions occurred. This, then, became another of many small rites of passage that brought me closer to acceptance among a people where small group dynamics can be overwhelming in their intensity.

THE DAILY ROUND: MEN, WOMEN, AND CHILDREN

The social and physical environment of the mission and its scheduled activities to a great extent tend to structure present-day Yuquí life. Yuquí children are required to attend school, and although the classes taught by Mariano Ichu are not part of the state educational system, the Yuquí academic year parallels that of other Bolivian schools. Not being part of a public system, however, Yuquí schoolchildren are not subject to the many interruptions that plague state education, such as teacher strikes. But having children in school five days a week inhibits Yuquí movement away from camp. Nonetheless, even during those periods when children are not in school, the tradition of taking a "long hunt" away from camp for several days seems to be declining.

Although the school year and its demands on Yuquí children's time account for some parental reluctance to leave camp for long periods during the day, there is also a tendency to simply leave children behind. I found a great deal of variation among women in terms of their willingness to go off on a hunt without their offspring. Some women never did this, preferring to remain in camp while their husbands hunted alone or with a male companion, or even as part of a mixed group. Other women frequently left their children in camp, at times in the care of another female, but just as often alone. No doubt individual relations with one's husband may have determined some of this behavior, particularly if a woman was concerned that her husband might commit adultery if he were left unwatched.

As a mother experienced in what unsupervised small children are capable of, I was always concerned about very young children left alone in camp to be watched over by siblings often not much older than themselves. But they fended well for themselves and knew how to satisfy their own needs for food and water. In this regard, children, once they have been weaned, are not really cared for by either parent, having to cook their own food when hungry and then jealously guarding it from other children or adults. Specific mealtimes are unknown. Hunger is satisfied when it occurs and meals are limited only by the availability of food. The Yuquí gather to eat communally or as a family when men return from the hunt. If this falls during the day when part of the group is gathered in the missionary area, the fish or game will be cooked and shared there. Normally, however, men do not return from the forest with their catch until shortly before dark or even after dark. This food, often consisting not only of meat but of other items such as honey and fruit, remains at the house of its owner, to be portioned out by the man's wife to family and others who request a share.

The Yuquí "hang out" most frequently in the shade in front of the long building that houses the store on one end and the clinic on the other. The clinic operates on a daily basis, usually starting at about 8:00 or 8:30 in the

Photo 25. The opening of the store is awaited by a group of Yuquí who are passing the time eating and chatting.

morning and remaining open until everyone needing attention has been seen. The clinic traditionally is operated by one of the mission women, excluding Helen Porter, who devotes all of her free time to translation work. Helen, who has been there the longest and is the most familiar with the medical histories of each Yuquí as well as having considerable expertise in treating their ailments, acts as a consultant when needed. John Porter is called upon when there are severe injuries, particularly wounds that need suturing.

The availability of health care is, of course, a novel experience for the Yuquí, who are now highly sensitized to their current state of wellness. Every ache and pain causes concern and is reason to wait patiently for a turn at the clinic. Like many lowland Bolivians and other Third World peoples, the Yuquí are mesmerized by patent medicines and feel that they have been cheated if they are not given some pill or ointment in response to their illness. The clinic is also a reason to gather socially and to interact with missionary women, who otherwise tend to remain in their houses during the day.

The store, once operated on a daily basis to hand out food and other items in order to keep the Yuquí at the mission, is now strictly a cash-and-carry business open three days a week. It, like the clinic, represents a structured situation when the Yuquí may interact with missionaries as well as each other.

In the often humdrum monotony of camp life, these occasions offer diversion and the hope that something unexpected and interesting may occur. The Yuquí want to know what others are buying or what particular ailments are being experienced. At the same time, those doing the buying or visiting the clinic are fearful that their relatives will find out too much and somehow use this information to their own advantage. Thus, such simple acts as visiting the clinic or store can suddenly take on an air of mystery and intrigue.

On any given day, many different activities will be going on. During the time I was with the Yuquí, not a single day passed, rain or shine, without some of the men out hunting or fishing, often accompanied by their wives and perhaps younger children. Others would be in the forest gathering honey, fruit, or *imbai* bark for the making of string. Those wanting to visit the clinic and store usually remained in this area most of the day, chatting, recounting stories of the hunt, delousing each other's hair, making string or fashioning it into some article, or cooking plantains, manioc, or some other small tidbit saved from the evening before. Working in pairs arranged with the missionaries, each weekday two women would receive flour, part of the supply the

Photo 26. Also awaiting the opening of the store, Antonia listens as one of her kinsmen relates a hunting story.

Photo 27. With flour provided by the mission as part of U.S. surplus food supplies, Yuquí women have learned to make bread.

mission requested from the Catholic Relief Service (CARITAS), the distributor of U. S. surplus food to Bolivia. This flour, a combination of wheat, corn, and soy grains, would be made into bread using the large communal oven behind the clinic and store. Each woman would take half of the bread for her family. By this pairing up, every family had bread once a week, which was greatly enjoyed by everyone but usually finished that same day.

In the spring (September–November), those few men who are interested in putting in a *chaco* will begin preparing their fields. Their preference often is to plant bananas (plantains and fruit bananas) and manioc, cutting down small areas that take neither a great deal of effort nor an exorbitant amount of time, and putting in the root and stem cuttings. Once the plants are established, they take little care and can simply be "gathered" like any other forest product.

In addition to daily subsistence activities or those centered around the store and clinic, the Yuquí take turns working in missionary homes or around camp providing such labor as mowing, cutting brush, washing dishes, or hanging up laundry. Some of the upper caste, the *saya*, dislike doing this type of work because it is obviously a form of servitude; but they also want to be able to earn money to spend at the store. A few of the Yuquí like Carolina, Timoteo, and Benjamin, because of their advanced age or former slave status, have regular "jobs" with the missionaries and are therefore assured a steady income to offset their inadequacies in otherwise providing for themselves.

Men and women also spend time at the river, something that in the past was impossible because of the threat of attack by Bolivian nationals. During midday, the beach is uncomfortably hot, but this is the best time to wash clothes and dry them on the sand. The women will build a small shelter out of sticks and palm or perhaps a dirty blanket or sheet awaiting washing. Because soap must be purchased, the women do not always have it; then they must wash their clothes with the grit of the river sand. Much of their clothing awaits washing wadded up on the floor of the house or even out in the elements, gathering mildew spots and an assortment of other stains. As a consequence, even "clean" clothes look dirty much of the time.

Late in the afternoon when the weather is nice and the river is not in flood, the Yuquí gather at the Chimoré to bathe. The older people, who do not swim, sit at the edge of the water, usually fully clothed (a rather typical result of the imposition of mission rules of modesty), washing themselves as well as their apparel. The younger Yuquí, all of whom swim, will venture farther out into the water, playing games of tag and racing to see who is the strongest swimmer. Often, a large tree will come to rest in the center of the stream, forming a small island. The children race out and then take turns jumping from the limbs into the river. As the sun begins to set, the Yuquí leave the beach, clothing drenched and each carrying a container with water. At dusk, John Porter walks back to camp for the evening prayer session, marking an end to the day's activities.

The rhythm of camp life consisting of hunting, fishing, gathering, planting crops, visiting the store and clinic, school, and other activities revolving around the mission are punctuated by events that are in some way unusual and bring diversity to Yuquí existence. Planes arrive a few times a month carrying supplies and perhaps visitors, an event that will always bring everyone rushing to the airstrip to watch the approach and landing. Arguments invariably spice things up for a while, with hostilities forcing people to remain in their houses or in other ways to avoid contact with their enemies of the moment. From time to time, groups of Yuquí will travel upriver along a well-used trail to visit with Francisco Blanco, the only neighbor in the area and the only form of outing that offers interaction with a known and therefore "safe" outsider. Finally, there are natural events that create uncertainties as well as excitement: The river may flood and overrun its banks; lightning may strike and set a tree on fire; a jaguar will wander into camp one night; or a huge herd of white-lipped peccaries will move into hearing distance and the cry goes out for a spontaneous hunt.

RELATIONS WITH EACH OTHER

Social and Spatial Arrangements

The spatial reorganization of Yuquí society that came with sedentism has brought about significant changes in their social interaction, but at the same time underscores the adaptations they have made to maintain old conventions. The establishment of separate dwelling places as opposed to a single camp has radically altered many customs, such as the ability of masters to continue to control slaves. It has also affected the distribution of meat, now considered a personal item to be secretly hoarded, if possible. In the past, all interaction took place in the base camp, the center of Yuquí life. Having separate dwellings now means that there is no common gathering place in the Yuquí living area at the other end of the airstrip. The camp was not planned with traditional Yuquí social patterns in mind; rather, it reflects the attitude of the missionaries, who were concerned about minimizing strife and illicit sex. The problem of a dispersed settlement inhibiting interaction is compounded by the fact that the camp is a newly cleared area so the ground is littered with fallen trees, and there is very little shade except around the houses of each individual family. With tin roofs, the houses are hot and uncomfortable during most of the day, forcing the Yuquí to look for more comfortable accommodations. What has developed, then, is the habit of using the Yuquí camp only as a place to cook at the end of the day, sleep, or remain during arguments or bad weather. It is not a place that inspires much socializing. The shady area near the store/clinic has become the Yuquí commons. This is where they remain most of the day to talk and to cook manioc, plantains, fish, and meat (when available). It is also what contributes to the Yuquí's image of being "mission Indians." "Mission Indian" is a generic term applied by anthropologists to indigenous populations that have been brought into a dependency relationship with a mission or other outpost through the supplying of consumer goods. The condition is characterized by people sitting for endless hours waiting for the day's handout, unwilling to fend for themselves. While the dependency relationship is certainly present, the hours spent in the shade of the store/clinic building and trees are as much a reflection of old patterns preserved as of new ones that have developed as the result of mission presence. When hunters and gatherers are not out foraging, they spend a great deal of time relaxing around camp. When this was fully understood by anthropologists, the life of the forager, formerly considered one of constant toil, had to be reevaluated. It is this inactivity that, when viewed in Western terms, creates the impression of laziness or lack of willingness to work. From the forager's perspective, work is not something to be admired, as it is by those who espouse the Protestant ethic. Thus, if a mission hands out food, the native will simply have more time to relax, preferably in the vicinity of that food source. In terms of cultural survival, of course, this can have devastating consequences on the group's integrity.

The Yuquí commons in front of the store/clinic, then, has become a recognized gathering place. In the past, if they were not in the forest looking for food, people normally would remain in camp making string, eating, talking, nursing babies, repairing weapons, and napping—precisely the things they now do by the store/clinic. As noted earlier, the store and clinic also operate at specific times during the day; for the Yuquí, who have not internalized Western schedules, it is a convenient place to await the opening of both. The closing of the store late in the afternoon usually marks the end of the day, when people go to the river to bathe or return to camp to see who has arrived with meat.

The missionaries at the Yuquí camp quickly taught the Yuquí that they would have to earn the money that could then be translated into goods purchased at the store, reducing to some degree their absolute dependency. One of the problems with this system, however, is the closed nature of the camp's economy. The Yuquí work for the missionaries, who supply the cash exchanged at the store for commodities. The missionaries also keep the store stocked with goods brought in by plane, goods the Yuquí now depend on. Unfortunately, the Yuquí have no real understanding of how these products came to be there. Without the presence of the missionaries, the system would cease to function. The Yuquí have marketed a few crops, but as yet are not proficient enough at this to ensure that their ongoing and growing needs will be met.

In addition to creating a dependency on the mission, money and consumer goods have increased both the frequency of theft and accusations that it has occurred. In the past, each Yuquí had what everyone else owned. Material possessions consisted only of those items that could be manufactured from the surrounding forest. Now there are "things," objects to be bought and coveted by others. Nonetheless, most stealing is done to spite the owner, since the taking of an article for later use is virtually impossible given the size of the group.

Carolina came to me in tears one afternoon because someone had stolen her plate and probably tossed it into the river. She had had words with one of the women that morning and was certain it was that individual who was responsible. The purpose of Carolina's visit was to offer to make a baby sling for me to earn some "quick" money to buy a new plate. It was always interesting to see the reaction of someone when a stolen article of clothing or cooking utensil was inadvertently discovered in the woods or at the time an area of tall grass near the airstrip was cut back. Normally, several months would have passed since the item's disappearance and by then animosities had been forgotten; however, the recovery of the stolen article inevitably would refuel the old argument.

Given the opportunity, the Yuquí do steal money from each other, with the express purpose of using it because the ownership of cash is impossible to establish. For this reason, women carry around the family savings in cans and jars. If someone has had money stolen recently and another is seen spending cash that cannot be accounted for, a bitter argument is bound to ensue, and, once again, the camp is thrown into an uproar.

The Yuquí are so prone to disagreements that at times I wondered if this was simply some peculiar form of entertainment for a people who have very little else to enliven their existence. The Yuquí are not the least reticent about jumping right into an argument, which, as more people gather around, becomes louder and more violent. The high-pitched staccato speech form (*iquio jasi*, to be fast; or *ju jasi*, to speak fast), particularly curious when employed by the men because they move into a falsetto, reaches ear-splitting proportions as people draw lines and take sides. If the argument persists, it may become physical and quite bloody, a combination of wrestling, strangling, hairpulling, and biting. There is also a great deal of crying among both men and women as emotions get the better of the group. When it is over, usually as suddenly as it began, the combatants glare at each other and stalk off to their houses to sulk. The participants and spectators gradually disperse, returning to their homes to speak of the event in whispers. The equilibrium of the camp is now upset, and the members of the band not directly involved in the dispute will begin to force a reconciliation. This usually involves working out an indemnity of food or money that is agreeable to both sides.

Arguments in camp are usually made known when the participants begin to yell and scream at each other. One morning Alicia, married to Alejandro, and her daughter Antonia, the wife of Lorenzo, began arguing over a missing chicken (chickens rarely last very long in camp). Alicia accused Antonia of having taken the chicken and eaten it. Although the problem was between the mother and daughter, the two men began to tussle, pulling and choking one another. People began to gather, and soon the air was filled with crying and screaming. The fight broke up with Lorenzo and Alejandro returning to their homes. For the next few days Lorenzo stayed in his house, a sign of embarrassment. When he finally went fishing, he gave part of his catch to Alejandro, an admission of guilt but also an apology. Relations between the two households remained cool for a while, but the hostilities eventually were forgotten.

One of the more interesting disputes of the many to occur during my stay involved three families. No one knew exactly what initiated the argument, but Justina had torn up one of Victor's better shirts and he had a number of bites and scratches on his face. She stopped by my house just long enough to say that he had strangled her (squeezed her windpipe) and made her mouth bleed. Then she marched off down the trail. When I went by to check on Victor, he looked morose. Justina had taken her mosquito net and moved in with her mother Carolina. Several days later, Justina was still angry at Victor. He took his bow out early one morning and shot a sackful of fish as a peace offering, but Justina would have none of it. When I went by Victor's place later to weigh his catch, he was sitting on the edge of his sleeping platform staring at his feet. He looked at me with tears in his eyes and said only, "Justina." Leonardo, Justina's brother, told me that she would stay mad at least a week. In the meantime, Felicia, Victor's daughter by Quenesí (who was abandoned by Victor when Justina set her sights on him), accused Gloria, Justina's daughter by the slave Juamia, of having stolen a plate. The animosities were now being carried into the next generation. There was a great deal of screaming and yelling as the two women hurled accusations and denials back and forth. Since Gloria had to walk through Felicia's yard to leave camp, Felicia's husband, Manuel, erected a fence to prevent Gloria and her family from using the trail. The fence was a ramshackle affair made of *chuchillo* tied with vines, but its presence was the ultimate insult to Gloria. Her husband,

Humberto, then cut a new trail around Manuel's fence so they could get to the river. To support his daughter Felicia, Victor also put up a fence, forcing Humberto to cut yet another circuitous trail. Victor's fence was a little better made and had a swinging gate made of some old boards and a couple of rusty hinges. I marveled at his ingenuity. And so it went as people took sides and fences began springing up across all the major trails. Since I was by now the only neutral person in camp, I was allowed to use the old trails, but at each house I had to ask permission to cross the fence, something that quickly became a nuisance as I tried to make my rounds each afternoon taking game counts. Victor stood vigil at his gate, and we would go through an elaborate ceremony as I was given access to the trail leading to the back of camp. I was beginning to see that it was imperative to get Justina back home. Everyone else as well was losing patience with the inconvenience of having to take alternate routes to their houses. Soon Victor made another offer of food that, fortunately for all of us, Justina accepted. The fences came down and camp life returned to normal.

The frequency of these fights and their patterns of occurrence began to interest me. I soon realized that meat and its relative abundance or scarcity had a visible effect on camp behavior. Some anthropologists contend that protein scarcity can cause aggressive behavior, but this presumably is something that develops over a long period of time (Divale & Harris 1976; Gross 1975; Harris 1974; Ross 1978). The Yuquí suffer periods of scarcity of fish and game, but these are rarely protracted, at least to the degree that one would expect some type of physiological response. Nonetheless, meat is the favored food, and its absence from a meal is perceived as real hunger. The failure of a man to provide meat reflects negatively on his status and prestige, leverage that women are quick to employ when there is no meat in camp. Thus, women use gossip and outright insults to force men into the forest to hunt. Lack of meat can create tensions between spouses and between mothers and sons, and ultimately may involve the group as a whole. A simple, straightforward argument over meat can quickly be subverted into a major camp disturbance as old transgressions are again dragged into the public arena. Before long the Yuquí are quite literally at each other's throats. On the other hand, when meat is plentiful and stomachs are full, days go by without major upset—people are happy and get along with each other. Meat, then, remains the common currency of Yuquí life. In this regard, the Yuquí are not much different from the members of an industrial nation, where money, or rather the lack of it, is often the seed of family disputes.

When the Yuquí lived as a single unit, tensions were lowered by merely shifting one's hammock to another tree on the other side of camp. Each night brought a different ordering of living arrangements, reflecting the alliances and disputes currently in effect. Having permanent houses now places greater stress on the Yuquí, since moving after an argument with a neighbor becomes impractical. Part of this problem has been resolved by allowing buffer zones of scrub to grow between the houses, providing both privacy and a certain degree of isolation. On the other hand, this separation often seems only to

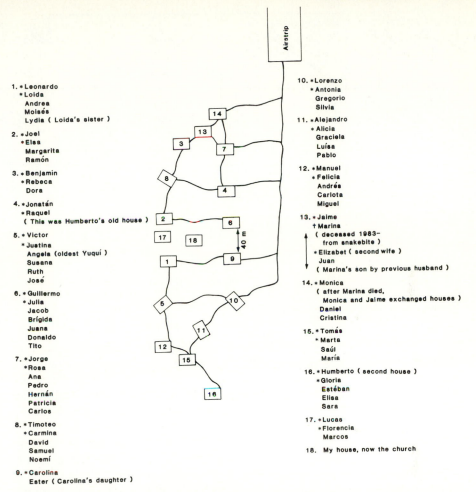

1. *Leonardo
   *Loida
   Andrea
   Moisés
   Lydia (Loida's sister)

2. *Joel
   *Elsa
   Margarita
   Ramón

3. *Benjamin
   *Rebeca
   Dora

4. *Jonatán
   *Raquel
   (This was Humberto's old house)

5. *Victor
   *Justina
   Angela (oldest Yuquí)
   Susana
   Ruth
   José

6. *Guillermo
   *Julia
   Jacob
   Brígida
   Juana
   Donaldo
   Tito

7. *Jorge
   *Rosa
   Ana
   Pedro
   Hernán
   Patricia
   Carlos

8. *Timoteo
   *Carmina
   David
   Samuel
   Noemí

9. *Carolina
   Ester (Carolina's daughter)

10. *Lorenzo
    *Antonia
    Gregorio
    Silvia

11. *Alejandro
    *Alicia
    Graciela
    Luisa
    Pablo

12. *Manuel
    *Felicia
    Andrés
    Carlota
    Miguel

13. *Jaime
    †Marina
    (deceased 1983-
    from snakebite)
    *Elizabet (second wife)
    Juan
    (Marina's son by previous husband)

14. *Monica
    (after Marina died,
    Monica and Jaime exchanged houses)
    Daniel
    Cristina

15. *Tomás
    *Marta
    Saúl
    María

16. *Humberto (second house)
    *Gloria
    Estéban
    Elisa
    Sara

17. *Lucas
    *Florencia
    Marcos

18. My house, now the church

Figure 8. Present Yuquí camp: Yuquí residents, 1982–1983. Houses numbered in order of construction. Population: 73, (*) heads of family, (†) deceased during research period.

encourage the Yuquí to devise more elaborate means to aggravate their enemies. The fence-building episode is a good example of Yuquí inventiveness in this regard.

Although the missionaries were instrumental in the planning and spacing of the camp at the end of the airstrip, the Yuquí themselves decided who would live where. Leonardo was the first to build his house in the new camp, with others following in the order in which each structure is numbered in Figure 8. Thus, Leonardo and his immediate family of mother and siblings form the "core" of the camp, with the other families occupying more peripheral sites. As marriages have occurred and new houses have been built, the tendency is for sons to build near their parents' residence, lessening the "ideal" distance between dwellings as conceived by the mission. Only one

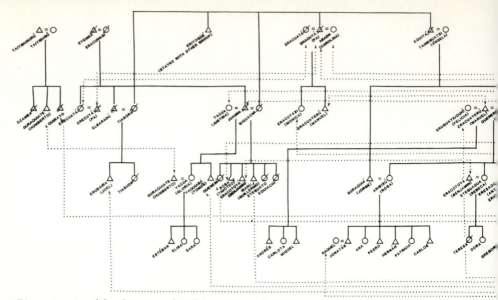

Figure 9. Yuquí kinship: Yuquí (Bía) at Chimoré, 1983

family, that of Humberto and Gloria, have moved their place of residence since the camp's establishment in 1982. Humberto, an ex-slave always at odds with his *saya* masters, found it impossible to live surrounded by those he formerly served. After months of tensions, the missionaries gave Humberto and Gloria the tin for a roof, enabling them to build a new dwelling at a site they chose on the south side of the settlement. This location placed them at the "back" of the camp, farthest from the river, the airstrip, and the continuous scrutiny of their kinfolk. What is interesting about this move is the physical space that now separates Humberto and Gloria from the rest of the group as well as their increasing social isolation. Humberto seems content with the arrangement and claims that he is now free from the demands of his former masters. Of the ex-slaves, he is the only one to hunt on a consistent and successful basis, another indication of Humberto's evidently lifelong desire to divest himself of the stigma of having been born a slave.

Kinship

In a large society such as our own, people have virtually unlimited opportunities to establish social relationships outside the family. From early childhood we are exposed to neighbors and schoolmates, most of whom are unrelated to us. As we reach adulthood, this network of interaction expands to individuals we meet in the job force, at parties, through other friends, and during any number of occasions where people are brought together. Kinship, the system of relationships established through marriage and family, is only one of the many facets of daily interactions that drive American society. We

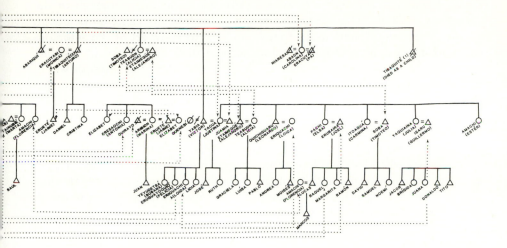

(Figure 9 continued)

are concerned about keeping family separate from much of our life, compartmentalizing our culture to ensure that kinship does not interfere in domains that we have designated as public, not domestic. For this reason, American society is permeated with rules such as those against nepotism or the hiring of kin to positions of authority in a business or institutional situation.

When one moves from a large, industrial society to a small, traditional one, it quickly becomes apparent that such distinctions are untenable. Small societies are by definition kin based, a concept that requires all social activities to be analyzed in terms of how people are related to one another. For this reason, when anthropologists first go into the field to study a particular culture, they often initiate their work with genealogies, systems of past and present interrelatedness. Napoleon Chagnon tells of his frustration in working with the Yanomamö when he discovered that, after almost six months' careful work, the Yanomamö had been purposefully deceiving him about their kin ties as part of an elaborate joke (1983: 19–20). Angry, Chagnon threw away all of his painstaking notations and began anew. He, like other anthropologists, knew that in order to understand the meaning and significance of behavior and events in Yanomamö society, he would first have to sort out the complexity of how people were related to each other.

The collecting of genealogies is normally a time-consuming, tedious task involving a great deal of cross-checking (how Chagnon eventually discovered he had been fooled) and backtracking. Even among most traditional peoples such as the Yanomamö, the population is large enough to make the tracing of kinship and descent a formidable task. In the case of the Yuquí, completing the genealogy did not involve all of the normal struggles usually accompanying such work. With only 14 households consisting of 27 adults and their children (in 1982 when I first visited the Yuquí), working out their kin ties did not present much of a challenge. In fact, after only a few hours' effort, it was obvious that the end result would be only *one* genealogy—that all of the Yuquí constituted a single extended family. The difficulty came in the design of the genealogical chart itself, that is, in how to show all of the interconnections in a way that did not produce a maze of lines and arrows. At one point in trying to develop a solution, I reflected on a "Star Trek" episode where Spock was playing three-dimensional chess and wished that I could do the same with my genealogy. The result, appearing as Figure 9, is only partially successful in presenting the reader with an immediate and clear image of how the Yuquí are all related. With any format developed, there is always the problem of "moving" people from one place to another to indicate marriage.

At times, when I sit and look at this graphic representation of the Yuquí, I am mesmerized by the anthropologist's dream come true: a complete documentation of the kinship ties of an entire society. Although I can never go back through all the generations of Yuquí, now erased from memory, the genealogy represents the Chimoré population known to exist at the time of contact. What I find even more gratifying, however, is the keeping of the genealogy itself, adding new names as children are born, drawing new linkages as marriages occur, and noting the inevitable deaths. In many respects, the genealogy is an affirmation of the reality of the Yuquí as a people, and its existence as a visible entity leads me to hope that the generations will continue. For me, it has become a symbol of their continuity and ability to survive. I would also like to think that many generations from now this document will still exist as a living record, giving the Yuquí not only an appreciation of their past but of their unique place in human history.

All interactions among the Yuquí, then, are shaped by kin ties. Every time there was an argument, I would check my genealogy to determine exactly who was involved and how this behavior was likely to evolve given the nature of the relationships of the participants. It was only through understanding the past and present linkages of Victor and Justina, for example, that the fence-building episode made any sense. On the surface, the subsequent argument between Gloria and Felicia would have seemed an isolated incident had I not understood the intricacies of family ties.

As people of Tupí-Guaraní origin, the Yuquí apparently fall into a kinship system common to other Tupian groups where marriage to one's cross-cousin (mother's brother's offspring or father's sister's offspring) is prevalent. The Yuquí also practice "avuncular marriage," or a man marrying his sister's daughter, which, among Amazonian peoples such as the Tupinamba, is considered as part of a general cross-cousin category (see Shapiro 1968; and Figure 10). In fact, among the Yuquí, this is the only "preferred" marriage pattern, the Yuquí expressing that it is "good" for a man to marry his sister's daughter. In actuality, this has occurred only twice: the marriage between Victor and Justina and that of Jorge and Rosa. Given the extremely small size of the group with its limited number of available marriage partners,

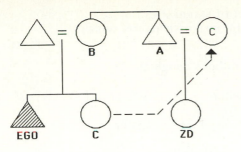

1) If a man (A) "should marry " his
   sister's (B) daughter (C) then:

2) EGO'S sister is the wife of his
   mother's brother. Therefore:

3) EGO'S sister's daughter (ZD)
   is also his CROSS-COUSIN :

   MOTHER'S BROTHER'S DAUGHTER
   (MBD=ZD)

Figure 10. Cross-cousin marriage to sister's daughter (ZD).

however, one would not expect the ideal pattern to be prevalent. Having
sorted out the Yuquí marriages where relationships are known (those Yuquí
present at contact), I found that 10, or 58 percent of all marriages, could be
classified as "cross-cousin" (see Figure 11). Nonetheless, unlike the Sirionó,
who have a specific label, *"yande"* ("potential spouse" = cross-cousin), for
this individual, the Yuquí have no such terminology. Still, the stated preference for marrying one's sister's daughter, along with the high number of
actual cross-cousin marriages, is a strong indication that at some point in their
history, the Yuquí had a "rule" for such a marriage system and perhaps the
terminology to go along with it. While the Yuquí may not have a specific
term denoting a marriage partner, they continue to employ what at first seems
to be a bewildering array of other kinship terms. In many regards, Yuquí
kinship terminology parallels that of the Sirionó. As mentioned above, however, there is no indication that mother's brother's children and father's sister's
children (cross-cousins) are differentiated from any other cousins of one's
own generation. Like the Sirionó, the Yuquí system of terminology is highly
classificatory, with many different individuals sharing the same term. Also
similar to Sirionó terminology, the Yuquí have two perspectives in using
kinship terms: one for address and one for reference. Thus the term "mother"
has two forms. If mother is present and being addressed, she is *"Taï."* But
if someone's mother is absent and being referred to, she is *"esi."* Actually,
all referential kinship terms are possessively marked. *Esi* means his/her
mother [e + si]; *eru* is his/her father [e + ru]. Many other categories of
words are also possessively marked. All parts of the body, for example, must
be expressed in the possessive. When I asked for the word "eye," I was given
"cheresa" [che + eresa], my eye. Yuquí kinship terminology, in its format
of terms of reference and address, is presented in Figure 12.

FIGURE 11. YUQUÍ MARRIAGES
(RELATIONSHIP OF THE MALE SPOUSE TO HIS WIFE)

1. Leonardo married to Loida:
   * Loida is Leonardo's mother's brother's daughter
2. Pa (deceased) to Carolina:
   + Carolina is Pa's brother's daughter
3. Joel to Elsa:
   * Elsa is Joel's mother's brother's daughter's daughter
4. Benjamin to Rebeca:
   * Rebeca is Benjamin's mother's brother's daughter's daughter
5. Humberto to Gloria:
   + Gloria is no relation to Humberto
6. Victor to Justina:
   * Justina is Victor's sister's daughter
7. Guillermo to Julia:
   *Julia is Guillermo's mother's brother's daughter
8. Jorge to Rosa:
   * Rosa is Jorge's sister's daughter
9. Timoteo to Carmina:
   * Carmina is Timoteo's mother's brother's daughter's daughter
10. Lorenzo to Antonia:
    # Antonia is Lorenzo's mother's sister's daughter
11. Alejandro to Alicia:
    + Alicia is Alejandro's mother's sister
12. Manuel to Felicia:
    # Felicia is Manuel's father's brother's son's daughter
13. Jaime to Elizabet (and her deceased sister, Marina):
    * Elizabet and Marina are Jaime's father's sister's daughters
14. Abariquí and Tibaquité (two brothers, both deceased) to Monica:
    # Monica is Abiriquí's and Tibaquité's father's brother's daughter
15. Jonatán to Raquel:
    * Raquel is Jonatán's father's sister's daughter's daughter
16. Lucas to Florencia:
    * Florencia is Lucas' father's mother's brother's daughter's daughter
17. Tomás to Marta:
    # Marta is Tomás' mother's mother's sister's daughter

Categories of marriages and number of each:

(*)   Cross-Cousin (mother's brother's offspring; father's sister's offspring; sister's daughter):
      10

(#)   Parallel Cousin (mother's sister's offspring; father's brother offspring): 4

(+)   Other: 3

Percentage of marriages that fall into the category of "cross-cousin": 58

FIGURE 12. YUQUÍ KINSHIP TERMS

Yuquí Terms of Reference

Esi: mother, grandmother (the older term for grandmother, *"Ari,"* has fallen from use; however, the term is still used by the Sirionó), great-grandmother, stepmother

Eru: father, grandfather, great-grandfather, stepfather, husband

Erinisi: wife (literally, child's mother; a contraction of [*"eriru̅"* (offspring) + *"dn"* (diminuitive) + *"si"* (mother)]

Eriru̅: offspring

Eriquiya: this term also means offspring but appears to have a more formal connotation. In keeping with the higher status of males among the Yuquí, no doubt deriving from a patrilineal system, sons will be referred to as *"Eriquiya,"* not *"Eriru̅"*; but a man's wife and daughters will be referred to as *"Eriru̅"*

Eribu̅: a term used by older boys and men when referring to younger females; sister; aunt. It is also used by males to refer to other younger male relatives (not offspring); brother; uncle. It may be employed by older girls and women to refer to younger female relatives; sister; aunt. It is never used by women to refer to younger males

Eriqui/Erquiẽ: a boy/man uses this term to refer to his older male and female relatives. Some Yuquí insist that when it is used to refer to an older female relative, the term should be *"Eriquiẽ."* This latter term is also preferred by women when they are referring to their older female relatives. The word *"Eriqui"* is used by women to refer to older male relatives

Ếbuyã: this term is equivalent to *"Eribu̅"* except that it must be used to refer to younger relatives of the *same sex* as the person being referred to. Thus it can be used to mean "his younger brother" but not "his younger sister"

Enetare: literally, "a bigger one of the same kind or thing." This is most typically a "female" term used by women to refer to their older female relatives, particularly older sisters. Some speakers use the term to refer to a boy/man's older male relatives, particularly brothers, but it is not the preferred choice

Egurigõ: literally, "a smaller one of the same kind or thing." Females or males use this term to refer to younger female and male relatives, respectively. It is used particularly when referring to younger sisters and brothers

Enongüe: literally, "his/her other; one like him/her." If the person being referred to is male, another male; if female, another female. It can also be used to refer to a person's wife or husband

Ererecua: a man with no sons or only one is referred to as his mother-in-law's *"Erecuã."* Once he has more than one son, he is referred to as his mother-in-law's *"Ererecua"* (not nasalized). The Sirionó use the term *"Ererecua"* to indicate the headman of the band

Ererecuamo: eldest male child; first-born son

Eruquiatũda: this word is equivalent to "relative" but does not refer to one's children, grandchildren, or immediate family

Eboa: those who are not in any way related to one. It connotes outsider and has only this form. A form such as *"Cheboa"* (my no one who is related to me) would be illogical

(continued)

Figure 12 continued

Yuquí Terms of Address

Taï: females use this term when addressing mother, grandmother, great-grandmother, woman who assisted in her birth, woman who nursed her at times during infancy, woman who nursed her mother or assisted in her mother's birth, stepmother, mother-in-law

males use this term when addressing all of the above except mother-in-law

Papa: females use this term when addressing father, grandfather, great-grandfather, stepfather, father-in-law, husband

males use this term when addressing all of the above except father-in-law, and, of course, husband

Yiti: child; a man will address his very young children and his wife by this term; he may also address a younger sister with this word. A woman employs the term when addressing her very young children or when referring to another man's wife or their small children. When referring to a group of children, adults will use the diminuitive form of "*biá*" (people), "*biadn*" (little people)

Yagua: females use this term when addressing adult males: brother, half-brother, mother's brother, father's brother, mother's sister's son, mother's brother's son, father's sister's son, father's brother's son, brother's son, sister's son, husband's brother, sister's husband

Aï: males use this term when addressing adult women; wife (if she has a child), sister, half-sister (shared mother), mother's sister, father's sister, mother's sister's daughter, mother's brother's daughter, father's sister's daughter, father's brother's daughter, brother's daughter, sister's daughter, wife's sister, brother's wife

Eyo: a reciprocal form of address used by *women* with all other older (postpubescent) female relatives

Erabiã: parents use this term when addressing a daughter or stepdaughter who has reached puberty; it is used by grandparents to address granddaughters or great-granddaughters who have reached puberty; it is also used to address one's daughter-in-law

Eteguayo: a man whose wife is childless addresses and refers to his wife with this term. She is referred to by others as "*Enemeguiarū*" (his wife without child). His mother-in-law is also referred to as "*Enemeguiarū*" which becomes "*Eneme-guiaru*" (not nasalized) once a child is born to the daughter and son-in-law. This word is an altered form of "*erebequiaru*," which means "the one he causes to eat meat." The man is expected to provide meat to both his wife and mother-in-law

Cherecuã: a woman who is childless addresses and refers to her husband with this term. It is also used by a woman to address and refer to her (childless) son-in-law. When the woman's daughter bears a child, the husband and son-in-law will then be addressed or referred to as "*Cherecua*" (not nasalized)

Itēē: a man without children uses this term to address his mother-in-law

Miasi: once a man has a child, he uses this term to address his mother-in-law

Biricuã: a man uses this form of address with his childless son-in-law. The son-in-law responds with "*Serecuã*" (a form of "*Cherecuã*")

Miaru: once a man has children, he and his father-in-law reciprocally use this term. Men who have shared the same wife will also use this form to address one another. Thus Timoteo and Alejandro call each other by this term since Alicia was married first to Timoteo and then to Alejandro

Figure 12 continued   SOCIAL RELATIONS   121

Biariqui: a man uses this term to address his sister's husband. His sister's husband responds with *"Serecua," "Cherecuā,"* or *"Cherecua"*

Yaqui: this form of address is used by males and females with all young offspring of their own and other close relatives who are no longer *"Yiti"*

Chiqui: males use this term of address with all those men who call them *"Yaqui"* except for father, stepfather, and grandfather

Yagō: young females use this term to address all those individuals who call them *"Yaqui"* with the exception of mother, father, stepmother, stepfather, grandmother, and grandfather. Following puberty, they will call the older women *"Eyo"* and the older men *"Yagua."* *"Yagō"* is also used by very young boys to talk about older female relatives who call them *"Yaqui"* except for mother, stepmother, and grandmother. These older females will later call them *"Yagua"* and will in turn be addressed as *"Aī"*

What is particularly interesting about all of the above is the Yuquí's focus on two primary distinctions: sex and generation. When taken together, most of the terms of address and reference are concerned with (1) the sex of the speaker or the person being referred to, and (2) whether that person is older or younger (ascending or descending generation) than the speaker. With regard to the latter, adulthood (marked by puberty and the bearing of children) is also built into the system, thus conferring recognition to those who have achieved adult status by giving them appropriate titles.

In addition, this rather formidable assortment of terminology is yet another indication of probable deculturation from a larger, more complex society. It is conceivable that this system may at one time have been even more elaborated; but when relationships narrowed as the group grew smaller in number, the terminology may have disappeared. This is apparent, for example, in the loss of the term *"Ari"* (grandmother) within the last 50 years. *"Ari"* is still remembered by the older Yuquí like Ángela, but has now been abandoned. It is intriguing to speculate on the possibility that "grandmother" may have fallen from use when the Chimoré Yuquí fissioned from the parent band and there were no grandmothers present in the new group. It was not for a number of years until the band's children had children; but by then the word had not been used for so long that it must have sounded strange. As the band size grew smaller, the social distance between grandmothers and grandchildren also must have narrowed, until grandmother occupied a position similar to that of mother and so was called *"Taī."*

The Yuquí Population

At the time of contact, the Yuquí were experiencing increasing pressure from colonists moving into their territory and had greater temptation to remain in areas of settlement to pilfer crops, and, as a consequence, hostile encounters with Bolivian nationals became more frequent. With both the growing threat of being killed outright as well as the Yuquí practice of selecting and killing

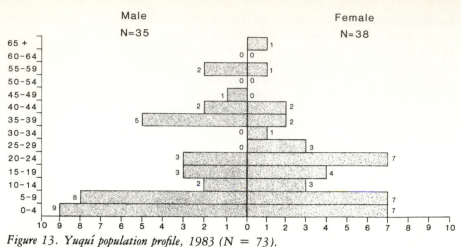

Figure 13. Yuquí population profile, 1983 (N = 73).

a companion to accompany the *saya* dead, the Yuquí population was continuing to decline. It was ultimately the Yuquí's leniency toward rules of incest
and the probable expansion of categories of marriageable partners to include
anyone not a sibling (by one's mother) or a parent that allowed the group to
continue to reproduce and survive. Even today, with mission scrutiny and
teaching against sex outside of wedlock, the Yuquí continue to practice old
patterns of sexual behavior.

One of the greatest problems now facing Yuquí women in particular is
finding a marriage partner. With the small size of the population, any im-
balance in the sex ratio becomes critical. In addition, the tendency for men
to take younger wives (although there were three cases of the reverse) leaves
unmarried those women who simply have no one available to them. In looking
at those age cohorts (see Figure 13) in which females are most likely to marry,
it is immediately apparent that some women will be left without spouses. In
the ages between 15 and 24, there are 6 males and 11 females. Several of
these women are married to older men, and several of the men are married
as well. Remaining unmarried, however, and unlikely to find a mate are
Susana and Ester, aged 22 and 21, respectively. Their only hope of securing
a husband would be for an older woman to die. But even in this case, it is
probable that the widowed man would select a much younger female. This
situation greatly increases the competition among the younger women for the
available men and at times fosters bitter disputes. In spite of not having
marriage partners, unattached women are sexually active, and when pregnancy results, they may decide to keep the child, particularly if it is a boy.
The spectre of a woman without a male to hunt for her still looms large,
overshadowing at times the mission sanction against children being born out
of wedlock.

The younger generation of Yuquí exhibits a more normal sex ratio pattern,
with slightly more males than females. With a typically higher mortality rate

for male children, by the time these cohorts reach marriageable age, the ratio should be about 1:1. The abnormal configuration of the Yuquí population pyramid for the older cohorts is a graphic representation of the toll taken on these people as the result of disease and skirmishes with settlers. Although the mission made every effort to provide health care at the time of contact, several of the Yuquí died from respiratory illnesses. The Yuquí, like all other Native Americans, have little resistance to European diseases, particularly colds and flu. Once the acute period of impact had passed, however, the population rebounded, with the help of vaccines and antibiotics, to continue to grow.

The problem of inbreeding due to the small size of the group has had only minimal visible effects thus far. Other than clubfeet, a trait common both to the Sirionó and Guarayo as well, birth defects are not frequent among children or adults (I am aware of one child born with a number of serious defects, who lived only a few hours). Although accurate statistics on miscarriages are not available, Yuquí women continue to produce healthy children in adequate numbers. If the remaining group of Yuquí are successfully contacted and brought to the Chimoré as planned, this new infusion of people will contribute to the existing gene pool. Then too, as more settlers move into the area, there is the increased possibility of intermarriage, a process that might strengthen the Yuquí in terms of genetic variability, but would threaten the group's cultural integrity. Whether they can continue to reproduce successfully as a small, isolated population will be a matter for history to determine. At present, however, the Yuquí are multiplying with the geometric progression of any population expanding at will, something that bodes well for their future as a people.

RELATIONS WITH THE ABÁ

The term the Yuquí apply to all non-Indians is *Abá* (often spelled *Ava* by Spanish speakers), a Guaraní word I have come across in other places and contexts but one I cannot fit precisely into Yuquí usage. The Yuquí believe that they are descendants of the first people on earth, who, according to their creation myth, were the *Abá*. Historian Thierry Saignes, writing about the Chiriguanos, the group that probably gave rise to the Yuquí and Sirionó (see Stearman 1984), states that:

> These migrants [the Chiriguano from Paraguay] share the Tupí-Guaraní view about their contemporaries, divided among Ava, "the supreme men," and tapuy, "the slaves," that is to say, the remaining peoples who were not Ava. (1985:4–5)

This concept meshes with the Yuquí pattern of hereditary slavery and also with the claim that the *Ava* were their ancestors. What transpired during the intervening generations of isolation to cause the Yuquí to begin calling Bolivian nationals and missionaries "*Abá*" can only be surmised. We know, for example, that the Yuquí believed until convinced otherwise that all "whites" were the spirits of dead Yuquí. Knowing only of the existence of their own kind, the Yuquí would have been faced with having to explain the intermittent presence of these strange pale intruders. Their odd physical appearance, attire, ability to fly inside great beasts (airplanes), and advanced technology (particularly firearms) would have contributed to the assumption that they were mythical beings, ancestral spirits from bygone eras, perhaps the *Abá* returning. The behavior of the "whites," who were at times friendly, offering food, but at other times ready to kill with their sticks that spewed fire and thunder, was entirely consistent with the Yuquí concept of the spirits of the dead as capable of meting out both good and evil. Thus, the term *Abá* as used by the Yuquí to refer to non-Indians carries a baggage of meaning that goes far beyond the simple translation of the word as "other" or "white." At the least, it inspires fear, awe, uncertainty, and, at times, contempt.

Today, the Yuquí have learned to distinguish among the *Abá*, trusting for the most part those individuals associated with the mission but remaining leery of strangers, particularly Bolivian nationals, who come into camp from time to time. The missionaries encourage this dichotomy of "mission vs. non-mission" in an effort to defend their hard-won territory from interlopers as well as to protect the Yuquí from the corrupting influence of the outside world. While some of the isolationism practiced by the mission is, therefore, quite self-serving, the missionaries are also cognizant of the abuses meted out to native peoples when left to the mercy of local *mestizo* populations. An obvious example of this occurred during our trip to Puerto Villarroel. During those several days in the port town, I witnessed numerous occasions when the townspeople attempted to cheat both the Yuquí as well as the much more acculturated Francisco Blanco. Most *mestizos* consider Indians as something less than human and therefore "fair game" in any business transaction. The Yuquí, masters in their own environment, were bewildered at being duped so easily by the town's residents and were angered at the obvious attempts to take advantage of them. Their frustration at times was overwhelming, particularly when cultural and language barriers prevented them from defending their own interests. These and other incidents where Bolivian nationals have taken advantage of them only serve to reinforce the Yuquí's perception of *mestizos* as untrustworthy and undeserving of respect. For this reason, Mariano Ichu constantly has to prove his worth and, like his wife, Leonarda, is frequently the target of derisive comments. Although Mariano and Leonarda are themselves native Amazonians, they are members of the Trinitario group, a highly acculturated people from the Beni. Just as Francisco Blanco is considered an *Abá*, the Yuquí tend to lump the Ichus together with other Bolivian nationals. The fact that they do not live in the missionary area strengthens the Yuquí's conviction that they are not to be accorded the same measure of respect as are the missionaries. This attitude was emphasized one afternoon when one of the men spotted a large group of white-lipped peccaries near the camp. The cry went out and all the men took up their guns. Mariano happened to be at my house and wanted to join in the hunt so I lent him my rifle. Later, he recounted that Manuel, leaving his house at the same time as

Mariano, told the teacher that he would not be his hunting partner. The reason he gave was an insult: Mariano did not know how to hunt (something Manuel had absolutely no knowledge of since he had never hunted with Mariano). When Mariano killed several animals with well-placed shots, Manuel was astounded. The story of Mariano's skill circulated through camp and greatly improved his standing. He now had demonstrated his worth in terms meaningful to the Yuquí.

Far from having the egalitarian world view expected of most foragers, the Yuquí are quick to rank people according their scheme of things. In the world of the *Abá* the Yuquí consider the missionaries to be people of high status, grudgingly submitting to the missionaries' wishes in most things because they recognize missionary power to supply the goods they want and need, and to protect them from the outside world. It is also significant that, given the Yuquí's attention to skin color, the fact that the missionaries are "white" while most Bolivians are "brown" reinforces their own cultural stereotypes and prejudices. After contact, many of the Yuquí admitted to having planned to steal the missionaries' blonde children to raise as slaves and eventual mates, admiring their fair skin and light hair. The Yuquí's preoccupation with being "*amachi*," "light skinned," has worked in the mission's favor in signalling the superiority of the Americans in the Yuquí system of prestige.

Even in terms of the missionaries themselves, the Yuquí rank each according to his or her perceived power *vis-à-vis* the other missionaries. Contrary to first impressions, the missionaries are seldom democratic in the governing of the camp. There is a definite hierarchy that becomes more evident when interactions are observed. The Yuquí, sensitive to any manifestations of ranking, were, for me, an excellent litmus test in determining how this system functioned. It was by observing the Yuquí's behavior toward and commentary concerning individual missionaries that I was able to confirm my own assumptions about power relationships among the missionaries.

The senior couple, the Porters, as a result of their length of residence among the Yuquí, their ability to speak the language, and John's authoritarian style, not only receive the greatest respect but tend to have the final say in all major decisions. Hank Monroe occupies the next position in the hierarchy; if he had a more aggressive personality, Hank would probably be the highest ranking individual in camp. Hank is the most senior member both in terms of age and tenure, but he does not appear particularly interested in having more than a supporting role in the mission's governance. The remainder of the missionaries, numbering from two to five at any given time, have come and gone over the years. Because there has been such flux, this group tends to occupy another niche altogether in the hierarchy; but its members are also ranked within this second category according to perceived qualities meriting respect: strength, aggressiveness, or other characteristics admired by the Yuquí.

For the most part, the camp and its mixed bag of residents constitute the Yuquí's most frequent interactions. Visitors are not welcome, unless they are members of the mission community. From time to time, river travelers will stop in, looking for a place to spend the night, to trade, or simply to satisfy their curiosity. All are encouraged to move on quickly. Only Francisco Blanco's homestead is within easy walking distance from camp, and it has tremendous drawing power for the Yuquí. Francisco's compound of houses, kitchens, and storage buildings is also open to Yuquí inquisitiveness, something they find intriguing since entry into mission homes is restricted. Francisco represents their first prolonged contact with an *Abá* whose lifestyle is within their comprehension. The missionaries, for the most part, have attempted to create a way of life akin to that in the United States, with many of the comforts and amenities of "home." For the Yuquí, this lifestyle is beyond anything they could hope to attain or, for that matter, would even desire. The rusticity of Francisco's homestead is also appealing to the Yuquí in that they do not feel quite so removed from their own way of life. Francisco's wife Concebida's kitchen and Leonarda's are equally inviting: Both are palm-thatched buildings with dirt floors where the Yuquí can sit comfortably and chat.

Francisco's homestead provides a useful model for the Yuquí since it demonstrates how a family can live quite comfortably and acceptably by planting different varieties of crops, hunting, fishing, and using primarily forest materials for shelter and other needs. At the same time, Francisco participates in the cash economy and forges his Bolivian identity through language and other cultural trappings he has acquired from the larger national society. The Yuquí seem to sense that what they need to know about the *Abá* world will ultimately be supplied by Francisco and not the mission, with its foreign culture and complex technologies. Francisco is a hardworking man and, with his indigenous understanding of the wilderness, an example of appropriate technology *par excellence*.

In spite of his many admirable qualities, I found Francisco frequently a poor role model in other regards. I was constantly disturbed by the opportunism and hypocrisy in his dealings with the missionaries and Indians. I was much less tolerant than the missionaries, who, knowing of his many transgressions, were nonetheless willing to welcome him back with each remorseful apology. Francisco had learned that by befriending the mission, he was able to tap into the mission's willingness to assist him not only spiritually but materially as well. Once out of sight of the missionaries, Francisco's Christian commitment was frequently forgotten in his encounters with the Yuquí. Francisco in this respect was no different from any other Bolivian national: He treated the Yuquí as objects of derision.

Because Francisco was always ready to take advantage of the Yuquí, working them for long hours and then handing over a few bananas in payment and, on occasion, physically abusing them, I thought they would eventually tire of visiting his homestead upriver. Particularly after the trip to Puerto Villarroel and all that happened, I was certain the link between the Yuquí and Francisco would be permanently strained. It was not. Granted, the Yuquí stayed away from Francisco for a while, but soon he was back hiring them for next to nothing as day laborers and complaining about their ineptitudes as farmhands. For their part, the Yuquí were back in Concebida's kitchen being given small gifts of food and attention. I came to realize that in spite of his abuses, the Yuquí admire Francisco for his spirit, grit, and ability to manipulate life to his own advantage, precisely those qualities they respect among their own. At the same time, they envy his freedom and knowledge to come and go as he pleases. The Yuquí were once nomads, free as well to roam at will. Although the mission offers safety and security, it is also tremendously confining, a constant reminder to the Yuquí that they are no longer in control of their own lives. Francisco's homestead is a brief escape into another, less constraining world.

5/Belief

The Yuquí normally go to bed shortly after dark, a habit that left the camp in silence by 8 P.M. Unaccustomed to going to sleep quite so early, I would read by lantern light as the evening grew cooler and then fall into that deep sleep that comes from a long day marked by heat, humidity, spurts of strenuous activity, and the constant drain of confronting new social situations. The forest is not quiet at night, but the sounds are comforting, lulling one quickly into unconsciousness: crickets chirping and frogs singing in their multi-voiced cacophony. Thus, it took some serious interruption of this forest Muzak to rouse any of us from slumber. One occasion was a shotgun blast when a jaguar came into camp, looking for something to eat. Monica's son, Daniel, heard the animal snuffing by his sister Cristina's mosquito net and fired his gun to scare it off. The other incident involved a call emanating from the forest that was loud enough to wake me from a sound sleep. It was a strange wail, seeming almost human. What disturbed me was that I could tell that it was not human, but it did not fit any of my known categories of animal calls. It also appeared to come from very far away and yet was loud and clear. I lay awake for a long time, trying to determine what exactly it was that I had experienced. I could also hear the Yuquí talking in their houses, the voices gradually growing weaker as they fell back to sleep. The next morning I asked several of the men and women what it was that we had heard but received no answer. They simply gave me an odd look and said they had no idea what the noise was. When I attempted to question them further, I was brushed off. All I managed to learn was that it was not an animal. The source of the call from the forest remained a mystery to me.

Nowadays, the Yuquí do not talk about their former beliefs since these are treated by the missionaries as something to be dismissed as part of the Yuquí's heathen past. Like the Yuquí views concerning death, the old ideas may have been shelved away as inappropriate in the mission environment, but it is unlikely they have been forgotten. Each time I queried one of the Yuquí concerning the strange sound we all heard that night, I had the feeling that there was something being concealed, something known to the others but no longer mentioned. In spite of years of effort on the part of the missionaries to teach Christian doctrine, the Yuquí still maintain much of their original world view. During the first years of contact, these beliefs were not hidden, but were talked about openly. In the mission's need to understand the Yuquí's concept of the supernatural in order to begin the process of proselytizing Christianity, a detailed record of these beliefs was kept in the "Culture File." Some of that record has been interpreted below, along with my own observations of Yuquí patterns of belief.

DEATH, GHOSTS, AND THE SPIRIT WORLD

The Yuquí universe is perceived as consisting of both the living and the dead, with the dead holding the upper hand in terms of relative power. The living are confined to their world, while the dead may move at will between their realm somewhere in the "sky" (*teruquia*) and that of the living here on earth. In their concept of the supernatural, the Yuquí are what Sir Edward B. Tylor (1958) termed "animists." Tylor postulated that animism was one of the earliest forms of religious expression, encompassing a pervasive "belief in supernatural beings." To the Yuquí, the world is filled with spirits, mostly of their own dead, who can enter animals or take other forms. Anything, for that matter, that is unusual in nature will be incorporated into their belief in spirits.

Like other peoples of the Amazon and elsewhere, the Yuquí greatly fear death and the transformation that occurs when the living give up that fragile and mysterious state of being. Also in keeping with many early beliefs that are found throughout human populations, the Yuquí equate breath with the life force. Writing of this phenomenon, William Howells (1962) tells of a case from ancient Rome: "The eldest son of a dying ancient Roman took this seriously (that the soul leaves the body in the breath), making an effort to breathe in his father's last outgoing breath, and so catch his soul" (149). Our word, "respiration," for example, was derived from the Latin term meaning "spirit." We might add to this that a synonym for "die" is "expire," which also has the same Latin origin in the concept of breath being linked with the soul. Howells goes on to explain that the Polynesians tried to save a dying man by stopping up his nose and mouth, to keep the spirit from escaping.

The Inuit, who are known for "rubbing noses," are actually sensing one another's breath, being touched by each other's souls, as it were. It is also believed that kissing, probably developed in India, is but a variation on this theme. Cats have the habit of lying close to one's face, and are attracted by warm breath. Out of this action grew the fear that cats were stealing one's soul, and henceforth they became associated with witches and acts of witchcraft.

From this, we can also interpret the importance of saliva, used in many curing practices worldwide. My colleague, David Jones, author of *Sanapia: Comanche Medicine Woman* (1968), recently told me that one of his first memorable experiences with Sanapia was having a mixture of well-masticated herbs thrust into his mouth by the Comanche healer and then having to lick the saliva off her finger. The efficacy of the treatment for a stomach problem he was suffering was not only in the herbs but also in the saliva, which carried the power of the medicine woman herself. Michael Brown (1985), writing of the Aguaruna Jivaro in the Peruvian Amazon, explains:

> Saliva and the act of spitting are important in many magical acts performed by the Aguaruna, and they also figure prominently in the mythical conjurations of Etsa, the sun. A special kind of saliva, called *kaag*, is the medium in which shamans reveal their spirit darts. (200)

Thus, the slang expression "swapping spit," in referring to a kiss, is not far from the original intent of the action of experiencing the soul of another person. In this context, then, the Yuquí customs of blowing on dying relatives, scooping saliva from their mouths, and even preventing vomit from reaching the ground as efforts to ward off sickness and death become understandable.

The Spirit World

The Yuquí believe that once the soul, or breath, has left the body, the spirit divides into two entities. This concept, also well known among other Amazonian groups such as the Chiriguano, the probable precursors of the Yuquí, is expressed in several forms. When a Yuquí dies, that person becomes two spirits. The first is called the *Biá agüe*, or *Biagüe*. The morpheme "*agüe*" means "used to be." Thus, a *Biagüe* is a "used to be person." Of the two spirit entities, the *Biagüe* is the most greatly feared and is thought to become an *Abá*, the mythical being from whom the Yuquí believe they are descended and who is manifest in Bolivian nationals, missionaries, or other "whites." It is the *Biagüe* who are capable of causing sickness and death, or bringing other misfortunes on the group. When Jorge was bitten by an alligator thought to be dead (and therefore harmless), the Yuquí blamed this unnatural event on the *Biagüe*. It is also interesting that the concept of malevolent *Biagüe* spirits being embodied in the *Abá* was strengthened by the spread of disease when the Yuquí would come in contact with Bolivian settlers.

The *Biagüe* live in the sky and are referred to as "*teruquiarinda*," the "ones across the sky" (*teruquia* = sky; *ri* = across; *nda* [nominalizer] = ones). There is water in the sky and that is where the *Biagüe* are to be found. Thus it is they who cause the rain and storms. They are also said to be unhappy about the people left behind and to cause sickness and death to remedy this situation. Thunder, feared because it presages the approach of a storm, is thought to be a drinking party of the dead, the *Biagüe* thinking about the ones still on earth.[7]

The other half of the soul becomes a *Yirogüe* (*yiru* = breath; *agüe* = used to be). A living person has *yiru*, breath (this word also means mouth and lower face, inside of mouth, and throat), but upon dying it leaves by the

---

7. The Yuquí at one time made mead from fermented fruit and honey. A mildly intoxicating beverage, it caused them to reflect on the dead and to call forth their spirits, and therefore was seen as a saddening experience. As the frequency of contact with Bolivian nationals increased, the Yuquí gave up the preparation of this drink since it jeopardized their alertness and safety and also because they rarely had the time necessary for it to mature properly.

mouth. The Yuquí also speak of "dying all the way somewhat" (*mano tuti ja yai*) to explain when someone appears mortally ill (comatose) but then miraculously returns to life. The "breath" appeared to have left the body but did not. The *Yirogüe* are ambivalent spirits in that they can both help and harm an individual. A man will call upon his deceased elder sister's *Yirogüe* to assist him in the hunt. It is the *Yirogüe* who are being asked to come and heal the sick when the *jirase*, the sickness chant, is being sung over someone seriously ill. The bones of the dead may also contain the *Yirogüe* and so are carried to protect the living. The *Yirogüe* of those who died in the prime of life have the greatest power. It is their bones that were painted red with *urucú* and then carried in a basket for years, being placed under the hammock of a close relative when the group camped. This latter belief in the curative power of bones, particularly those of people who in life had great prestige, is widespread in Amazonia. The Guaraní, also culturally linked to the Yuquí, were convinced that the souls of the dead would return to inhabit that individual's bones, which could then advise and heal relatives (Métraux 1963b:569).

The *Yirogüe*, unlike the *Biagüe*, who inhabit the sky, are to be found among the living most frequently in the form of two small birds, the *gurai* and the *tiruru* (species unknown). Both of these birds are darters, flying at one suddenly as if out of nowhere. I remember my first encounter with a *gurai* when it flew at my head and then was gone. The experience was uncomfortable and left me a bit unnerved. Both of these birds are also notable in that they have small red markings, red having mystical power for the Yuquí as well as for most other Amazonian peoples. The red, blood-like colorant *urucú* is used as a body paint (as is animal blood at times) to ward off evil in addition to being used as a protection against snakebite. Snakes and jaguars (perhaps the only two animals in the Bolivian forests that are deemed a threat to human life) are the other animals in which the *Yirogüe* may take up residence. The *Yirogüe*, therefore, can cause harm to as well as protect the living. Like the *Biagüe*, they too may come and take the living with them, but are pacified if another person is sacrificed to accompany the spirit of the dead. However, the *Yirogüe* of someone who is killed is more dangerous than it would be if he or she had died from other causes. In this regard, the *Yirogüe* of slain slaves were often blamed for illness or death that the group experienced shortly after those individuals had been sacrificed.

In addition to the dual entities representing the spirits of the dead, the Yuquí also believe in other more malevolent beings that have no real form but are "shades" or "shadows" that inhabit the forest. These beliefs, also found among the *mestizo* population in lowland Bolivia, center around two categories of supernatural beings: the *Iguanda* (igua = next to, close by; *nda* [nominalizer] = ones) and the *Chochoi*.

The *Iguanda* are beings that cannot be seen, although the Yuquí believe that those who lived a long time ago could see them somewhat. They are always evil spirits and come during the night to abduct the unwary. When animals are found dead in the forest, it is believed that it was the *Iguanda* that killed them. Therefore, even if the meat is still good, the Yuquí will give these animals a wide berth. The *Chochoi* is similarly an unseen creature of the night and can be identified by its loud, shrill call (was this what the Yuquí believed we heard late that night but that would not be mentioned?). It also comes to take people, and is fond of going for the eyes. While I was living in the lowland village of San Carlos, I often heard parents threaten misbehaving children with the *Cocoi*, a bogeyman who would come in the night to carry them off.

Chanting

The spirit world is dealt with primarily through the use of chants. In addition to being an act of supplication, David Jones (1987) notes, "Chanting functions to relax, focus attention, regulate breathing and emotional states, and coordinate thinking. These functions are generally ignored in most anthropological accounts." Alfred Métraux also tells us:

> Chanting is, of course, closely linked to and accompanies all religious ceremonies throughout South America. Its importance as a means of averting impending dangers is well-illustrated by the behavior of the Apapocuva-Guaraní who at the slightest difficulty or even because they felt depressed, resorted to chanting. (Métraux 1963b:583)

The Sirionó were known for their chanting, and I was able to record several of these old songs that are still repeated by the elderly. The Sirionó were fond of welcoming the dawn each day and would sing their morning song, a melodious but plaintive chant, repeated over and over until the sun was at last above the horizon.

Like the Sirionó and other Guaraní peoples, the Yuquí also had a penchant for chanting and some still do. The chant for death or impending death is called the *jirase*. Whenever there was a threat to life, this chant would be sung. If a child fell down and began to bleed, while he was being treated for his wound the *jirase* would be softly chanted over him. The *jirase* was sung to appease the spirits of the dead, to convince them not to carry away the living. Since the spirits were watching, they had to be properly impressed. Thus, the *jirase* was carried out with great fervor, accompanied by shrieks, screaming, and crying. As noses ran profusely, they would be wiped with long strands of Yuquí hair.

In addition to the *jirase*, the remaining Yuquí chants, the *iyusumano* and the *amayaquia*, were to protect the people from wind and storms. The Yuquí inhabit a region that is plagued with bad weather, no doubt due to its nearness to the Andes Mountains. Having lived in Florida as well as eastern Bolivia, I was accustomed to unsettled weather; but during the time I spent with the Yuquí, we experienced storms of a violence I had not known previously. One night in particular, the winds were so strong I worried that the roof of my house would be torn off. It is no wonder, then, that the Yuquí would chant until the storm abated, often becoming hoarse from the effort or even spitting up blood.

The *iyusumano* is chanted to protect the band from the high winds that are capable of felling large swaths of forest. The shallow-rooted trees fall easily, converting the normally safe cover of forest into a death trap. This chant is dedicated to the spirits of the dead, the *Biagüe*, calling on them to stop the fury. While the chant is in progress, the men hold their bows and arrows and beat them together, increasing the urgency of the act. The *ama-yaquia* is also chanted to the dead; it is directed toward the thunder and lightning that accompany rainstorms. The lightning in this area is of ferocious frequency and power, each discharge bringing a tremendous crash of noise and a sudden, blinding flash.

Taboo

The need to manipulate the power that the spirit world exercises over the fate of those on earth is expressed not only through chanting but also through a wide range of taboos. By observing these taboos, one may avoid angering the ever-present spirits with their unpredictable intentions toward the living. Taboo also helps explain the occurrence of ill fortune, since rules of conduct may be inadvertently violated either by oneself or through the negligence of another.

Some of these taboos have already been discussed in other contexts, particularly those that surround women and men during pregnancy and childbirth. This is a dangerous time for all involved, and so many things can go wrong that pre- and post-natal taboos are a cultural universal, found not only among indigenous peoples such as the Yuquí but among Western societies as well. For example, our Anglo-American departmental secretary, in reminiscing about her first pregnancy, related the story of her mother warning her not to look at anyone with a physical deformity lest this affect the unborn child.

Food taboos also infuse Yuquí belief, affecting not only pregnant and parturient women and their husbands (they must not eat twin fruits, or deer heads with their runny noses), but also most other segments of the society at one time or another. A great deal has been written about the function of food taboos in aboriginal society as a means of limiting the hunting of certain species, and this may pertain to the Yuquí as well. It also is indicative of the relative importance of people within the band, however, since it is most often children and old women, not adult males, who are subjected to food taboos. Small children are not supposed to eat white-lipped peccaries, animals that run in large herds and, when captured, supply large amounts of meat. In addition, children may not eat collared peccaries, capyguara, paca, and cicero monkeys. It should be pointed out that several of these species typically have a high fat content, leaving a coating of grease in the mouth, which is what the Yuquí believe causes thrush in children (a fungus that leaves a white, pasty coating on the mucous membranes of the mouth).

Menstrual taboos are also prevalent among the Yuquí as they are among many groups throughout the world. All body fluids are considered to have power since they carry an essence of that person's spirit; but none is so powerful as blood, which is synonymous with life itself. Hence, menstruating women are seen as highly threatening in that they are able to bleed from an internal source, something that normally signifies impending death, and yet they do not die. Menstruation, obviously but "inexplicably" part of being female, is therefore viewed as potentially harmful to men, who do not have this capability. It is interpreted as dangerous and polluting, and contact with the menstrual flow or the women who are experiencing it will cause men to weaken and possibly die.[8] This contamination can be transferred to others as well, or even to their weapons. Thus, a woman is isolated in a "menstrual hut," she is put "behind leaves" in the *queesa* during menstruation and childbirth so that she will not endanger the men in her group or their hunting capabilities. If a woman is nursing a male child, he may not accompany her into the *queesa* since being in contact with a menstruating woman is potentially harmful to the young male. Female children are under no such constraints and may continue to suckle even while their mother is confined "behind leaves."

Only men who are older than a menstruating or parturient woman may hunt for her, presumably because their greater age protects them from harm. For this reason, not only do men have a preference for younger, more "attractive" women as mates, but women prefer to marry men who are older than they so they will be assured of having meat while confined to the *queesa*.

Concern with the power of blood is also seen in other taboos that prohibit the consuming of any meat that is undercooked. It is believed that swallowing blood, either that from an animal or one's own, will cause illness and parasites. During a prayer meeting one afternoon, Manuel's small son fell against a tree stump and bit his lip. His father jumped up and grabbed the boy by his legs, turning him upside down so that the blood would drain out of his mouth, not down his throat. For the next several minutes while the group resumed its meeting, Manuel carefully swabbed out the boy's mouth with his finger and shirttail until he was satisfied that the blood flow had stopped.

All meat must be well cooked, and it was not uncommon for anyone visiting me while I was roasting meat or fish to caution me not to eat it until all trace of blood was gone. Having been brought up in a society where meat is said to be ruined if it is overcooked, I often found Yuquí meat, smoked until it was dry and often like shoe leather, not terribly palatable. But if anyone happened upon me while I was eating a piece of meat that was only slightly pink in the center, it would be grabbed out of my hand with stern warnings and thrown back on the fire. The Yuquí have forever jaded that feeling of bliss I once experienced when I cut into a medium-rare steak.

8. Shortly after contact, when these beliefs were still current, if someone purchased food at the store for the mother of a newborn or for a menstruating woman, the entire lot of a particular item would be considered contaminated. Thus, when a can of sardines was purchased for a menstruating woman, the remainder of the case was considered "spoiled" and would not be touched.

Food taboos, particularly abstinence, are prevalent following the death of a close relative. While in mourning, the Yuquí will slap their stomachs, to indicate that they are flat, without food.[9] Other taboos that must be observed at death include not using a dead man's hunting trail or any of his personal items. For this reason, bows, cups, or other personal possessions were destroyed at the owner's death or left with the corpse. In this regard, the most personal possession of all, one's name, must also be "destroyed" by deleting it from verbal exchange.

During the first years of contact, the missionaries queried the Yuquí about many of their taboos, asking them why the missionaries did not suffer any ill effects from ignoring these rules of behavior. The Yuquí responded that it was because they were *teruquia gurinda*, "people under the sky," while the Yuquí were *osenda*, "people of the forest." From the perspective of the Yuquí, they and the missionaries belonged to different worlds and therefore were subject to different sets of rules.

THE YUQUÍ CREATION MYTH

All societies have creation myths, stories that are explanatory in function and incorporate the supernatural in describing the origins of the world. It is also typical for creation myths to describe the primacy of one's own people in the scheme of things based on supernatural preference. Thus, the name individual groups give themselves often means "true men" or "the people," placing all others into a lesser category or even perhaps one that is not quite human. The Yuquí as well refer to themselves as "the people," *Biá*, while non-Yuquí are *Abá*.

The Yuquí creation myth, as related by those who remember it, falls within a range of similar myths found throughout native South America that focus on the role of the sun and moon in the origin of the world and the people who inhabit it. In the case of the Yuquí, however, it was their early ancestors, the mythical *Abá*, who created the sun, moon, and stars:

> The first living things on the earth were the *Abá*. Some very old animals that were with them were the tapir, jaguar, white lipped peccary, and the deer. Then the *Abá* gave birth to the *Erebeya*, then the *Erebeya* gave birth to the *Biá*.
>
> It was dark, there was no sun or moon. Because it was dark, the *Abá* heated up his grease—alligator, jaguar, peccary, tapir. When it was hot, he poured it out. That was the sun. Some splashed around, making the stars. The rest stayed in the round pot, getting hard. That was the moon.

From all appearances, Yuquí cosmology consists of little more than their belief in spirits and this old story of the origin of their people and how the sun, moon, and stars came to be. In writing about the Sirionó, Holmberg also noted that:

9. In mourning the dead, the Yuquí will go without food during the day. They feel they are free to eat at night, however, since the spirits cannot see them in the dark.

> Native religion has not reached a high degree of elaboration among the Sirionó. One of the reasons for this may be that the Indians are forced to devote most of their time and energy to the immediate struggle for survival. Both shamans and priests are lacking. (1969:238)

In his explanation of the simplicity of Sirionó belief, Holmberg did not consider the possibility that the Sirionó had experienced deculturation, as now appears to have been the case. But he was probably quite correct in assuming that the lack of elaboration he describes was due to their acute struggle to survive. The Yuquí as well have experienced this same hardship and as a consequence have had little opportunity to preserve or develop an elaborate ritual life. As was true for the Sirionó, the Yuquí have no religious specialists, no shamans who are the keepers of old secrets and preside over all activities that involve the supernatural. Consequently, belief is maintained by everyone within the band and is subject to idiosyncratic interpretation and recall. Because no one was specifically charged with the responsibility of remembering the complexities of Yuquí cosmology, it has eroded with each successive generation. Knowledge of healing, usually linked with shamanism, is also rudimentary and remains in the common domain. The Yuquí have no intricate pharmacology, no extensive inventory of the magical as well as curative powers of plant and animal substances. Without this knowledge, they were even more enslaved by the whims of the spirit world, against whose power there was little recourse except to observe taboos and chant songs of propitiation.

LEARNING TO BE CHRISTIAN

Anthropologists and missionaries have a long history of being at odds with one another, stemming from our differing perspectives concerning cultural relativism. Cultural relativism is "the thesis that because cultures are unique, they can be evaluated only according to their own standards and values" (Haviland 1987:45). The imposition of another value system, therefore, such as Christianity, inevitably denies the innate worth and integrity of the values of the target population. Modern missionaries, aware of many of the criticisms of anthropologists and others, insist that they are not "forcing" the doctrine of Christianity but simply "making it available" to native peoples. What they fail to recognize is that Christianity is the ideology of a more technologically sophisticated culture and that it is this advantage that unfairly sets the stage for the dominant-subordinate roles that inevitably follow.

Technological superiority cannot be underestimated in the process of attracting native peoples like the Yuquí to the mission environment. Through the supplying of trade goods and creating a dependency relationship based on the provision of firearms, ammunition, food, and clothing, the Yuquí were convinced to remain with the mission for longer and longer periods. Once that dependency was firmly established, their fate was sealed. They are now inextricably linked with the mission and their lives are in large part determined by the demands of mission life.

In spite of over ten years of living at the mission encampment, however, the Yuquí remain largely indifferent to conversion, at least in terms of how the missionaries define their version of Christianity. Given that Yuquí numbers are so low, particularly regarding adults, and that the missionary-to-Yuquí ratio has always been quite high, one would expect that mission impact on the Yuquí's spiritual life would have been greater. As a cultural relativist, I took comfort in the fact that the Yuquí had managed to demonstrate such remarkable resistance to change. But as an anthropologist familiar with the processes of acculturation, I was also curious to discover what factors had led to what I was beginning to perceive as a religious stalemate between missionaries and Indians. Much of this, I determined, lay not only within the complexity of Yuquí culture, but within that of the missionaries as well.

While I had not gone to the Yuquí camp to study missionaries, they were as much a part of the total social environment as were the Indians. Most of the Yuquí's daily interactions involved mission personnel to some degree. These interactions were usually quite structured, however, leaving both missionaries and Yuquí isolated in their own domains much of the time. The particular "style" of the mission contributed enormously to the continuing integrity of the Yuquí as a cultural entity, although I doubt that this was consciously intended by mission personnel. The evolution of the camp as a social system, largely a product of earlier hostilities and fears, has underscored the discreteness of each group. Once these initial patterns of interaction had been established, they became solidified over time. It also should be pointed out that, at least in terms of this particular mission group, preparation for living with people like the Yuquí was largely lacking. The emphasis was on religious, not necessarily cultural, expertise. Several of the missionaries had received some instruction in ethnographic techniques, primarily to assist them in compiling a data base concerning the ideology of the native peoples they were attempting to contact. Beyond this, however, there was little preparation for the huge cultural chasm that would confront them. Operating from their own Western value system and the position that any deviance from Christian teaching was reprehensible, the missionaries' first few years of contact with the Yuquí predictably resulted in culture shock. Much of this was dealt with by "circling the wagons," creating a separate mission area where the Yuquí would visit but not live. From this evolved the rather rigid system of interaction that persists to the present day. In addition to the spatial factors affecting acculturation, the philosophy of this mission has encouraged greater cultural resistance to conversion. The missionaries do not accept the premise that culture is integrated, that belief is simply part of a larger system and does not exist in isolation of everything else. In addition, the missionaries operate with the expectation that at some point in time each Yuquí will "receive the Spirit," experience salvation, and become a "new person" through the direct intervention of God. Thus, I was often told by John Porter that the role of the mission was to concern itself primarily with the religious aspects of Yuquí life—teaching the word of God as revealed in the Bible. All efforts are hinged to Helen Porter's translation of the Old and New Testaments. Therefore, Porter explained, such realms as subsistence, technology, and political and social organization were only of peripheral interest to the mission. This ideology in many respects explains the lack of concern about the camp's spatial division and missionary isolation, since the missionaries see themselves only as catalysts in the conversion experience. It also affects the Yuquí's ability to survive in the modern world, however, as will be discussed in the following chapter.

Unlike the Jesuits and the Franciscans who successfully spread Christianity across Latin America by taking advantage of logical compatibilities with native religions, the missionaries at the Chimoré want to begin with a "blank slate." They view present-day Catholicism in Latin America with all its syncretism of indigenous and European beliefs as a subversion of Christian doctrine, and in most respects not even worthy of being called Christianity. The blank-slate approach to religious conversion is, of course, an impossibility since all adults are products of years of enculturation that cannot simply be wiped away, even if we desire to do so. Thus, the frustrations experienced by the missionaries at the Chimoré when Christian teachings are consistently reinterpreted in traditional contexts are understandable. The missionaries, believing that Christianity is indeed a universal concept, work under the assumption that, with divine intervention, the Yuquí ultimately will come to see things "correctly."

For now, God is *Papaguatsu*, "Big Father," a term coined by the missionaries and introduced into the Yuquí cosmology as a benevolent/wrathful entity. This concept has been readily accepted, given the former Yuquí belief in the dichotomy of the soul and the ambiguous roles of spirits. The Devil, or Satan, is a more interesting character in that he presides over the Yuquí realm of malevolent spirits who were always much more active and willing to intervene in the affairs of men and women. Satan is referred to by the Spanish term, *Satanás*, but this combination of sounds is difficult for the Yuquí to pronounce so it has become *Sasanás*. I found, as I am certain the Yuquí did as well, that this collection of sibilants, resembling the hissing of a snake, was an appropriate name for the Devil.

Just as spirits in the past could be invoked during or blamed for unusual events, God and the Devil have similar functions. During arguments it was common to hear the word "*Papaguatsu*" being used as a threat against another person. I cannot help but recall a marvelous line used by Bea Arthur in the television series, "Maude." Each time someone worked against her wishes she would respond by saying, "God will get you for that!" While *Papaguatsu* is frequently invoked by the Yuquí during periods of stress or intense hostility, *Sasanás* is spoken of less openly and with the same sense of fear and dread that the *Biagüe* and *Yirogüe* formerly elicited. I remember listening with a growing sense of amazement when yet another missionary earnestly explained to me how the mission had "freed" the Yuquí from their domination by evil spirits.

In a classic situation of a less technologically complex society being over-whelmed by one that tests the limits of comprehension, the Yuquí spirit world pales before the likes of *Papaguatsu, Jesucristo*, and *Sasanás*. The mission-aries' considerable control over natural events contributes not only to the Yuquí's perception of the power of their supernatural entities but also to the missionaries' ability to effectively manipulate those entities through suppli-cation and magical acts. This is particularly true in terms of health care and the provision of vaccines, medications, and antivenin, which miraculously prevent sickness and which are perceived by the Yuquí as restoring life. In the pragmatic way of the Yuquí, and most other native peoples for that matter, it would be irrational not to recognize, respect, and embrace the greater authority of the *Abá* spirits. Beyond this, however, Christianity and what it demands in terms of behavior do not particularly capture Yuquí interest.

The greatest inroads in teaching Christianity to the Yuquí have been made with Julia and Leonardo, two of Equitá's grandchildren selected at an early age to be the conduits of mission efforts. As a girl of 12, Julia was identified by Helen Porter as having the quick intelligence and curiosity that would make her a good informant. Working with Julia on an almost daily basis, Helen learned the language and began her translation work. Julia continues to participate in this activity and spends two to three hours a day with Helen in the missionary's home. Although she has made a profession of faith, Julia continues to participate in Yuquí life in much the same manner as her peers. She is known to "backslide" now and then, something that gives Helen Porter as well as Julia great pain when it must be discussed and analyzed. In this context, Julia often seems caught between two worlds: wanting to please her mentor who has offered her a taste of another way of life but at the same time being tied to her people and their ways. The stress of this existence was apparent in fleeting moments of distraction and was manifest in frequent headaches and other undefinable illnesses that plague Julia's life.

Julia's brother, Leonardo, is the man the missionaries preferred to replace Equitá as leader of the group, although, as noted earlier, his acceptance by the Yuquí is not yet complete. Leonardo assists John Porter with the afternoon prayer sessions, but beyond this has little real authority except when supported by Porter. John Porter expresses a desire to see Leonardo truly lead his people one day, but as yet is not willing to give up his own control over the camp. On the other side of the question is a general reluctance on the part of the Yuquí to submit to the authority of anyone, including John, which they bridle under when it is imposed.

Like his sister Julia, Leonardo frequents the Porter house to work with John on language study and to receive religious instruction. Leonardo's re-lationship with the Porters seems much less emotionally dependent than that of his sister. This, in part, is a result of the Yuquí male's self-image of strength and independence and because he spends much less time there. Also, he is quite aware that he is being groomed for leadership; if he is ultimately to receive the respect of his people, Leonardo cannot show too much deference to anyone.

Religious teaching for the general Yuquí population at the Chimoré camp follows a pattern of holding daily prayer meetings shortly before dusk in the Yuquí settlement. These sessions are usually presided over by John Porter or, in his absence, Hank Monroe. None of the other male missionaries has been there long enough to have gained adequate language proficiency to conduct these gatherings. These meetings were usually well attended, although there was no real pressure to attend. Like me, the Yuquí seemed to look forward to the diversion the gatherings offered and the sense of comraderie they generated. We spent much of the half-hour or so singing hymns that had been translated into Yuquí by Helen Porter. In keeping with the pattern of camp segregation, these were "Yuquí" sessions and were rarely attended by anyone except the particular missionary leading the meeting. The missionaries conducted their own service on Sunday mornings in English, or Spanish if the Ichu family and Francisco were present. The Yuquí were welcome to attend these services, but few did.

Following the singing of hymns, John Porter would discuss a passage from the Bible. The Yuquí listened attentively as John made an effort to put events from two thousand years ago that happened in a place thousands of miles away into some familiar and meaningful framework. The meeting ended with one of the men, usually Leonardo or perhaps Jorge, praying for the group, for those who were sick, and for other more mundane needs of the moment, such as a broken riding mower that kept the airstrip serviceable. These spontaneous prayers, however, had a well-rehearsed, chant-like quality with many repetitions. Watching Jorge pray, eyes closed and rocking back and forth in rhythm to his chant, I was once again reminded that culture, that ephemeral entity that molds behavior, is a powerful and often relentless force in our lives that is not easily suppressed, let alone erased.

6/The Mission, the Yuquí, and Cultural Survival

In this final chapter, I would like to consider the problem of Yuquí survival, not only as individuals but as a people with a special ethnic identity. It is a complex issue and one that is facing many groups like the Yuquí as they confront the modern world, its technology, and its ideologies. In some regards, however, the Yuquí are unique in that they are so few in number, making the question of their survival particularly acute. Unlike native peoples with large populations, the Yuquí cannot absorb the loss of even a score of their members, whether through death or assimilation. The Yuquí people are also unusually vulnerable in that they come from a tradition of foraging with adaptations based on mobility. Their material culture was limited to only those things that could be easily transported. Thus, they are easily impressed by the wealth of new commodities and technologies offered by a larger, more complex society. Their social and political organization also reflects their having lived in small bands of related members. And with the disruption of contact, they no longer have patterns of leadership that would help them to meet the world head on and to develop strategies necessary to preserve their cultural integrity. In short, because the outside world has more than adequately demonstrated its technological superiority and power to dominate those from simpler traditions, the Yuquí are experiencing cultural disorientation, and they have doubts and misgivings about the ultimate worth of their own ways.

At the same time, they also show a stubborn resistance to submitting to the will and whim of outside manipulation. Much of this stems from the Yuquí personality itself, however, and not from any conscious effort to preserve their cultural integrity. This is a concept, I have found, that is largely missing from foragers like the Yuquí and Sirionó, who, not belonging to a people with a specific "tribal" identity, simply accepted who they were without much consideration of the matter. Overall, the Yuquí are trying very hard to live up to the expectations of this more powerful society that has come to restructure their lives, but patterns of viewing the world in their particular style are firmly entrenched and are not easily discarded.

I find myself thinking often of the Yuquí and weighing their chances for cultural survival. Much of this reflection often is focused on the New Tribes missionaries—not only their role in bringing the Yuquí into contact with the outside world, but their religious philosophy as it influences the process of acculturation itself. Having been around more liberal Catholic missionaries for many years, I frequently found myself in opposition to the New Tribes' interpretation of Christian belief and how this was affecting the lives of the Yuquí. Particularly distressing and distasteful to me was the concept being propagated that all those in the world who are unaware of, or do not accept, Christian teachings are forever doomed to an eternity in hell. The New Tribes Mission, as well as other fundamentalist groups working among native peoples, espouse and teach the doctrine of the unending punishment of the unsaved.

The ethical question of whether the Yuquí should have been contacted at all is, of course, now moot, but deserves comment nonetheless. As an anthropologist coming from a tradition of cultural relativism, I believe that all people have the right to live out their lives according to their own values and beliefs. Unfortunately, the world does not often work that way. At the time of the Yuquí contact, there was no one to lobby for their right to remain in the forest unmolested. The larger issue, however, is that they were not unmolested to begin with. The Bolivian government, through its policy of aggressive colonization of the "vacant" lands of the *oriente*, saw the Yuquí as an impediment to this process. From the perspective of the colonists, the hostile Yuquí were a threat not only to their success as pioneers, but to life itself. The political philosophy of Bolivia, and other Latin American nations as well, is one of "national integration"—that people such as the Yuquí need to be brought out of the forest and taught to become sedentary farmers and consumers in the national economy so that they may take their place with the rest of the peasantry. In this way, so it goes, they will be able to participate fully in national life.

Had the Yuquí not been contacted by the New Tribes missionaries, the only people at the time willing to risk their lives in this process, it is certain that they would have been killed off or taken as "*criados,*" a euphemism for lifelong slavery as servants in the homes of Bolivian nationals. My preference, and no doubt that of all concerned with cultural survival, would have been that some other group, one more attuned to the issues and problems of indigenous rights, have made that initial contact and remained with the Yuquí to help them confront the problems of living in the modern world. But no such group was available; and the fact of the matter is that very few people who do not have the driving zeal of the missionary are willing to put their lives on the line in a contact effort and to then devote the remainder of their existence to the difficult process of acculturation.

At present, the mission is a refuge. It may be a "golden cage," as ethnographer Erland Nordenskiold (1924) described mission life more than 60 years ago; but given the Yuquí's fledgling abilities to cope with the modern world, it is better than the other options currently available. However paternalistic, confining, and unenlightened the mission environment may be, my "worst case" scenario regarding the immediate future of the Yuquí would be for them to lose this protection.

While recognizing the positive role the mission plays in protecting the

Yuquí from assimilation, I must also question the mission's position regarding the needs of the Yuquí in their quest to take their place in the modern world. The New Tribes Mission does not construe its role as one that should aggressively address adaptive strategies necessary to preserve Yuquí cultural integrity. It was often explained to me that conversion, not cultural survival, was the mission's primary objective. Their purpose in being there was to save souls, not "culture," particularly one that in their eyes was so primitive and lacking in anything worth saving. I recall a confrontation I had with one of the missionaries one afternoon when I was expressing my concern that the Yuquí were having great difficulty in trying to reclear the previous year's *chaco* for this year's planting. Exasperated with my intrusion into "mission" affairs, the missionary's anger led him into being perhaps more forthright than he intended: "They don't have to learn to farm, we'll feed them!" When I was discussing this later with a biologist friend of mine, he responded with characteristic cynical humor. Paraphrasing from the old 1960s peace movement slogan, "better Red than dead," he quipped, "Are the Yuquí better fed than dead?" I would like to think they are, because as long as the group continues to exist, there is hope that ways will be found to ensure their survival as a cultural entity. And for the present, at least, much of this will depend on the New Tribes missionaries working with them.

With regard to the crucial area of political activism, however, the mission is severely limited by its philosophy concerning interactions with the state. In Latin America, where Catholicism is often a state-sanctioned religion, Protestant missions have managed to gain a precarious foothold by supporting the *status quo*, by providing the service of pacifying hostile Indians who stand in the way of eminent domain, and by refraining from entering into situations of potential conflict. They will support any government in power that does not threaten their own survival. This stance, they claim, is "dictated" by Scripture. However, as journalist Norman Lewis has pointed out in discussing the Summer Institute of Linguistics (SIL), a sister organization of the New Tribes Mission and one that shares many of the same philosophies,

> It may be in acknowledgement of this official cooperation (SIL is part of the Bolivian Ministry of Education and Culture) that the biblical text that features most prominently in the SIL's well-produced promotional literature is Romans 13:1, offered in Spanish and eight Indian translations. The Institute's text is at variance both with that of the English Revised version of the Bible, and its Spanish equivalent. "Let every soul be subject unto the higher powers" becomes, "Obey your legal superiors, because God has given them command", while the SIL quite remarkably re-translates "the powers that are ordained by God" as "There is no government on earth that God has not permitted to come to power." (1978:12)

Catholic missionaries, who as a result of historical precedent and the presence of a national clergy hold a much more secure position in Bolivia and risk less in taking on the government, operate from a very different perspective from that expressed above. Many do not accept the doctrine that governments are in place because of divine right, and are willing to tackle unpopular and often dangerous issues affecting the rights of native peoples. For this reason, many anthropologists do not necessarily see missionaries as a generic group but tend to classify them as "liberal, progressive" Catholics and "conservative, repressive" Protestant fundamentalists (see also Salamone 1977).

In my experience with the New Tribes missionaries at the Chimoré camp, I found much of the above to be true, but I also discovered that changes in attitude are possible and that fundamentalist missions, while extremely conservative, are capable of reevaluating their position, albeit cautiously and only after great deliberation. There is tremendous fear and suspicion of those who are not members of the mission community or its home supporters, an expected reaction from any group that finds itself in an embattled minority position. Any criticism leveled at mission personnel or policy by an outsider is viewed as an attack. These individuals are commonly labeled "communists" and are considered members of "Satan's army," which is bent on thwarting the efforts of the mission to reach the unsaved. Thus, it was extremely difficult for me to attempt to discuss the Yuquí's future with the missionaries or even to be given a fair hearing. Attempts at dialogue or constructive criticism from an outsider who was also an anthropologist were simply unacceptable. This problem was compounded by the fact that I am a female and, from the missionary perspective, not only was unlikely to have the competence to confront such problems but should not have concerned myself with issues that are more properly dealt with by males. But while I may have been ignored at the time, there is indication that some of my suggestions may have found fertile ground. One of these was land rights.

The integrity of any indigenous people is ultimately bound to the land. Without land, without a home territory, there can be no hope for group survival. But this quickly becomes a "political" issue because it involves interacting with those Bolivian agencies charged with land distribution. Thus, the mission is hesitant to press the case to the point that it might bring them into conflict with existing authority and therefore jeopardize their position as guests of the government. On the other side of the question, however, is the survival of the mission itself. If it is overrun with settlers, the work will come to an end, a harsh reality facing people who have invested significant financial resources and a large part of their lives in a single effort. Thus, regarding the Yuquí land question, the mission is truly faced with a dilemma.

When I broached the question of Yuquí land rights, John Porter told me that one of the missionaries in Cochabamba, accepting the responsibility for "these types of matters," had been working for years to have land secured for the Yuquí, but with little success. I pushed harder, at first while I was in camp and later by mail, but received no response. Then, in a long, detailed letter from John dated September 28, 1985 (quite a surprise since it is Helen who usually corresponds with me), I was told of the most recent efforts they themselves had undertaken to ensure the sovereignty of Yuquí territory. The Agrarian Judge in Cochabamba, an attorney, and a government representative from Indigenous Affairs were brought to the Chimoré camp by mission plane. A meeting was held with the missionaries, several of the Yuquí, and the visiting dignitaries. The proceedings were tape recorded by the Agrarian Judge, and several documents, prepared beforehand, were read and explained to the group. About a month later, a surveyor was brought in to delineate the land solicited by the mission in the name of the Yuquí. After reviewing topographic maps, it was determined that the Yuquí would be eligible under the laws of the Agrarian Reform for 7800 hectares, or about 17,000 acres. While this may seem a great deal of land for so few people, it is less than ten by ten kilometers, not much by foraging standards. Nonetheless, it assures the Yuquí of having a home territory.

The problem now at hand is securing a title, something that is extremely difficult in present-day Bolivia. It will also be difficult for the mission to press its case since there is growing reluctance to allow foreign churches to secure land ostensibly for the use of native groups. Unfortunately, the Yuquí still lack both the critical mass and the political skills to deal effectively with public officials themselves, a problem faced by many indigenous peoples of Bolivia and elsewhere. In response to this need, a grass-roots group, CIDOB (Committee of Indian Peoples and Communities of the Bolivian Oriente), has formed a coalition of several lowland indigenous communities specifically to confront such issues as land rights and titling. Given their fear of losing influence over the Yuquí, however, it is highly unlikely that the missionaries would risk inviting an outside organization like CIDOB into the camp.

Although the question of securing a clear title to Yuquí land has not yet been resolved, the filing of a formal solicitation with the office of Agrarian Reform gives the Yuquí some security for the present. According to Porter, the limits of Yuquí land have been surveyed and trails have been cut with *mojones* (large posts that mark land boundaries) set in strategic places. Bolivian law will honor the Yuquí claim to their land as long as they are able to keep it free of squatters. This will require constant vigilance, placing tremendous stress on the Yuquí with so few people and so many kilometers of boundary to protect. It will also become increasingly difficult to protect this territory as more settlers move into the area, hungry for land and unwilling to defer to a small group of people they consider savages who are selfishly keeping so much virgin forest from "productive" use.

In addition to assuring the Yuquí of having access to land in perpetuity, another important issue is that of economic self-sufficiency. While in a moment of anger the posture of extreme paternalism regarding the Yuquí's need to become food producers may have been taken, in reality there has been some effort over the years to address this issue. Inhibiting the growth of Yuquí economic self-sufficiency, however, are many problems, again largely attributable to mission organization and philosophy.

First, there is the inevitable conflict that arises between the mission's fear of losing influence over the Yuquí on the one hand, and wanting them to stand on their own economically on the other. Without the paternalism of safety and consumer goods, the glue that appears to be holding the Chimoré camp together, the missionaries worry that they would lose their hold on the

Yuquí. In actuality, the Yuquí now are irrevocably part of the outside world, if only marginally so, and express only distaste for their former existence. Unlike other groups that have enjoyed isolation to continue their own way of life, for generations the Yuquí were a beleaguered people. While the Yuquí resent their loss of self-determination, life at the Chimoré camp is their first respite from pursuit in perhaps almost three hundred years. They are also aware that there is still much to learn about Bolivian society before they will be able to function adequately in it; but at the same time, I witnessed frustration that the mission was moving so slowly in teaching them the skills needed to achieve this self-sufficiency and, with it, greater independence.

Second, many of the skills, such as farming, carpentry, and other useful technologies that are now beginning to interest some of the Yuquí, are not taught on a consistent basis because of a lack of trained personnel to do so. Other than the Porters and Hank Monroe, who are urban people with little background in these areas, there has been an almost constant turnover in mission workers at the Chimoré. It is also not the policy of the New Tribes Mission to train people in rural development, and such concerns as appropriate technology are not part of mission curricula. Missionary training focuses on biblical knowledge, doctrinal purity, and survival skills taught at a "boot camp" in some wilderness area in the United States. Any knowledge of farming or other practical skills that a missionary may bring to the field are simply fortuitous. Unfortunately, even those who may have some background in agriculture have approached it from a strictly temperate zone perspective, never questioning that this technology might be inappropriate not only for the Yuquí but for the tropics as well. When these methodologies fail, there is discouragement and a tendency to blame the failure not on the approach but on the Yuquí's lack of ability or willingness to learn. Again, because the mission does not see this as a priority and will not seek technical assistance, the move to achieve economic self-sufficiency has been a series of fits and starts lacking any planning or direction; this inevitably leaves the Yuquí as well as the missionaries with tremendous self-doubts and frustrations.

At present, a few of the younger Yuquí men are beginning to farm on their own, but for the most part are following established peasant patterns of monocropping rice and corn primarily for cash purposes. It is unfortunate that there have not been more efforts to encourage the growing of nontraditional as well as traditional crops that may not follow typical lowland cash cropping patterns. In addition, more ecologically sound systems such as intercropping (growing several varieties that are interspersed in such a way as to make maximum use of the land as well as to reduce erosion, leaching, and the need for weeding) and long-term succession resulting in tree crops could be introduced. Because of not having any tradition of agriculture whatsoever, the Yuquí are in an ideal situation to try some innovative techniques. In this sense, the paternalism of having food supplies available through the mission offers a safety net until they can develop strategies that best fit their own needs. Because the Yuquí are still able to supply many of their dietary requirements from foraging, they have the time to invest in long-term projects such as the development of tree crops. While swidden farming should not affect the integrity of their lands as long as the population is small, a much more profitable course would be to encourage better use of these swiddens, culminating in the cultivation of perennial crops that require little attention and are ecologically compatible with the local environment. In addition, it will be several generations before the Yuquí can be expected to accept the demands of the intensive farming practices of peasants, something that may not even be desirable given their particular environment. Peasant farmers are locked into the market economy and therefore must produce a cash crop at the end of their first year on a piece of land. With the typical lowland pattern of shifting cultivation, cropping the land until it no longer will produce rice or other cash crops in satisfactory amounts, and then moving on to yet another patch of forest to begin the cycle again, the peasant is unwilling or unable to invest the time and effort in permanent cropping patterns. Thus, there is little incentive to locate and plant good fruit tree stock, cacao, coffee, or other species of tree crops being developed. The planting of hardwoods, especially mahogany, is also avoided because it will be 25 to 50 years before the trees mature.

The Yuquí, on the other hand, have the opportunity to invest in future generations who, as game inevitably becomes harder to find, will begin to depend more and more on plant resources for their dietary and economic sustenance. If the Yuquí are not to fall into the traditional lowland pattern of abusing the land for immediate profit, which leads to displacement, economic marginalization, and poverty, innovative strategies for land use will have to be developed quickly.

And finally, because the Yuquí are not being taught the skills they require to provide for many of their needs, they will become increasingly dependent on the outside economy, something that will lead only to their willingness to leave camp and hire out to local farmers, ultimately becoming locked into debt servitude as are so many other lowland peoples. Again, this appears to be a problem of training in appropriate technologies. The Yuquí could be taught to make manioc flour, candles from beeswax, soap from ash and animal fat, sugar and syrup from cane; to cut lumber for their housing and furniture needs (tables, stools, shelves); and numerous other skills that are still to be found in rural areas and that would encourage their self-sufficiency. But, since it is much easier to supply kerosene, surplus flour, sugar, milled lumber, bar soap, and other commodities readily available in the marketplace and transported by plane, this type of knowledge has been largely overlooked or viewed as superfluous. Then too, other than Mariano and Leonarda Ichu, who receive no real encouragement to pursue the teaching of traditional technologies, there is no one to train the Yuquí in these skills. If there were greater recognition that this is indeed important, an effort could be made to bring in local people to teach a number of these technologies to the Yuquí.

Years ago, one of the missionary women taught the Yuquí women to make macramé items from *imbai* string, something they continue to do on a regular basis to earn cash. This is an indication that the Yuquí are open to acquiring new skills. The men, for example, expressed an interest in learning carpentry, and on several occasions we worked together on small projects. But unlike the first year I was in camp, the availability of tools is now restricted. By the time of my return visit a year later, the old shed where we had cut and shaped machete handles, repaired gun stocks, and made the canoe paddle, was rebuilt, reorganized, and then padlocked. This became missionary domain for the maintenance of their camp and homes and was not open to the Yuquí. No doubt the locking of the shed was the result of having tools carried off and not returned, something for which the Yuquí are infamous. Nonetheless, there were no organized activities or even times when supervised use of tools was possible to replace the former freedom of entry.

Having a home territory and achieving economic self-sufficiency are both critical to cultural survival, but added to these is the question of community solidarity as expressed through ethnic identity and self-awareness. Because the missionaries are so intent on erasing old ideologies, preserving what is Yuquí is seen as counter to the mission's ultimate objective of conversion.

Ethnocide can be a slow, insidious process, the gradual eating away of a people's culture until they are no longer distinguishable from the society around them. Not only is it a loss of diversity, something precious to humanity, but it is frequently accompanied by all of the side effects of losing one's cultural identity: alcoholism, social disorganization, apathy, violence, suicide, prostitution, and marginalization. I saw much of this in the remnants of Sirionó villages where people were stripped of their cultural integrity and left to the forces of a world all too ready to use and abuse them. As long as these villages were under the protection of the missions, in this case Catholic, they provided a safe environment for the Sirionó within. Once that protection was withdrawn, however, there was little to buffer the Sirionó from the outside world. Because no effort had been made to develop a sense of identity and ethnic consciousness, the Sirionó quickly succumbed to the pressures of more powerful groups around them. They were easily seduced into patterns of life that are now leading to their destruction not only as a cultural entity but as individuals as well. The one exception to this was at the mission of Ibiato, where a different ideology prevailed. Here, the preservation of the Sirionó language was paramount, and traditional patterns of leadership were preserved. The missionaries, in this case Four-Square Gospel and later SIL, were interested in recording many of the old stories and myths of the Sirionó, giving them a sense of their own past and importance in the scheme of things.

It cannot be assumed that the Yuquí will receive the benevolent protection of the New Tribes Mission in perpetuity, nor is that in any sense something to be encouraged. Yet, one would hope that the missionaries would consider the future of these people beyond their simply becoming Christians. Helen Porter will have invested most of a lifetime in the translation of the Bible into Yuquí, a monumental effort that will have been wasted if there are no future Yuquí to read it. Although Helen's efforts to preserve the Yuquí language are to effect religious conversion, the act of recording the language is nonetheless an important contribution to Yuquí cultural identity. Still, there are no overt actions on the part of the missionaries to underscore the importance of the language as something valuable beyond simply being a means to communicate Christian beliefs. Spanish is being taught by Mariano Ichu to Yuquí children, an important tool for survival in the world at large; but bilingual education to foster literacy in Yuquí is sporadic and does not include an appreciation of its intrinsic worth as a language.

Because the missionaries fail to see the value of Yuquí culture and are fearful that preserving it will interfere with their efforts at conversion, there have been no attempts to record Yuquí ethnohistory and old stories in the Yuquí language. Once the older people die off, this knowledge will have disappeared forever, leaving the Yuquí without a sense of ethnic continuity. Added to this are oversights stemming from a lack of sensitivity to indigenous issues or the need to preserve an indigenous past. For example, when the Yuquí were taken to Cochabamba for medical treatment, no thought was given to the fact that they would have to fill out documents and be given surnames. On the spur of the moment, Spanish surnames were chosen at random, so that all now have taken these names as their own. Unlike other groups, including the Sirionó, who took their own or antecedents' indigenous names as surnames, the Yuquí have lost yet another link to their identity as a people.

Ethnic identity is also preserved and reinforced through community-wide forums and decision-making activities, neither of which are being promoted among the Yuquí. Again, following the leadership pattern of the New Tribes Mission, which has been described as a "theocracy" where a board of directors makes decisions and then disseminates them downwards (Stoll 1984), the Yuquí are not being organized according to participatory democratic principles. At present, John Porter makes the final decisions affecting the camp, including the Yuquí as well as the other missionaries.

John is training Leonardo for leadership, and from all appearances the expectation is that Leonardo will at some future time assume a similar role of influence. The Yuquí are often disgruntled by this and on occasion resist submitting to John's and especially to Leonardo's authority. Although the headman Equitá claimed certain prerogatives as leader, the group followed a more typical foraging pattern of fluid, consensual leadership. Women as well as men had input into decisions, which were made as a matter of course as the band gathered together in a single camp. Lacking an accepted leader and suffering the disorganization of mission life, the Yuquí are hard pressed to reinstitute former patterns of leadership and direction. Thus, recognizing the greater power of the missionaries, they await direction from the outside. It is still not too late, however, to begin an active program of participatory leadership among the Yuquí, something that would foster their own solidarity, improve Leonardo's chances to develop a following, and better prepare them for the onslaught of national society. Having the experience of meeting regularly as a community to openly discuss issues and needs as well as to confront specific problems would not only strengthen the Yuquí as a political body but also encourage the growth of ethnic awareness—that they are not simply a collection of related individuals but are, in fact, a distinct cultural entity that must defend itself in order to persevere.

Up to this point I have dealt with the New Tribes missionaries and their dealings with the Yuquí from the perspective of specific issues and not as people living with one another. While I often questioned the missionaries' philosophy, their lack of willingness to critically evaluate their own presence among the Yuquí, and their stubbornness in coming to accept new ideas, I never doubted that they cared about the Yuquí as human beings. Although they live very separate lives, the missionaries have devoted years to the Yuquí and are genuinely interested in their well-being. Whether this is a reflection of changing attitudes of the mission as an institution or is simply a matter of individual missionary differences, I cannot speculate. At any rate, the missionaries at the Chimoré do not fit the pattern described by anthropologist Jürgen Riester in his encounter in 1962 with a missionary entrusted by the Bolivian government with the pacification of the Ayoreo:

> The missionary allowed more than 150 Ayoreos to die in cold blood, after establishing contact with them. The Indians were dying of a respiratory disease accompanied by high fever, and the missionary held back medicine, using the following argument: "In any case they won't allow themselves to be converted. If I baptize them just before they die, they'll go straight to heaven." (quoted in Lewis 1978: 13)

When speaking of the Yuquí, the missionaries at the Chimoré will remark that they are "like family," perhaps slipping into a bit of self-deception but nonetheless sincerely so. When a Yuquí falls ill or injured, every effort is made to provide help, including, if deemed necessary, flying the individual to a hospital in Cochabamba or Santa Cruz. Preventive health care is also part of mission procedure, including tetanus shots, vaccinations, worming, and an annual visit by an itinerant mission dentist. The death of a Yuquí is extremely painful for the missionaries because it not only represents the loss of one of the precious few and someone they may have known for many years, but signifies failure in that yet another of their flock has gone to hell. Curiously, I found that in discussing with the missionaries the Yuquí who died in recent years, there is a tendency to rationalize that because these individuals' lives had changed so much since contact, perhaps they really were "saved" after all. It is an interesting contradiction but one that indicates the missionaries' reluctance to admit that someone whose death is grieved will suffer eternal damnation. This is the point where one's adherence to a strict doctrine of salvation becomes severely strained when confronted with the reality of human emotions and caring.

But simply caring about the physical and spiritual well-being of the Yuquí is not enough. The New Tribes missionaries accepted the responsibility of bringing the Yuquí into the modern world and so they must also confront the long-term consequences of this action. The Yuquí have a right to survive as a people, and that right is now entrusted to the mission.

Guide To Yuquí Pronunciation

The Yuquí language is Tupí-Guaraní in origin. The consonant and vowel system is very similar to that of Spanish, for example:

/r/ is "flapped." The word *piri* (hunting) is pronounced "pidi."
/y/ is pronounced with a soft "j" sound. The word *yiti* (child) is pronounced "jiti."
/h/ is written with the Spanish symbol "j" as in *jinoquio* (basket), pronounced "he-no-ki-oh."

Diphthongs are written with the symbol [¨] as in *nenongüe* (one like you), pronounced "neh-nohng-gwe."
The vowels, /a/, /e/, /i/, /o/, and /u/ are as follows:

/a/ as in f*a*ther
/e/ as in l*e*t
/i/ as in b*ee*t
/o/ as in b*oa*t
/u/ as in b*oo*t

Sounds peculiar to Yuquí are:

/s/ is pronounced with a soft "ts" sound except when preceded by /i/.
"Nasalized" vowels, which are written with the symbol [˜], are common in Yuquí and often change the meaning of a word (nasalization is phonemic). The word for mother, "*Taĩ*," for example, is pronounced "Tain." The unnasalized form of this word, *tai*, means house, roof.
/b/ and /d/, particularly when in an initial position, are nasalized and are pronounced "mb" or "nd" as in (m)Biá (people) and (n)dió (manioc).

Yuquí words of two or more syllables are frequently stressed on the final syllable (Biá, dijá). These accents have not been written in all cases.

151

Glossary of Yuquí and Spanish Terms

Abá: (Yuquí) Used to indicate non-Yuquí as well as their ancestors. Probably is derived from the Chiriguano term, AVA, a name they use for those of high caste

Amachi: (Yuquí) To be light-skinned

Amayaquia: (Yuquí) The chant to appease the spirits that bring forth storms

Antajisa: (Yuquí) "Anteater foot", i.e., clubfooted

Ari: (Yuquí) Grandmother, old woman. Now discontinued from use

Arroba: (Spanish) A dry measure of 25 pounds

Biá: (Yuquí) "The People," what the Yuquí call themselves

Biá agüe; Biagüe: (Yuquí) One of the two forms that the spirits of the dead assume

Carpir: (Spanish) To weed a field using a flat-bladed shovel, or scuffling hoe, called a PALA

Chaco: (Spanish) A "garden" or field planted by using swidden horticultural techniques

Chapapa: (Spanish) A platform built up in a tree as a hunting blind

Cheresa: (Yuquí) "My eyes" [che + eresa]

Chimbó: (Yuquí) A type of barbasco vine used to poison fish

Chochoi: (Yuquí) A forest creature, bogeyman that abducts people

Chori: (Spanish, but of unknown indigenous origin) A lowland Bolivian term used to indicate the Sirionó and Yuquí. It is equated with "savage"

Chuchillo (*Gynerium sagittatum*): (Spanish) A rattan-like reed that grows along the banks of rivers or in areas formerly occupied by a river. The stem is used in construction and the flower staff for making arrows

Commandante: (Spanish) The naval commandant of a port town

Compadre: (Spanish) In the system of godparenthood, the term that the parents and godparents of a child use when addressing one another, if the person being addressed is male (if female, COMADRE)

Criado: (Spanish) Literally, someone who is brought up by an adoptive parent. In reality, it is a euphemism for "servant," since this is the role these individuals are commonly given

Dijá (*Genipa americana L.*): (Yuquí) The fruit and the blue-black dye from it that is used as a body paint

Ejene: (Spanish) A miniscule biting fly (Species unknown)

Enembaco: (Yuquí) Slave

Erasi: (Yuquí) Sick

Erebeya: (Yuquí) In their cosmology, the people who came after the Abá and gave birth to the Biá (present-day Yuquí)

Ererecua: (Sirionó) First-born son. The Sirionó use this term in referring to their headman

Erua: (Yuquí) Incest

Esi; Eru: (Yuquí) The terms of referral for mother and father

Eturã biti: (Yuquí) "It isn't good." An expression used when angry

Eyibasi: (Yuquí) To be meat hungry

Gringo: (Spanish) Foreigner

Gurai: (Yuquí) Small, darting bird (Species unknown)

Iguanda: (Yuquí) "One who is next to you," a greatly feared forest spirit

Imbai (*Cecropia spp.*): (Yuquí) The tree and the fiber that is taken from the bark to be used in the construction of string for hammocks, bows, and baby slings

Iogüe rusudn: (Yuquí) "Fat thighs." An explanation for why some women fail to become pregnant

Iquio jasi; Ju jasi: (Yuquí) To be fast; to speak fast. Terms to describe the Yuquí speech pattern of quick, high-pitched, staccato speech used when angry or upset

Iruu: (Yuquí) A basket made by folding a palm mat and then weaving the halves to close the bottom and side

Iyusumano: (Yuquí) The wind chant. Used to protect the Yuquí against the destruction caused by high winds

Jesucristo: (Spanish) Jesus Christ

Jinoa: (Yuquí) Palm leaves, fronds

Jinoquio: (Yuquí) A backpack made of woven palm, usually hastily constructed

Jirase: (Yuquí) The death and sickness chant

Jirayruu: (Yuquí) A basket made to be used to scoop up mudfish from a shallow pond

Jirisue tai: (Yuquí) "The corpse house," a shelter of palm built over the dead (jirisue = corpse; tai = roof)

Juez Agrario: (Spanish) The Agrarian Judge, a Bolivian official located in each Department (state) and charged with the responsibility of carrying out the Agrarian Reform Decree of 1953

Mano tuti ja yai: (Yuquí) "To die all the way somewhat," the Yuquí's way of expressing apparent death, or soul loss, followed by the return to life. An explanation for such occurrences as unconsciousness, coma, or having the wind knocked out

Mestizo: (Spanish) "Mixed," the term applied to most Latin Americans who are of mixed European and Indian heritage

Mojon: (Spanish) A large post set upright in the ground to mark a boundary line

Monte: (Spanish) The wilderness or virgin forest

-Nda: (Yuquí) a suffix used to nominalize a word, "one who . . ."

Oriente: (Spanish) "The east," in Bolivia, the lowlands

Osenda: (Yuquí) "People of the forest," i.e., the Yuquí

Pachiuba (*Socratea exorrhiza*): (Spanish) A tall, thin palm whose trunk is split for boards. The leaves are also used for thatching

Pala: (Spanish) A sharp-bladed shovel, or scuffling hoe, used for weeding fields and digging post holes

Papa: (Yuquí) "Father, husband." Also the term of address for the headman

Papaguatsu: (Yuquí) The term for God; "big father"

Patrón: (Spanish) The landlord of a large landholding who made use of debt peonage to work his property

Pilua: (Spanish, but probably of indigenous origin) A lowland term for a large container built of wood or other materials to store rice, corn, or other crop

Queesa: (Yuquí) Nest, "menstrual hut"

Quietá: (Yuquí) A grill made of green sticks, usually triangular or rectangular in shape

Reducción: (Spanish) The term given to Catholic missions whose purpose was to consolidate dispersed nomadic indigenous groups into a mission environment, or "reduce" these people to form a single, settled community

Satanás: (Spanish) Satan, the Devil; the Yuquí pronounce this word "sasanás"

Saya: (Yuquí) Upper, or ruling caste

Seso: (Yuquí) The term applied to URUCÚ when it is used in a magical context

Surazo: (Spanish) A "souther," the cold winds that blow across the Bolivian lowlands from the Antarctic

Tacõ siquio: (Yuquí) "To break the child"; the Yuquí act to abort the first pregnancy by kneeling on the woman's abdomen (tacõ = infant; siquio = to break)

Tacú: (Spanish, but probably of indigenous origin) A lowland term for a large, wooden mortar

Taĩ: (Yuquí) The term of address for mother

Tapuy: (Ava Chiriguano) Slave

Teicua biasu: (Yuquí) Burial basket formed from three mats woven together (teicua = mat; biasu = for Biá)

Teruquia: (Yuquí) Sky; open place

Teruquia gurinda: (Yuquí) "People under the sky." The terminology applied to those who do not live in the forest, i.e., non-Yuquí

Teruquiarinda: (Yuquí) "Those across the sky," i.e., spirits of the dead

Tiruru: (Yuquí) Small bird that darts through the forest (Species unknown)

Toria i: (Yuquí) To be hungry, all food except meat

Urucú (*Bixa orellana*): (Tupí-Guaraní term widely used throughout the Amazon) A bush-like tree that produces pods with red seeds inside. The seeds are a source of red dye

Yande: (Sirionó) Potential spouse

Yaqui: (Yuquí) Son, young man; perhaps the origin of the local name of this group, YUQUÍ

Yequaquiú: (Yuquí) To come of age, a girl's first menses

Yerequió: (Yuquí) Adultery

Yeyú detsá: (Yuquí) "Fish eye"

Yirogüe: (Yuquí) One of the two spiritual forms taken by the souls of the dead

Yiru: (Yuquí) "Breath, or spirit"; also mouth, lower face, inside of mouth, throat

Zarpe: (Spanish) Permission to leave port

References Cited and Consulted

Bodley, John H.
1982 *Victims of Progress*. Second Edition. Palo Alto: Mayfield.

Brown, Michael F.
1985 *Tsewa's Gift: Magic and Meaning in Amazonian Society*. Smithsonian Series in Ethnographic Enquiry. Washington, DC: Smithsonian Institution Press.

Chagnon, Napoleon
1983 *Yąnomamö: The Fierce People*. Third Edition. Case Studies in Cultural Anthropology. George and Louise Spindler, General Editors. New York: Holt, Rinehart and Winston.

Clad, J.
1984 "Conservation and Indigenous Peoples: A Study of Convergent Interests." *Cultural Survival Quarterly* 8(4):68–73.

Cochrane, Thomas T.
1973 *El Potencial Agrícola del Uso de la Tierra en Bolivia. Un Mapa de Sistemas de Tierra*. Misión Británica en Agricultura Tropical. Ministerio de Agricultura. La Paz: Editorial Don Bosco.

Davis, Sheldon H.
1977 *Victims of the Miracle. Development and the Indians of Brazil*. New York: Cambridge University Press.

Divale, William T. and Marvin Harris
1976 "Population, Warfare, and the Male Supremacist Complex." *American Anthropologist* 78:521–538.

Duguid, Julian
1931 *Green Hell: Adventures in the Mysterious Jungles of Eastern Bolivia*. New York: The Century Company.

Garland, Mary
n.d. "Yuquí Pedagogical Grammar." Typescript.

Gross, Daniel
1975 "Protein Capture and Cultural Development in the Amazon." *American Anthropologist* 77(3):526–549.

Hames, Raymond B.
1979 "A Comparison of the Efficiencies of the Shotgun and the Bow in Neotropical Forest Hunting." *Human Ecology* 7(3):219–252.

Hames, Raymond B. and William T. Vickers
1983 *Adaptive Responses of Native Amazonians*. New York: Academic Press.

Harris, Marvin
1974   *Cows, Pigs, Wars, and Witches: The Riddles of Culture*. New York: Random House.
1977   *Cannibals and Kings. The Origins of Cultures*. New York: Random House.

Haviland, William A.
1987   *Cultural Anthropology*. Fifth Edition. New York: Holt, Rinehart and Winston.

Holmberg, Allan
1969   *Nomads of the Long Bow*. Garden City, NY: The Natural History Press.

Howells, William
1962   *The Heathens. Primitive Man and His Religion*. American Museum of Natural History. Garden City, NY: Doubleday and Co.

Johnson, Allen
1982   "Reductionism in Cultural Ecology: The Amazon Case." *Current Anthropology* 23(4):413–418. Additional discussion: 418–426.

Jones, David
1968   *Sanapia: Comanche Medicine Woman*. Case Studies in Cultural Anthropology. George and Louise Spindler, General Editors. New York: Holt, Rinehart and Winston.
1987   Personal Communication.

Kelm, Heinz
1983   *Gejagte Jagar*. Teil 2. Die Mibia in Ostbolivien. Frankfurt am Main: Museum fur Volkerkunde.

Lee, Richard B. and Irven DeVore (eds.)
1968   *Man the Hunter*. Chicago: Aldine Publishing Co.

Leung, Wu and M. Flores
1961   "Food Composition Table for Use in Latin America." Bethesda, MD: INCAP-ICNND.

Lewis, Norman
1978   *Eastern Bolivia: The White Promised Land*. International Work Group for Indigenous Affairs. No. 31. Copenhagen.

Margolis, Maxine L.
1984   *Mothers and Such. Views of American Women and Why They Changed*. Los Angeles: University of California Press.

Maybury-Lewis, David
1967   *Akwe-Shavante Society*. London: Oxford University Press.

Métraux, Alfred
1963a   "Tribes of Eastern Bolivia and the Madeira Headwaters." In *Handbook of South American Indians*. Julian Steward, ed. Smithsonian Institution, Bureau of American Ethnology Bulletin 143, vol. 3. New York: Cooper Square Publishers.
1963b   "Ethnography of the Chaco." In *Handbook of South American Indians*. Julian Steward, ed. Smithsonian Institution, Bureau of American Ethnology Bulletin 143, vol. 1. New York: Cooper Square Publishers.

New Tribes Mission
1955–1976   "A History of the New Tribes Mission Project to Evangelize the Yuquí Indians." Typescript.
n.d.   "Culture File." Typescript.

Nordenskiold, Erland
1917   "The Guaraní Invasion of the Inca Empire in the Sixteenth Century: An Historical Indian Migration." *Geographical Review* 4(2):103–121.
1924   *The Ethnography of South America as Seen from Mojos in Bolivia*. Comparative Ethnographical Studies 3. Elanders Boktyckeri Aktiebolag. Gotegorg.

Parsons, James J.
1976   "Forest to Pasture: Development or Destruction?" *Revista de Biología Tropical* 24 (suppl. 1):121–138.

Porterfield, Bruce E.
1978   *Commandos for Christ*. Sanford, FL: Brown Gold Publications.

Redford, Kent H. and John G. Robinson
1985   "Hunting by Indigenous Peoples and Conservation of Game Species." *Cultural Survival Quarterly* 9(1):41–44.

Riester, Jürgen
1985   "CIDOB's Role in the Self-Determination of the Eastern Bolivian Indians." In *Native Peoples and Economic Development: Six Case Studies from Latin America*. No. 16. Theodore MacDonald, Jr., ed. Cambridge, MA: Cultural Survival, Inc.

Ross, Eric B.
1978   "Food Taboos, Diet, and Hunting Strategy: The Adaptation to Animals in Amazon Cultural Ecology." *Current Anthropology* 19(1):1–36.

Saignes, Thierry
1985   "Una Cultura de Conquistadores." *Presencia*. August 25. Segunda Sección, pp. 1, 4. La Paz.

Salamone, Frank
1977   "Anthropologists and Missionaries: Competition or Reciprocity?" *Human Organization* 36(4):407–412.

Scheffler, Harold W. and Floyd G. Lounsbury
1971   *A Study in Structural Semantics: The Sirionó Kinship System*. Englewood Cliffs, NJ: Prentice-Hall.

Shapiro, Warren
1968   "Kinship and Marriage in Sirionó Society: A Reexamination." *Bijdragen Tot de Taal-, Land-, en Volkerkunde* 124:40–55.

Siskind, Janet
1973a   *To Hunt in the Morning*. New York: Oxford University Press.
1973b   "Tropical Forest Hunters and the Economy of Sex." In Daniel R. Gross, ed. *Peoples and Cultures of Native South America*. New York: The Natural History Press.

Sponsel, Leslie
1986   "Amazon Ecology and Adaptation." *Annual Review of Anthropology* 15:67–97.

Stearman, Allyn MacLean
 1984 "The Yuquí Connection: Another Look at Sirionó Deculturation." *American Anthropologist* 86(3):630–650.
 1987 *No Longer Nomads: The Sirionó Revisited*. Lanham, MD: Hamilton Press.

Steward, Julian and L.C. Faron
 1959 *Native Peoples of South America*. New York: McGraw-Hill.

Stipe, Claude
 1980 "Anthropologists versus Missionaries: The Influence of Presuppositions." *Current Anthropology* 21:165–179. Additional discussion: 22:89, 181, 297–298; 23:338–340; 24:114–115, 242–243; 25:124–126.

Stoll, David
 1982 *Fishers of Men or Founders of Empire?* London: Zed Publications.
 1984 "All Men Will Hate You Because of Me: The Controversies over the Summer Institute of Linguistics and the New Tribes Mission in Latin America." Typescript.

Turnbull, Colin
 1972 *The Mountain People*. New York: Simon and Schuster.

Tylor, Edward Burnett
 1958 *Primitive Culture*. Original 1871 publication reprinted in two volumes: Vol. 1, *The Origins of Culture*; Vol. 2, *Religion in Primitive Culture*. New York: Harper Torchbooks.

Index